International Law as Constructive Resistance towards Peace and Justice

International Law in Japanese Perspective

Series Editor

Yuji Iwasawa

VOLUME 16

The titles published in this series are listed at *brill.com/iljp*

International Law as Constructive Resistance towards Peace and Justice

Edited by

Makoto Seta and Yota Negishi

BRILL | NIJHOFF

LEIDEN | BOSTON

Library of Congress Cataloging-in-Publication Data

Names: Mogami, Toshiki, 1950- author. | Seta, Makoto, 1983- editor. | Negishi, Yota, editor.
Title: International law as constructive resistance towards peace and justice / edited by Makoto Seta and Yota Negishi.
Description: Leiden ; Boston : Brill, 2024. | Series: International law in Japanese perspective, 0929-7111 ; volume 16 | Includes bibliographical references and index. | Summary: "Professor Toshiki Mogami, the featured figure of this memorial edition, has developed his academic career in international law and politics. Professor Mogami's original normative and analytical framework is characterized by himself as Jus Contra Anarchism et Oligarchism: international law against interstate and institutionalised violence. The editors extract the very essence of his teachings from Professor Mogami's masterpieces, specifically, International Law as Constructive Resistance towards Peace and Justice"– Provided by publisher.
Identifiers: LCCN 2024015805 (print) | LCCN 2024015806 (ebook) | ISBN 9789004681460 (hardback) | ISBN 9789004681477 (ebook)
Subjects: LCSH: International law. | Peace. | United Nations. Security Council. | Jurisdiction (International law) | Constitutional law. | Restorative justice. | Law and globalization. | War (International law) | International organizations.
Classification: LCC KZ5538 .M64 2024 (print) | LCC KZ5538 (ebook) | DDC 341–dc23/eng/20240409
LC record available at https://lccn.loc.gov/2024015805
LC ebook record available at https://lccn.loc.gov/2024015806

Typeface for the Latin, Greek, and Cyrillic scripts: "Brill". See and download: brill.com/brill-typeface.

ISSN 0929-7111
ISBN 978-90-04-68146-0 (hardback)
ISBN 978-90-04-68147-7 (e-book)
DOI 10.1163/9789004681477

This book is printed on acid-free paper and produced in a sustainable manner.

Contents

Introduction
International Law as Constructive Resistance towards Peace and Justice 1
Makoto Seta and Yota Negishi

PART 1
(De-)Constructive Resistance for Alterity in International Law

1 The Phenomenological Embodiment of International Lawyers: the Gaze at People Living 'in This Corner of the Beautiful World' 15
Yota Negishi

2 For Belated Justice in International Law: Righting Historical Wrongs in East Asia 36
Kohki Abe

PART 2
(Re-)Constructing Peace and Justice in International Law

3 Gender-Based Violence against Women in International Law: Transformative Possibility of International Law 59
Miho Omi

4 The Right to Peace Revisited: beyond an Aspiring Norm 80
Yasue Mochizuki

PART 3
Constructive Resistance in International Law from Below

5 Treaty on the Prohibition of Nuclear Weapons as Legal Correction of International Injustice
Issues of Normalization of 'Human Security' and Creation of World Law 113
Masashi Nakayama

6 Enemy or Disobedience? Paradigm Crisis on the Use of Lethal Force in Occupied Territory 142
Kyo Arai

PART 4
Constructive Resistance through International Legal Institutions

7 International Organisations and Contestation: Reconsidering Democratic Control in Global Constitutionalism 165
Ryuya Daidouji

8 Legal Control for the UN Security Council: toward *jus contra oligarchiam* as Critical Global Constitutionalism 186
Masami Maruyama

PART 5
Constructive Resistance in International Law by Sovereign States?

9 The United Nations and the Big Powers at a Time of 'Patriotic Unilateralism' and 'Global Governance' 217
Tetsuya Yamada

10 The Role of Universal Jurisdiction in Achieving International Legal Justice: a Global Constitutionalism Perspective 230
Makoto Seta

Index 251

Introduction

International Law as Constructive Resistance towards Peace and Justice

Makoto Seta and Yota Negishi

International law has developed around *anarchically* structured interstate violence and *oligarchically* institutionalised global power. In the history of international law, the use and threat of force between sovereign States were not prohibited until the indescribable tragedies of the two world wars unfolded. Even after the birth of the UN Charter prohibiting interstate violence, humanity has still been stuck in the threat of devastation by nuclear weapons and weapons of mass destruction. On several occasions, the prohibition of the use of force under the UN Charter has been manipulated by hegemonic powers for their political purposes.

Admittedly, unilaterally exercised violence has been partially restrained by virtue of the role of international organisations, particularly the most global one, the United Nations. Nonetheless, it should not be underestimated that the Security Council, which is endowed with the primary responsibility for international peace and security, is controlled by the permanently entrenched oligarchic membership. The P5's veto power has been allegedly abused to categorically exclude certain problems from the Council's mandate. Even in reverse cases of authorisation under Chapter VII of the Charter, the Council was criticised for the excessive mobilisation of its authorised power, which has implications for the rule of law and human rights.

Professor Toshiki Mogami, the featured figure of this memorial edition, has developed his academic career against these issues. Professor Mogami's normative and analytical framework was greatly nurtured in rich encounters with the members of the World Order Models Project (WOMP), represented by Saul Mendlovitz, Richard Falk, Johan Galtung and his mentor Yoshikazu Sakamoto.

His original normative and analytical framework is characterised by himself as *Jus Contra Anarchiam et Oligarchiam*: international law against interstate and institutionalised violence. The *Festschrift* in honour of Professor Mogami aims to situate his great academic achievements in the genealogy of international legal scholarship and to disseminate his intellectual legacy to the whole world. All contributors to this book share the intention not only to celebrate his milestone birthday but also to retrace his entire academic works and thereby advance his vision for future research in international law.

 | DOI:10.1163/9789004681477_002

Having traced the path of Professor Mogami's entire life by reading his masterpieces and holding dialogues with him, the editors extract the very essence from his teachings, namely, *International Law as Constructive Resistance towards Peace and Justice.* This part begins by briefly introducing the doctrinal trajectory of Professor Mogami for readers (1), and then explains the structure of this edition (2).

1 Tracing the Trajectory of Professor Toshiki Mogami's *Jus Contra Anarchiam et Oligarchiam*

1.1 *International Organisation as Catalyst for International Order*

Throughout his academic life, Professor Mogami has engaged in theorising the dynamic phenomenon of international organisations as a focal point of international law and politics.[1] In contrast to the existing literature that descriptively explicates the authorities and functions of international organisations that actually exist, Professor Mogami's analysis is normative and critically addresses the conceptualised phenomena of utilising international organisations and/or multilateralism for the international order.[2] Among his original conceptual inventions, the term *in-organisational counter-hegemony* proved useful to describe a revolutionary momentum that occurred within the United Nations during the Cold War.[3] In fact, the newly independent states, less powerful outside the United Nations, gained more influence within the organisation, particularly in the General Assembly, compared to those who maintained their oligarchical hegemony in the Security Council. This counter-hegemonic action stemmed not from hard military or economic power but from the normative and democratic legitimacy conferred by the principle of sovereign equality. To describe such an overturn of the hegemonic structure with normative power, Professor Mogami coined the notion of *non-violent*

1 Professor Mogami finished his doctoral thesis in 1980 on the dynamic regional integration of the European Community. His theory on international organisation is summarised in the textbook titled *Kokusai-kiko-ron Kogi* [*Lecture on International Organisation*] (Iwanami Shoten 2016).

2 Toshiki Mogami, 'On the Concept of International Organization: Centralization, Hegemonism, and Constitutionalism' in Madeleine Herren (ed), *Networking the International System: Global Histories of International Organizations* (Springer 2014) 43–52.

3 Toshiki Mogami, 'The United Nations System as an Unfinished Revolution' (1990) 15 Alternatives: Global, Local, Political 177–197; Toshiki Mogami, 'Grafting the Past onto the Future of the United Nations System' in Richard A Falk, Robert C Johansen and Samuel S Kim (eds), *The Constitutional Foundations of World Peace* (SUNY Press 1993) 129–146.

revolution, drawing inspiration from the seemingly paradoxical terms 'creative destruction' coined by Joseph Schumpeter and 'creative anarchy' by Rajni Kothari.[4] This circumstance could equally be described as a form of anarchic structuring. Unlike Hedley Bull's assertion that it permits inter-state conflicts, it instead facilitates a pursuit of 'universality from below' by various stakeholders attentive to mutual considerations.[5]

1.2 *Normative Multilateralism against Anarchical Unilateralism*

Concurrent with his research on international organisations, Professor Mogami published several works that illuminate the various aspects of *violence* at the international level. In the middle stage of his career, the first aspect of his analytical framework, *Jus Contra Anarchiam*, emerged. It criticises the direct form of violence the *direct* form of violence, namely, the use and threat of force between States. Professor Mogami consistently pays careful attention to the interaction between the UN Charter (Article 2(4)) and the Constitution of Japan (Article 9), the amalgam of which is labelled by himself as 'the norms of common destiny'.[6] In the case of the Gulf Crisis, in which the Security Council Resolution 678 '[a]uthorize[d] Member States to use all necessary means [...] to restore international peace and security in the area', Professor Mogami lamented the Japanese Government's involvement in a coalition, and proposed it to be a *conscientious objector State*.[7] When the administration of Shinzo Abe assertively promoted what was alleged to be an unconstitutional reinterpretation of the constitution through interpretation for collective self-defence in 2014, Professor Mogami asserted that the right to collective self-defence under international law cannot be invoked to justify such a political decision.[8]

Professor Mogami's insights extend from the direct use of force by States to the *indirect* form of violence caused by the distortion of social structures. The paper on the *right to peace* in the early stage of his career, for example, shrewdly detected its emerging character to challenge the structural barriers preventing

4 Toshiki Mogami, The Crisis of the UNESCO and the World Order: International Organisation as Non-Violent Revolution (Token Syuppan, 1987) [in Japanese] 169–198.

5 Toshiki Mogami, *Beyond the United Nations System* (Iwanami Shoten 1995) [in Japanese] 177, 185–186.

6 Toshiki Mogami, 'Normativity: Domestic and International Dimensions' (1987) 12 *Peace and Change: A Journal of Peace Research* 39–50.

7 Toshiki Mogami, 'For a Testimony of Conscientious Objector State: Seeking the Cornerstone of Post-Cold War Security' (1990) 547 *Sekai* 23–34 [in Japanese].

8 Toshiki Mogami, 'International Law Is Not the Imperial Standard' (2015) 873 *Sekai* 62–70 [in Japanese].

'a social and international order in which the rights and freedoms [...] can be fully realized' as promulgated in Article 28 of the Universal Declaration of Human Rights.[9] In the textbook of his lectures concerning human rights and humanity carried by Japan's public broadcaster NHK, Professor Mogami redefined the concept of peace through the lens of *structural* violence coined by Johan Galtung, from the absence of inter-state violence (negative peace) to that of any type of violence (positive peace).[10] The need to overcome the structural obstacles is of particular weight, as Professor Mogami warns, for vulnerable and marginalised peoples whose suffering is continuing under the structure of international law such as hibakusha (victims of nuclear bombs) in Hiroshima and Nagasaki, the population of Okinawa/Ryukyu, which remained under US military presence even after the occupation ended in 1972, and so-called comfort women in East Asia during the WWII.[11]

Drawing from his observations countering the unilateral use of force by States and the structural violence caused by multiple international actors, Professor Mogami embarked on elaborating an original concept of *normative multilateralism*. For him, multilateralism has by nature a normative agenda that designates certain fundamental modes of action, namely, collective making of decisions and actions based on common norms. This normative aspect of multilateralism is thus essentially tied with several different components of *the rule of law*. Its multilateral character should not be equated with multi-State but rather encompass the roles of non-State actors that challenge the State-centric idea under international law and politics.[12] He particularly directed his criticism at the unilateral use of force by the US and its allies without clear legal bases: one against Afghanistan after 9/11 terrorist attacks in 2001 based on the right to self-defense against non-State actors;[13] and another against Iraq for

9 Toshiki Mogami, 'The Right to Peace' (1989) 40 *Freedom and Justice* 33–39, included in *The Era of International Constitutionalism* (Iwanami Shoten 2007) [in Japanese].

10 Toshiki Mogami, 'Redefining Peace: Peace for Humanity' in *What is Peace Now? Nine Stroies Around Human Rights and Humanity* (Iwanami Shoten 2006) [in Japanese]. See also, Johan Galtung, 'Violence, Peace, Peace Research' (1969) 6 *Journal of Peace Research* 167–191.

11 Mogami Toshiki, 'Japan' in Simon Chesterman, Hisashi Owada and Ben Saul (eds), *The Oxford Handbook of International Law in Asia and the Pacific* (Oxford University Press 2019) 320–340.

12 Toshiki Mogami, 'Non-State Actors and International Law: A Tentative Theorization on the Conversion of the Principle of the Legal Order' (2009) 108 *Journal of International Law and Diplomacy* 117–143 [in Japanese].

13 Toshiki Mogami, 'The Legal Structure of Justice and Humanity: What Determines the Legal Justness?' (2002) 74(6) *Horitsu Jiho* 5–10, included in *The Era of International Constitutionalism* (Iwanami Shoten 2007) [in Japanese].

the allegations of weapons of mass destruction (WMDs) in 2003 based on the prior authorisation from the Security Council.[14]

1.3 *Critical International Constitutionalism against Oligarchical Hegemony*

In the process of pursuing normative multilateralism, Professor Mogami explicates the core essence of *international constitutionalism*.[15] An outline of international constitutionalism was already presented in 1995, celebrating the 50th anniversary of the UN and the bicentenary of Immanuel Kant's *Zum Ewigen Frieden*.[16] As his critique focused on the illegitimate exercise of international public power within the realm of international constitutionalism, Professor Mogami consciously addressed the second aspect of his analytical framework, *Jus Contra Oligarchiam*. The law against oligarchy is primarily directed to the unrestricted legislative power of the Security Council, represented by its Resolutions 1373 on counter-terrorism and 1540 on counter-WMD proliferation. In the particular case of targeted sanctions, the European Court of Human Rights (e.g. *Behrami and Sramati*) and the European Court of Justice (e.g. *Kadi*) revealed a certain kind of disobedience to put the limits on the Security Council's public authority.[17] Even though these judicial reactions originated primarily from Europe, Professor Mogami argues that such disobediences imply the legitimacy for seeking a constitutional system of international law based on universal human rights principles.[18] In other words, such challenges represent a form of *constructive resistance* that relativises the established hierarchical structure of power 'from above', and thereafter seeks to establish alternative universal principles 'from below'.[19]

---

14 Toshiki Mogami, 'Multilateralism and the Rule of Law: A Reflection on the Position of the Norm on the Prohibition of Use of Force' (2004) 23 *Yearbook of World Law* 93–123, included in *The Era of International Constitutionalism* (Iwanami Shoten 2007) [in Japanese].

15 Akihiko Kimijima, 'Japan's Contribution to Global Constitutionalism' (2009) 4 *Societies Without Borders* 105–116.

16 Toshiki Mogami, '<Two Hundred Years> of the United Nations: A Memorandum on International Constitutionalism' (1995) 67(6) *Horitsu Jiho* 44–50, included in *The Era of International Constitutionalism* (Iwanami Shoten 2007) [in Japanese].

17 Toshiki Mogami, 'Towards *Jus Contra Oligarchiam*: A Note on Critical Constitutionalism' (2012) 55 *Japanese Yearbook of International Law* 371–402.

18 Toshiki Mogami, 'Universal Public Power and Universal Legal Order: On the Judicial Review of the Resolutions and Actions of the United Nations Security Council' in Takeo Matsuda, Norio Tanaka, Kimio Yakushiji and Sigeki Sakamoto (eds), *Thoughts and Structure of Contemporary International Law, Vol II: Environment, Sea, Criminal, Dispute and Foresight* (Toshindo 2012) 371–404 [in Japanese].

19 Toshiki Mogami, 'A New Horizon of International Constitutionalism: Hierarchy, Heterarchy, De-Europeanization' (2013) 85(11) *Horitsu Jiho* 6–12 [in Japanese].

In his recent works, Professor Mogami more explicitly adopts the concept of *critical constitutionalism* to critically examine the existing literature of international or global constitutionalism. Behind the emergence of critical constitutionalism, there already existed epistemic and methodological diversity and norm proliferation around the notion of international constitutionalism, and thereby its conceptual framework became seriously ambiguous. Professor Mogami reflects that this ambiguity is not novel, having been observed in the WOMP, which preceded contemporary debates on global constitutionalism.[20] Against this background, Professor Mogami consciously disciplines his own position not to envision an all-encompassing order construction but to zero in on the legal rectification of allegedly illegal actions and illegitimate institutions according to constitutional principles (regarding *jus contra anarchiam* and *jus contra oligarchiam*).[21]

1.4 *Essence: International Law as Constructive Resistance towards Peace and Justice*

The foregoing introduction of Professor Mogami's main pieces does not cover his entire academic life and works. His analytical framework is still under development as mentioned in his latest papers on *Global History*[22] and *Effectiveness*[23] of international law. Even at this stage, however, the editors discern the essence of his doctrine from the comprehensive overview provided above, that is, *international law as constructive resistance towards peace and justice*. The '*contra*' aspect of *jus contra anarchiam* and *jus contra oligarchiam* demonstrates the attitude of *resistance* against international hegemonies, as reflected in Professor Mogami's innovative notions such as *non-violent revolution* and *conscientious objector State*. It does not mean, however, that such opposition to arbitrary authority devolves into a form of radical relativism, which would

20 Toshiki Mogami, '*Perpetuum Mobile*: Before and After Global Constitutionalism' in Takao Suami, Anne Peters, Mattias Kumm and Dimitri Vanoverbeke (eds), *Global Constitutionalism from European and East Asian Perspectives* (Cambridge University Press 2018) 29–57.

21 Toshiki Mogami, 'Criticism of International Constitutionalism and Critical International Constitutionalism' (2014) 33 *Yearbook of World Law* 1–32 [in Japanese].

22 Toshiki Mogami, 'The Relocation of Multilateralism: Prolegomenon' in Noboru Kashiwagi *et al* (eds), Comparative Law Seen from Japan and Brazil: Festschrift in Honour of Professor Masato Ninomiya's 70th birthday (Shinzansya 2019) [in Japanese].

23 Toshiki Mogami, 'The Effectiveness of International Law and International Legal Scholarship: A Preparatory Consideration' in Yuji Iwasawa and Masataka Okano (eds), *International Relations and the Rule of Law: Festschrift for Judge Owada Hisashi in Commemoration of his Retirement from the International Court of Justice* (Shinzansya 2021).

ironically result in the victory of factual powers; they instead inherit a *constructive* character to uphold core legal principles, as evident in his foundational theories including *normative multilateralism* and *critical international constitutionalism*. Ultimately, Professor Mogami advocates for the pursuit of constructive resistance in aspiring for universally recognised values such as *peace and justice*.

2 The *Festschrift*'s Structure

The Festschrift is an academic endeavour to contextualise the significant contributions of Professor Mogami within the lineage of international legal scholarship, with the intent to promulgate his intellectual legacy globally. Throughout his distinguished career, Professor Mogami has been dedicated to formulating theories and concepts with the potential for universal application and acceptance. Regrettably, except for certain periods, there has been a notable paucity in the exposition of Professor Mogami's profound insights in the English language, both by himself and by his Japanese peers. To address this and facilitate the global dissemination of his universally resonant ideas, the editors have engaged a diverse array of esteemed Japanese scholars, whose expertise spans from public international law and constitutional law to the social sciences and peace studies.

The Festschrift, drawing on an innovative interdisciplinary approach, allows for the perpetuation and adaptation of Professor Mogami's distinctive theories and concepts, tailored to the specialisations of the individual contributors. These acolytes of Professor Mogami's scholarly work, including the editors themselves, strive not only to present his fully developed ideas to an international readership but also to critically evaluate their normative underpinnings, with an eye towards propelling future scholarly inquiry.

The memorial book is partitioned into five thematic segments, each featuring paired scholarly works. Part 1 encompasses a philosophical treatise by Yota Negishi alongside a historiographical critique by Kohki Abe. Both pieces collectively endeavour to rectify epistemological prejudices inherent in contemporary international legal discourse, thus fostering the emergence of alternative conceptualisations of peace and justice.

Part 2 is composed of Miho Omi's exploration of gender-based violence and Yasue Mochizuki's examination of the right to peace, shedding light on the underpinnings of structural violence and the barriers impeding the actualisation of peace and justice.

Part 3 juxtaposes Masashi Nakayama's scrutiny of the Treaty on the Prohibition of Nuclear Weapons with Kyo Arai's analysis of the application of lethal force in occupied territories. These contributions highlight the essence of grassroots activism in shaping peace and justice, with the former appraising the pivotal role of civil society in the formulation of treaties, while the latter delineates the legal frameworks governing, and potentially safeguarding, civilian opposition to occupation forces.

Part 4 is dedicated to the study of international organisational dynamics, featuring an examination of inter-organisational relations by Ryuya Daidouji and an inquiry into international regulatory mechanisms by Masami Maruyama. These studies focus on the capacity of international entities and juridical institutions to challenge oligarchic dominion, advocating for the realization of peace and justice.

Finally, Part 5 presents Tetsuya Yamada's dissection of what he terms 'patriotic unilateralism' exercised by major powers, in conjunction with Makoto Seta's research on the backlash faced by the International Criminal Court. This concluding section grapples with the legitimacy of state-level resistance to international organisations or juridical entities, probing its potential to contribute constructively to the global discourse on peace and justice.

2.1 *Part 1: (De-)Constructive Resistance for Alterity in International Law*

Chapter 1: Yota Negishi, 'The Phenomenological (Dis-)Embodiment of International Lawyers: the Gaze of Peoples Living "in This Corner of the Beautiful World"'

Negishi draws inspiration from Professor Mogami's phenomenological intuition of international law as described in his essay 'In This Corner of the Beautiful World.' He first introduces the concept of phenomenological reduction to bring international lawyers back to their lifeworld, the foundation upon which the scientific field is built. The author then gives a phenomenological account in which international lawyers, situated within their lifeworld, cast 'the gaze to the beauty of the world' through aesthetic sensibilities that form the basis for logical activities. He ultimately demonstrates the embodied intentionality, or intercorporeality, among international lawyers, which emerges through the lived experiences of others, allowing their aesthetic sensibilities to connect 'beyond the beauty of the world for me'. Through these phenomenological lenses, international lawyers strip away the rational guise from ideas and reconnect with their lived realities, where aesthetic sensibility is passively intertwined with that of others.

Chapter 2: Kohki Abe, 'For Belated Justice in International Law: Righting Historical Wrongs in East Asia'

The reparation for past injustices has gained momentum since 1980s as if it is an underground stem stretching throughout the world. Brought into the public arena are people's memories forcibly silenced by the dominant legal and political discourse. The initial driving force behind the momentum was an institutional response to grave human rights violations in the immediate past in the name of 'transnational justice'. It is widely known that a comprehensive framework for truth, justice, reparation and non-recurrence has been rapidly developed after the model pioneered in Latin American countries in their transitions away from authoritarian rules. East Asia is no exception to the emerging global calls for righting historical wrongs. Against this background, this paper aims to illuminate the contemporary development in East Asia as it is related to the global dynamics for belated justice. Particular references will be made to the international law implications of past injustices imposed on Ryukyu/Okinawa and Korea, two of territories colonially dominated by the Imperial Japan. It thus critically portrays the contemporary interplay of colonialism and international law in East Asia.

2.2 *Part 2: (Re-)Constructing Peace and Justice in International Law*

Chapter 3: Miho Omi, 'Gender-Based Violence against Women in International Law: Transformative Possibility of International Law'

The feminist approach is not just a methodology to apply female experience and knowledge to various academic fields. It also means to challenge the core mindset of each academic field and propose a possible solution by utilizing feminist theory as a fundamental concept. Such feminist analysis is an attempt to connect the resistance and construction which Prof. Mogami seeks. In the area of international law, the feminist approach can be used to change international law which is established by the male-dominated States, to be more inclusive to cover females and other invisible people. Against this background, this paper focuses on the interfaces between international law and violence against women which are categorised as international injustice.

Chapter 4: Yasue Mochizuki 'The Right to Peace Revisited: beyond an Aspiring Norm'

This research aims at (re)-identifying the concept of the right to peace by examining the treaty provisions which stipulate the right. This paper examines the backgrounds and motives to lay down the right to peace in treaties, the content of the right to peace, and if there is any obligation to respond to it and the objectives of these provisions. The research then analyzes whether the treaty provisions have any significance in facilitating rights to peace as a universal norm or whether it remains as the right within the regional context. By exploring the rights to peace provisions, this paper will revisit the concept of the right to peace and to investigate its legal/political significance in the current international community.

2.3 *Part 3: Constructive Resistance in International Law from Below*

Chapter 5: Masashi Nakayama, 'Treaty on the Prohibition of Nuclear Weapons as Rectifying International Injustice: Challenges for Norming "Human Security" and Forming a Global Law'

Although nuclear weapons have been accepted to maintain the current global security system on the basis of nuclear deterrence theory, this system itself is injustice from the perspective of the right to peaceful life. This idea is one of the reasons the international community requires the Nuclear Weapon Ban Treaty based on the presumption that human rights, humanity and human security should be secured at the global level. When adopting this treaty, the contribution of the civil society should not be overseen, because it plays an essential role to put the concept of human security into the international norm. This paper aims to demonstrate the above argument and concludes that the establishment of the rule of law in the international community is a non-violent resistance which labels nuclear weapons not as a necessary evil, but as an absolute evil.

Chapter 6: Kyo Arai, 'Enemy or Disobedience? Paradigm Crisis on the Use of Lethal Force in Occupied Territory'

Under the traditional law of occupation, an occupying State shall have effective control over the occupied territory, and stably exercise its authority which can be assimilated to the police power of a sovereign State. Sometimes, the people in the occupied territory do not obey the occupying authority and engage in resistant activities. Traditionally, these people are punished as a criminal unless they satisfy the requirements to be a prisoner under Geneva Convention III. Recently, however, there have been some situations where both international and non-international armed conflict cumulatively exist as shown in the Tadic case. In such a context, the people in the occupied territory might not have a sense of belonging to the occupied State, but they have the one to the other armed group. How does the law of occupation work, and how does it not, in this situation? The paper tries to answer these questions, by referring to the concept of resistance which Prof. Mogami articulates.

2.4 *Part 4: Constructive Resistance through International Legal Institutions*

Chapter 7: Ryuya Daidouji, 'International Organizations and Contestation: Reconsidering Democratic Control in Global Constitutionalism'

This contribution explores the role of IOs in the process of contestation against hegemonic IO, with the lens of IOR. Amongst the different kinds of non-state actors, such as individuals and non-governmental organizations (NGOs), IOs aggregate and organise their opinions, voices, or information, which are otherwise not easily heard. They may utilise such information gained on the ground to demand policy change in other IOs, thereby contesting them (Daidouji, forthcoming). In this sense, this process may be termed 'organised contestation', which may serve as a factor to constraint a powerful IO. This contribution elaborates this notion by briefly examining the fundamental rights protection in the EU's asylum policy and counterterrorism policy, thereby claiming that the frameworks from IR – including norm contestation and IOR – and global constitutionalism can potentially complement each other.

Chapter 8: Masami Maruyama, 'The Legal Control for the UN Security Council: towards *jus contra oligarchiam* as Critical Global Constitutionalism'

In researching the value and possibility of international constitutionalism for an international organisation, especially the Security Council, it is essential to refer to the mindset of critical constitutionalism proposed by Professor Mogami. One of the most important values of international constitutionalism is to justify the strengthening and expansion of the authority of international organisations when they respond to the changing international society. This idea resonates with the idea of *jus contra oligarchiam* which is emphasised by Professor Mogami. This paper aims to reconsider the value of critical constitutionalism by comparing various arguments on international constitutionalism and clarifies the challenges which currently international organizations have when engaging in judicial review or legal (judicial and non-judicial) control.

2.5 *Part 5: Constructive Resistance in International Law by Sovereign States?*

Chapter 9: Tetsuya Yamada, 'The United Nations and the Big Powers at a Time of "Patriotic Unilateralism" and "Global Governance"'

This chapter focuses on the current situation where several Big Powers are showing attitudes of what could be called 'Anti-' or 'Non-multilateralism'. On the one hand, the current 'patriotic unilateralism' in the position of the US and in some European states is a clear violation of rules of international law or the withdrawals from existing international organizations and régimes. On the other hand, the Chinese diplomacy towards the UN would also undermine the UN's innovative and progressive aspects. The possible resulting influence of this on the UN will be made clear. This explanation would make it possible to predict the future of other international organizations as well as the world order. In addition, such an explanation leads to a reconsideration of the significance of Global Governance, both as a theory and as a practice.

Chapter 10: Makoto Seta, 'The Role of Universal Jurisdiction in Achieving International Legal Justice: a Global Constitutionalism Perspective'

In his article named 'Introduction of Universal Jurisdiction' in 2009, Professor Mogami, emphasises universal jurisdiction as an effective tool to universally realise legal justice, but at the same time, considers it as a transitional tool before a permanent international criminal tribunal which has wider and more universal criminal jurisdiction is established. The ICC was established on the way to establish such court, though its jurisdiction is limited. Certainly, from a historical perspective, it is clear that universal jurisdiction has been supported by the norm of *jus cogens*, which is based on the existence of universal justice, as Professor Mogami pointed out. Meanwhile, African States have strengthened its criticism on not only the exercise of universal jurisdiction by the Western States, but also the ICC activity, as a form of new imperialism. Then, finally, African States decided to introduce a regional criminal court to prosecute and punish some specific crimes within its human rights court. In Asia, in a similar vein, The Philippine decided to withdraw from the ICC, since the ICC initiated its investigation for the so-called drug war. How should we evaluate these facts? Do these facts mean that in Africa and Asia, 'regional justice' which is different from 'universal justice', as developed by the Western States would be established? Or are they just a temporary backlash on the way to establish the international criminal tribunal which can realise universal justice? This paper tries to answer this question.

PART 1

(De-)Constructive Resistance for Alterity in International Law

CHAPTER 1

The Phenomenological Embodiment of International Lawyers: the Gaze at People Living 'in This Corner of the Beautiful World'

Yota Negishi

1 Introduction

In his last masterpiece *The Crisis of European Sciences and Transcendental Phenomenology*, Edmund Husserl, the father of phenomenology, lamented that science has lost its meaning for *life*. Husserl found the cause of this crisis to be the mathematically substructured world of idealities that is substituted for our everyday *lifeworld* (Lebenswelt) – the only real world that is actually given through perception and that is ever experienced and experienceable.[1] In the natural scientific manner, the lifeworld, constantly portrayed to us as actual in our concrete lives, is measured for a 'well-fitting garb of ideas, that of the so-called objectively scientific truths'.[2] The garb of ideas making the life-world is dressed up as objectively actual and as true in nature such that 'we take for *true being* what is actually a *method*'.[3]

The crisis of science highlighted by Husserl is *redivivus* over generations in the discipline of international law. In their traditional approaches, international lawyers have elaborated rational theories based on the reason to order and validate the supremacy and objectivity of international law over other sources of law. As a result of the method of positivist reduction, international lawyers have ironically confined themselves within the precepts of the garb of ideas, and their experienceable lifeworld has sunk into oblivion. To overcome the futile state of international lawyers, the present paper, placed as the first chapter in the ceremonial edition for Professor Toshiki Mogami, amplifies this

1 Husserliana (hereinafter Hua) VI: *Die Krisis der europäischen Wissenschaften und die transzendentale Phänomenologie* (Nijhoff 1954) 48–53. For English translation, Edmund Husserl, *The Crisis of European Sciences and Transcendental Phenomenology: An Introduction to Phenomenological Philosophy, translated by David Carr* (Northwestern University Press 1970).

2 ibid 51.

3 ibid 52 (emphasis in the original text).

 | DOI:10.1163/9789004681477_003

phenomenological conception of the international law employed in the aesthetical essay *In This Corner of the Beautiful World*.[4]

> *Behind academic paradigms and objective concepts*,[I] there exist the lives of people, longing for improvement, angry because of oppression and sad about poverty, at which Saint-Exupéry gave a cherished gaze from the giant sky during the Night Flight. In real life, all people wish to protect their happiness and to escape from unfortunate situations. For such people, there must be a beautiful world and, if realized collectively, it would be made the universal beautiful world.
>
> Furthermore, <the objective truth> is not at all opposite to <subjective beauty>. […] Propositions and hypotheses about social science can be as beautiful as poetry, depending on the direction at which they gaze, and perhaps not remain simple subjectivity. This is because when a proposition goes *beyond the <beauty for myself>* [III] to the <beauty of the world>, there must be some objectivity. […]
>
> Then, there is no reason why social scientists should be held away from beauty. Instead, […] we should keep our *gaze somewhere else – i.e. at the <beauty of the world>* [II]. There seems to be a social science sensibility based on empathy with others.

This impressive *passage* reflects at least three core ideas of phenomenology to counter the loss of life caused by positivist reduction. First, the expression '*behind academic paradigms and objective concepts*' exposes the reality of people's lives, including emotions and desires behind which international law is conceptualised (2). Second, as is implied in the expression '*the gaze to <the beauty of the world>*', psychological aspects correlated to our bodies, which have been overly ignored in international law, can be an object of analysis in this academic field (3). Third, the expression '*beyond <the beauty of the world for me>*' depicts how subjective aesthetical judgments on international law should be shared with others (4). This contribution unpacks the potential of Professor Mogami's phenomenological insight to embody international lawyers situated in their experienceable lifeworld.

---

4 Toshiki Mogami, 'In This Corner of the Beautiful World (1): The Gaze at the Beauty of the World' (2012) 41 *UP* (University of Tokyo) 22–27, 24–25.

2 'Behind Academic Paradigms and Objective Concepts'

2.1 *Positivist Reduction Disembodying International Lawyers in Idealities*

According to the traditional approach to international law, rationality or reason plays a major role as an ordering and validating factor that asserts the supremacy and objectivity of international law over other sources.[5] Indeed, international scholars who have adopted traditional approaches have contributed to providing the necessary work of rationalisation and systematisation that makes legal materials eventually appear orderly and coherent.[6] However, the reason-constructing framing transforms international lawyers into prisoners of small thinking by impoverishing idealities and limiting their ability to examine realities.[7] As a result, exercising political power becomes a legal-technical matter, instead of an ethico-political matter, as illustrated in the debate on *the Fragmentation of International Law*.[8] In a nutshell, the lifeworld of international lawyers has been covered with a well-fitting garb of ideas by means of a dual positivist reduction: '*a*-political and *a*-moral *epoché*' and 'a contractual and liberal *epoché*'.[9]

Such an intellectual manipulation results in the *disembodiment* of international lawyers by disguising them in a garb of ideas. In general, cognitive science maintains the traditional belief that intelligent behaviour, including the ability to perceive, think and use language, need not to arise from any specific bodily form.[10] The mainstream accounts of rationalised international law, which are deeply influenced by the Kantian moral theory, also exclude the body as a part of nature that is characterised by emotions conceptualised as external forms of determination and a lack of freedom, thus taking us away from the path of the pure person.[11] This 'dispassionate' approach, which inspires scholars

5 Andrea Bianchi, *International Law Theories: An Inquiry Into Different Ways of Thinking* (Oxford University Press 2016) 30–33.

6 ibid.

7 ibid.

8 Martti Koskenniemi, *From Apology to Utopia: The Structure of International Legal Argument, Reissue with a New Epilogue* (Cambridge University Press 2006) 82.

9 Anthony Carty and Anna Irene Baka, 'Sources in the Meta-History of International Law: From Liberal Nihilism and the Anti-Metaphysics of Modernity to an Aristotelian Ethical Order' in Jean d'Aspremont and Samantha Besson (eds), *The Oxford Handbook of the Sources of International Law* (Oxford University Press 2017) 245–263, 249–258.

10 Raymond Gibbs, *Embodiment and Cognitive Science* (Cambridge University Press 2012) 2.

11 Anna Grear, *Redirecting Human Rights: Facing the Challenge of Corporate Legal Humanity* (Springer 2010) 41–42.

to identify more concrete, objective or empirically-sound research projects, pays attention to the over-emphasis of emotion that can lead to a solipsistic personalisation of analysis or to broken bodies or a kind of victim pornography.[12]

This disembodying approach remains the mainstream in international law, but it is occasionally challenged, especially in terms of *psychology*. Andrea Bianchi and Anne Saab reviewed the traditional idea that cognition and decision-making processes are exclusively controlled by reason.[13] While paying attention to the role played by fear, they claim that 'emotions are part of the cognitive process that informs and triggers the making of decisions' on international law.[14] Anne van Aaken and Tomer Broude, the editors of the symposium *the Psychology of International Law*, also advocate departures from rational choice assumptions, through scientifically inspired experiments that can have 'high internal validity and the potential to uncover causal effects' as to how actors actually behave.[15] Van Aaken and Broude employ natural scientific methods of experiments to empirically observe actors' cognition and real preferences, and as a result, they confer a high degree of internal validity to their findings in controlled circumstances.[16]

Nonetheless, if international law is solely based on the psychological data collected by analogising a descriptive natural science, then we would eventually encounter the Scylla of *psychologism*, not just the Charybdis of *logicism*. Husserl's criticism is directed not only to natural science itself, but also to descriptive psychology – i.e. 'an "exact" psychology, as an analogue to physics (i.e. the dualistic parallelism of realities, of methods and of sciences), is an absurdity'.[17] Anthony D'Amato once attempted to describe 'international law as psychological data' but then realised that we 'were left with the problem of our inability to enter into the minds of national decision-makers to determine the exact objective content of this data'.[18] Since this inability is a given

---

12 Naz K Modirzadeh, 'Cut These Words: Passion and International Law of War Scholarship' (2019) 61 *Harvard International Law Journal* 1–64, 53.

13 Andrea Bianchi and Anne Saab, 'Fear and International Law-making: An Exploratory Inquiry' (2019) 32 *Leiden Journal of International Law* 351–365. See also, Ian Ward, 'The Play of Terror' in Oren Ben-Dor (ed), *Law and Art: Justice, Ethics and Aesthetics* (Routledge 2011) 177–187; Anne Saab, *Narratives of Hunger in International Law: Feeding the World in Times of Climate Change* (Cambridge University Press 2019).

14 ibid.

15 Anne van Aaken and Tomer Broude, 'The Psychology of International Law: An Introduction' (2019) 30 *European Journal of International Law* 1225–1236, 1227.

16 ibid.

17 Hua VI 224–227.

18 Anthony D'Amato, *International Law Studies: Collected Papers Volume Two* (Kluwer Law International 1997) 311–317 (Chapter 22 Phenomenology of International Law).

and cannot be overcome, D'Amato decided to take the next step, which was 'to consider the *phenomenology* of international law as perhaps pointing the way towards getting our subject-matter on a studier scientific footing'.[19] The phenomenological attitude that focuses on the correlation between the subjectively psychological mind and the objectively logical data would provide a novel epistemic that is 'no less than scientific methodologies that can shape the work of professional legal scholars and our relation to the many realities that we seek to study and the many institutions and publics to which we are called to account for'.[20]

2.2 *Phenomenological Reduction Re-embodying International Lawyers in Realities*

The objectivity of international law has been re-examined by critical scholars in the camp of New Approaches to International Law, particularly under the influence of Martti Koskenniemi.[21] In his masterpiece, *From Apology to Utopia*, Koskenniemi famously demonstrates a battle of legal minds on two fronts in examining the objectivity of international law: on the one hand, the 'concreteness' of the law by distancing it from theories of natural justice and, on the other hand, the normativity of the law by creating distance between it and actual state behaviour, will or interest.[22] There was always a 'descending' argument that attempted to ensure the law's normativity, and this was always countered by an 'ascending' argument that provided for the concreteness of the law. The former went beyond state will in a manner that seemed vulnerable because it was non-concrete in nature (utopian), while the latter led to particular state will and seemed unacceptable because it was non-normative (apologist).[23]

After employing the deconstructive criticism of objectivism in the first seven chapters, in the eighth chapter, titled 'Beyond Objectivism', Koskenniemi emphasises that the critical approach neither entails anarchy nor cynical nihilism as a necessary consequence; instead, it implies a normative project.[24] More concretely, as Koskenniemi clarifies in the New Epilogue, *From Apology*

19 ibid [emphasis added].

20 Anne Orford, 'Scientific Reason and the Discipline of International Law' (2014) 25 European Journal of International Law 369–385.

21 José María Beneyto and David Kennedy (eds), *New Approaches to International Law: The European and the American Experiences* (Springer 2012).

22 Koskenniemi (n 8) 17–23.

23 ibid 514.

24 ibid 533–548.

to Utopia looked beyond the descriptive purpose and has the normative project to 'provide resources for the use of international law's professional vocabulary for critical or emancipatory causes'.[25] The very last paragraph of the New Epilogue elaborates this point well, asserting that 'The purpose of that book was [...] to show how individual lawyers [...] have worked in and sometimes challenged the structure sketched there and how they have acted in a conceptual and professional world'.[26]

It is remarkable that Koskenniemi concludes his thesis by noting that 'situationality, as Outi Korhonen puts it, is a key aspect of legal practice'.[27] The concept of *situationality* refers to a certain feature in human existence that breaks the duality of the mind and body and reconnects the human person to the spatio-temporal continuity of the world.[28] Situationality is, as Korhonen rightly opines, the opposite of solipsistic existence, only that it encompasses concrete matters (e.g. sex, race, genes, physical environment, home, work, other persons, etc.) as well as abstractions (e.g. culture, tradition, upbringing, education, profession and economic and social conditions).[29] In the context of international law, as a result of the ultimate denial of solipsism, 'an international lawyer is faced with the entire situational interconnectedness – both in terms of other disciplines of scholarship and in terms of his own personal being'.[30] The task of international lawyers is therefore to hold on to the situatedness of the practice without resorting to nihilism.[31]

Jean d'Aspremont, in his monograph *Epistemic Forces in International Law,* adopts the functional situatedness of international lawyers who deploy argumentative techniques about the fundamental doctrines of international law, rather than the above-mentioned socio-historical situatedness.[32] This type of situatedness is more deeply amplified in his most recent masterpiece, *International Law as a Belief System*. In relation to this book title, d'Aspremont uncovers a belief system in which international lawyers experience a sense of

25 ibid 589–590.
26 ibid 617.
27 ibid 616.
28 Outi Korhonen, 'New International Law: Silence, Defence or Deliverance?' (1996) 7 *European Journal of International Law* 1–28. See also, Outi Korhonen, *International Law Situated: An Analysis of the Lawyer's Stance Towards Culture, History and Community* (Kluwer Law International 2000).
29 ibid 5.
30 ibid 14.
31 Andrea Leiter, 'Review Essay: Is International Law International? by Anthea Roberts' (2018) 19 *Melbourne Journal of International Law* 413–422, 421.
32 Jean d'Aspremont, *Epistemic Forces in International Law* (Edward Elgar 2015) 6–9.

constraint towards fundamental doctrines, and therefore, they do not wish to recognise due to the fear of exposing themselves to charges of arbitrariness, naïve objectivism or dogmatism.[33] One of the main functions of the international belief system is to provide 'a comfort zone where international lawyers can afford debating about the content of the fundamental doctrine without having to inquire about the foundations of their fundamental doctrines'.[34] Having revealed the entire structure of the belief system, d'Aspremont ambitiously persuades international lawyers to 'temporarily suspend' the *illusion* to allow them engage in an exercise of 'unlearning' the understanding of the fundamental doctrines that they have been trained to continuously reproduce and respond to.[35]

Although the potential of suspending the belief system of international law remains unexplained by d'Aspremont, such an ambition can be more profoundly explicated in terms of phenomenological reduction. In contrast to positivist reduction, phenomenology requires an attempt of suspending judgments; i.e. an *epoché*, based on the objective validity of the truth, would establish the ultimate ground for realities. In his early masterpiece, *Ideas toward a Pure Phenomenology*, Edmund Husserl once adopted the so-called 'Cartesian way' that leads to the 'transcendental ego' in one leap, which has been severely criticised as solipsism.[36] In fact, as explained by Husserl in his last lecture, *Crisis*, the Cartesian *epoché* has a major shortcoming – 'it brings this ego into view as apparently empty of content, since there can be no preparatory explication'.[37] The new way that Husserl attempts to open up in *Crisis* tends to withhold the natural, naïve validities that are already in effect – 'an *epoché* of all participation in the cognitions of the objective sciences and *an epoché* of any critical position-taking which is interested in their truth or falsity, even any position on their guiding idea of an objective knowledge of the world'.[38]

Anthony Carty, one of the influential advocates of international legal phenomenology, advocates that the positive dimension of the phenomenological approach to international law aims to provide a pathway to the 'de-objectification' of an entity through understanding the self-embedded in

33 Jean d'Aspremont, *International Law as a Belief System* (Cambridge University Press 2017) 47–54.

34 ibid 94.

35 ibid Chap 5.

36 Hua VI 156–158.

37 ibid.

38 Hua VI 138–140.

relationship with others, namely, through the notion of 'intersubjectivity'.[39] In their insightful co-authored paper, Anthony Carty and Anna Irene Baka adopt the transcendental phenomenological method to 'expose the primordial empirical data that had given rise to the concept of international law in general and the idea of the sources of international law in particular'.[40] To return to the lifeworld of international lawyers, Carty and Baka explain that *phenomenological reduction* inspires their decision 'to revisit the whole dimension of legal modernity in a rethink of' the theories of international law.[41]

3 'The Gaze to the Beauty of the World'

3.1 *Relative Aesthetics of International Lawyers with the Lifeworld*

The purpose of phenomenological reduction (*epoché*) is to return from the objective world to the so-called *lifeworld* – i.e. the world that is always already there (*immer schon da*) as the ground (*Boden*) where we live under the practical interest of daily life.[42] In contrast to the objective and true world as a theoretical-logical substruction, the subjective-relative lifeworld is *actually perceivable and experienceable*.[43] Ulrich Claesges sharply discerns the ambiguous aspects of the lifeworld: the return to lifeworld through phenomenological reduction contributes to both to *diagnosing* the dangerous situation of academics and to *therapeutically* treating such an academic crisis. Differently put, this implies that the diagnostic function reveals the *ground* that objective sciences have sweep in oblivion (*Boden-Funktion*), whereas the therapeutic function remedies the crisis of academics by *giving guidance* to transcendental phenomenology (*Leitfaden-Funktion*).[44]

According to Husserl, *Lebenswelt* is 'concerned with the disparaged *δόξᾰ* [*doxa*], which now suddenly claims the dignity of a foundation for science, *ἐπιστήμη* [*episteme*]'.[45] Admittedly, for scientists in orientation towards the

39 Anthony Carty, 'Scandinavian Realism and Phenomenological Approaches to Statehood and General Custom in International Law' (2003) 14 *European Journal of International Law* 817–841, 820.

40 Carty and Baka (n 9) 258.

41 ibid. 248.

42 Hua VI 145–146.

43 ibid 130–132.

44 Ulrich Claesges. 'Zweideutigkeiten in Husserls Lebenswelt-Begriff' in Ulrich Claesges and Klaus Held (ed), *Phaenomenologica Perspektiven transzendental-phänomenologischer Forschung, für Ludwig Landgrebe zum 70. Geburtstag von seiner Kölner Schülern* (Martinus Nijhoff 1972) 85–101.

45 Hua VI 158–159.

objective truth, the lifeworld bears a mere subjective-relative stamp that entails the disdainful colouring of *doxa* supposed to be overcome.[46] However, the subjective-relative world with life is still functioning even for such objectivist scientists – 'not as something irrelevant that must be passed through, but as that which ultimately grounds the theoretical-logical ontic validity for all objective verification'.[47] In other words, 'no conceivable human being, no matter how different we imagine him to be, could ever experience a world in manners of givenness that differ from the incessantly mobile relativity'.[48] The world of human life, which as a matter takes up into itself all practical structures, is therefore related to subjectivity throughout the constant alteration of its relative aspects.[49]

In the introduction of *From Apology to Utopia*, Koskenniemi opines that the language of international law 'conveys to us a certain interpretation of the social reality to which it is addressed, under the veil of objectivity or naturalness' and 'opens up a possibility for alternative descriptive – and simultaneously normative – characterizations of the world in which States live'.[50] By providing an insider's view to legal discourse, such an approach might produce a 'therapeutic effect' on lawyers frustrated with their inability to cope with the indeterminacy of theory and the irrelevance of doctrine.[51] Therefore, the therapeutic epistemology guided by ethics is concerned about '[t]he problem of what a lawyer should do in an inherently conflictual reality of international life' or 'whether and how one can *live* in and through [international law]'.[52] As a more direct mention to phenomenology, Koskenniemi attempts to cancel the objective way of thinking and reveal the 'sensibilities' of international lawyers – in *The Gentle Civilizer of Nations* – as follows: 'Like any social phenomenon, international law is a complex set of practices and ideas, as well as interpretations of those practices and ideas, and the way we engage in them or interpret them cannot be dissociated from the larger professional, academic or political projects we have. [...] International law is also a terrain of fear and

46 ibid 126–129.

47 ibid.

48 ibid 168–170.

49 ibid 173–176.

50 Koskenniemi (n 8) 13.

51 ibid. For an examination of the therapeutic effect in terms of the links between Koskenniemi and French psychoanalyst Jacques Lacan, Matthew Nicholson, 'Psychoanalyzing International Law(yers)' (2019) 18 *German Law Journal* 451–510.

52 ibid 548.

ambition, fantasy and desire, conflict and utopia and a host of other aspects of "the *phenomenological* lives of its practitioners".[53]

In a similar vein, Jean d'Aspremont and Sahib Singh, by referring to Martin Heidegger's phenomenology and hermeneutics, deeply delve into the surface of the indissociability that 'conceptual worlds are pre-reflectively disclosed to us through international law's pre-existing concepts and categories, and only then are these worlds reflectively disclosed *through* us'.[54] In other words, '[h]ow we today live in, see, understand, think about and know international law through its concepts has been constantly reoriented and transformed on the shifting and entwined terrains of *aesthetics*, politics and ethics'.[55] They argue that aesthetics, as one of these terrains, 'not only moulds the work of the various scholars, but also shapes our contemporary sensibilities (in their living, seeing, understanding and reflective thinking and knowing).[56] International lawyers unconsciously tend to find and direct legal concepts through the lens of a given and accepted aesthetic and, as an undesirable result, develop a particular fetish in their disciplinary silos.[57]

Only a few exceptional works, especially those focusing on the relationship between literature and law, prove the actual relevance of *aesthetics* in international legal discourse. Ed Morgan's *The Aesthetics of International Law*, which is one of such rare *oeuvres*, illustrates the fact that legal texts 'must be read as a fantasized work of art, while literature can be read as a straightforward, explanatory guide to the law'.[58] Morgan uses the analogy of 'a hall of mirrors effect' to explain his study, and he admits that through its seemingly exhaustive repetition, international law is effectively replenished.[59] From the aesthetics perspective, literature tends to remind us that international law cannot be elaborated without context and historical background; therefore, it must be

53 Martti Koskenniemi, *The Gentle Civilizer of Nations: The Rise and Fall of International Law 1870–1960* (Cambridge University Press 2001) 7 [emphasis added].

54 Jean d'Aspremont and Sahib Singh, 'Introduction: Concepts for International Law: Contributions to Disciplinary Thought' in Jean d'Aspremont and Sahib Singh (eds), *Concepts for International Law: Contributions to Disciplinary Thought* (Edward Elgar 2019) 1–24, 16.

55 ibid 19–20 [emphasis omitted].

56 ibid.

57 ibid.

58 Ed Morgan, *The Aesthetics of International Law* (University of Toronto Press 2007), 5. See also Ed Morgan, 'Yom Kippur in Hell: The Empty Life of International Law' in Russell A Miller and Rebecca M Bratspies (eds), *Progress in International Law* (Martinus Nijhoff Publishers 2008) 119–131.

59 ibid 6.

situated within human conditions.[60] In this sense, Nicolas Bourriaud's concept of *relational aesthetics*, which regards the artwork as a 'social interstice',[61] may also be transplanted to the field of international law. Based on this idea, critical lawyers and activist artists can be involved in solving the same problem and come up with common solutions to facilitate respectful encounters and encourage self-reflective ways of being together.[62]

3.2 *Lived Bodies of International Lawyers in Passivity*

In phenomenology, the constitution of space and time implies the presence of various bodily predispositions experienced in the *aesthetic* forms of *sensibility*. In his early lecture, titled *Thing and Space*, Husserl differentiates the aspect of a lived, sensing and moving body (*Leib*) from the aspect of a physical body (*Körper*): 'On the one hand, the lived body is a thing as well as a physical thing as other things. [...] It is a thing midst other things. On the other hand, this thing is just a lived body, the bearer of I. [...] The constitution of physical things is intertwined with the constitution of my lived body (*Ichleib*) in a strange correlation'.[63] Given this distinction, my lived body is not a simple thing among other things; instead, it is an organ of *kinaesthetical* senses with which I can see, hear, feel, smell, go and move.[64] The term *Kinästhese* here is an important coinage by Husserl, and it is composed of Greek notions of 'movement' (*kinesis, κίνησις*) and 'sense' (*aesthesis, αἴσθησις*). It is not an empty logical possibility; it is the capability (*Vermöglichkeit*) motivated by 'I can go' with my kinaesthetic lived body, which accompanies the horizon as a playing space (*Spielraum*) of the possible and physical experience.[65]

It is particularly important to note that such a kinaesthetic experience is a result of *passive synthesis* as opposed to the activity of ego. In *Analyses Concerning Passive and Active Synthesis*, Husserl sailed to an uncharted 'sphere of experience in which the "ego" is not active, i.e., does not creatively participate or actively orient itself in the constitution of sense'.[66] The notion of

---

60 Andrea Bianchi, *International Law Theories: An Inquiry into Different Ways of Thinking* (Oxford University Press 2016) (Chapter 14: Law and Literature) 287–310.

61 Nicolas Bourriaud, *Relational Aesthetics* (Les Presse Du Reel 1998) 45.

62 Peter Goodrich, 'On the Relational Aesthetics of International Law' (2008) 10 *Journal of the History of International Law* 321–341, 341.

63 Hua XVI: *Ding und Raum: Vorlesungen 1907* (Nijhoff 1973) 162.

64 ibid 158.

65 Shinji Hamauzu, 'On Dis/Ability in Husserl's Phenomenology' (2017) 19 Clinical Philosophy 79–94, 86–87.

66 Anthony Steinbock, 'Translator's Introduction' in Edmund Husserl, *Analyses Concerning Passive and Active Synthesis: Lectures on Transcendental Logic* (Springer 2001) xxxviii–xliii.

passivity therein is basically equivalent to *perceptual, pre-predicative, pre-reflective and pre-linguistic* experiences while active processes denote making judgments, predicating something of an object, reflection and linguistic acts.[67] The Husserlian formula of passive synthesis challenges the Kantian schism between sensibility and understanding. For Kant, while understanding (*Verstand*) has the spontaneous character of *active synthesis* that holds together and connects the sensuous manifold according to rules, sensibility (*Sinnlichkeit*) has the character of passivity that the inner and outer senses merely receive sense data.[68] From this Kantian perspective, pre-meaningful accomplishments of sensibility are understood to constitute objects of knowledge.[69] In contrast, Husserl's formula of passive synthesis suggests that the origin of meaning must be sought in the sphere of aesthesis (passivity) as the foundation for logos (activity).[70]

Just a few contributions in the existing literature discern the passive synthesis of corporeal sensibility in the actual practices of international dispute settlement.[71] Thomas Schultz and François Ost, who edited the symposium *Shakespeare and International Dispute Settlement,* get a hint for an aesthetical form of international law from the ritual role of *masques* (or *persona* in Greek) that assign roles in theatre and relate to *the desire* 'to be perceived in a certain way, to be respected and obeyed'.[72] The masquerade of international law helps translate the story of death-seeking passions into logics of life that are easy to deal with rationally – the translation in which 'law is there to regulate desire and, regulating it [...] arouses desire'.[73] In a similar way, Marina Aksenova aesthetically characterises the process of international adjudication as a form of ritual that matters not only the material result of the work of international courts, such as textual judgment or legal procedure, but also the process through which this outcome is achieved.[74] Emphasis is put on the ritual

67 ibid.

68 ibid.

69 ibid.

70 ibid.

71 Mary Ellen O'Connell, *The Art of Law in the International Community* (Cambridge University Press 2020).

72 Thomas Schultz and François Ost, 'Shakespearean Legal Thought in International Dispute Settlement' (2018) 9 *Journal of International Dispute Settlement* 1–27, 18. Remarkably, they also note in this context that '[p]henomenologists would probably concur: we have no direct access to reality; reality always comes masked; law is one such mask'.

73 ibid 19.

74 Marina Aksenova, 'Introduction to the Symposium on Art, Aesthetics, and International Courts' (2020) 114 *AJIL Unbound* 103–107, 105.

details, including the robes worn by international judges, rhetoric adopted by the parties, layout of the courtroom and architecture of an international court such as stained glass, gavel, screen and so on – all of which 'contribute to the perception of international justice by those intimately involved with it and also by those following its developments from the "outside"'.[75]

The difference between passive and active syntheses can also be used to explain the mysterious relationship between preambles and main texts of treaties. According to Article 31(2) of the Vienna Convention on the Law of Treaties, the *context* for the purpose of interpretation of a treaty shall comprise, in addition to the text, its preamble and annexes. Having reviewed a wide variety of treaties, Jan Klabbers points out that over the years, it became customary for treaty preambles to add a list of *desiderata* (wishes and hopes), in combination with a *testimonium* (names and positions), of contracting parties.[76] In fact, texts from the preambles of various international legal documents show how the sorrow from the scourges of war and how the shock of human conscience from crimes against humanity led states to adopt international treaties and conventions that are the core of international law.[77] As a representative example, the formula of 'conscience of humanity', which evokes the 'dictates of public conscience' and the 'laws of humanity' enshrined by the Martens Clause, has been the primary foundation for developing human-centred fields of international law.[78]

4 'Beyond <the Beauty for Myself>'

4.1 *Universal Correlation of International Lawyers with Lifeworld*

Although phenomenological reduction leads us to the relative-subjective sphere of *doxa*, the lifeworld still retains the *universality* to seek a new type of

75 ibid. Daniel Litwin, 'Stained Glass Windows, Peace Palace, the Hague' in Jessie Hohmann and Daniel Joyce (eds), *International Law's Objects* (Oxford University Press 2018) 463–477; James Parker, 'Gavel' in ibid 214–224; Christine Schwobel-Patel and Wouter Werner, 'Screen' in ibid 419–430.

76 Jan Klabbers, 'Treaties and Their Preambles' in Michael J. Bowman and Dino Kritsiotis (eds), *Conceptual and Contextual Perspectives on the Modern Law of Treaties* (Cambridge University Press 2018) 172–200, 176–182.

77 Vesselin Popovski, 'Emotions and International Law' in Yohan Ariffin, Jean-Marc Coicaud and Vesselin Popovski (eds), *Emotions in International Politics: Beyond Mainstream International Relations* (Cambridge University Press 2016) 184–203, 196.

78 Margaret deGuzman, *Shocking the Conscience of Humanity: Gravity and the Legitimacy of International Criminal Law* (Oxford University Press 2020).

episteme. Husserl notes that 'the lifeworld does have, in all its relative features, a universal structure [...] to which everything that exists relatively is *bound*'.[79] Put differently, however the lifeworld changes or is altered, it still holds to its essentially lawful set of types, 'to which all life, and thus all science, of which it is the "ground," remain *bound*'.[80] The identical world of life 'constituted throughout all its relative aspects as a unity' serves as 'an intentional index for the multiplicities of appearance' through which all subjects are oriented towards a common world and the things in it.[81]

The universal *a priori* of the lifeworld is explained using the universal *a priori* correlation of *intentionality*, without which the objects and the world would not be there for us; instead, they 'exist for us only with the meaning and the mode of being that they receive in constantly arising or having arisen out of those subjective accomplishments'.[82] Therefore, the universal and invariant correlation of the lifeworld and intentionality enables us to navigate between the Scylla of psychologism and the Charibdis of logicism.[83] Husserl was originally concerned with the level of *static phenomenology* and the most general, *a priori* background presuppositions of an intentional experience – the sense-giving side of intentionality (*noesis*) animates the sensory component of a perception (*hyle*) as a phenomenon of the objective-sense (*noema*) relating to an object.[84] At this stage, intentionality was simply understood as the unique characteristic of experience to be consciousness of something (*Bewußtsein von etwas*).[85]

---

79 Hua VI 142.
80 ibid 176.
81 ibid 173–177.
82 Translation 159–160.
83 Frank M Kirkland, 'Immanuel Kant' in Lester Embree (ed), *Encyclopedia of Phenomenology* (Springer, 2013) 377–381. See also, Maurice Merleau-Ponty, 'Phenomenology and the Science of Man' in *The Primacy of Perception: And Other Essays on Phenomenological Psychology, the Philosophy of Art, History, and Politics*, translated by William Cobb and edited by James Edie (Northwestern University Press, 1964) 55–56 ('always between the Scylla of psychologism and the Charybdis of logicism that Husserl steers his course.'); Jacques Derrida, *Writing and Difference*, translated by Alan Bass (University of Chicago Press, 1978) 158 (Husserl 'had to navigate between the Scylla and Charybdis of logicizing structuralism and psychologistic genetism (even in the subtle and pernicious form of the "transcendental psychologism" attributed to Kant).').
84 For the concept of intentionality, see in general Ronald McIntyre and David Woodruff Smith, 'Theory of Intentionality' in Jitendranath N Mohanty and William R McKenna (eds), *Husserl's Phenomenology: A Textbook* (Center for Advanced Research in Phenomenology and University Press of America 1989) 87–152.
85 Hua III/1: *Ideen zu einer reinen Phänomenologie und phänomenologischen Philosophie: Ergänzende Texte (1912–1929)* (Nijhoff 1976) 188.

However, the analysis of intentional synthesis was enlarged to the sphere of *genetic phenomenology* that uncovers the temporal becoming and the temporal relationship of one experience to the next, thereby revealing a 'temporal depth' of any experience, which cannot be achieved through static analysis.[86] In developing the ontology of the lifeworld in *Crisis*, Husserl emphasises that every perception has a *horizon* belonging to its object: '[i]n seeing I always "mean" it with all the sides which are in no way given to me, *not even in the form of intuitive, anticipatory presentifications* [*Vergegenwärtigung*]'.[87] As regards the constitution of *time*, perception is only related to the living present [*lebendige Gegenwart*], which always has an endless past behind it [*Retention*] and an open future before it [*Protention*].[88] As regard the constitution of *space*, an individual thing in perception not only has an internal horizon [*Innenhorizont*] such as what is actually perceived, but also an external horizon [*Außenhorizont*].[89]

The phenomenological correlative principles seem to amplify the idea of *international legal intentionality*, which is implied in a few critical legal writings.[90] Gleider Hernández illustrates the *co-constitutive* process in which international law is simultaneously constituted by and constitutes the community of international lawyers 'who come to create, interpret and render operative the international law with which they engage in their professional practice'.[91] He further opines that 'certain argumentative rules pervade the international legal discipline, thus generating background ideas that come to constitute, or at least structure, the professional vocabularies of all international lawyers'.[92] Such a correlational constitution between international law and individual lawyers is articulated in a different way by Jessie Hohmann, who asserts that '[i]nternational law does not have *a* "life" as a singular entity'; instead, it 'has thousands of lives in that it interacts in myriad ways with countless individuals

86 Janet Donohoe, *Husserl on Ethics and Intersubjectivity: From Static and Genetic Phenomenology* (University of Toronto Press 2016) 30–37.

87 Hua VI 159–161 [emphasis added].

88 ibid 161–163.

89 Ibid 163–167.

90 In the field of legal philosophy, Hans Lindahl follows Husserl in inventing the correlative concept of *legal intentionality*. See Hans Lindahl, *Fault Lines of Globalization: Legal Order and the Politics of A-Legality* (Oxford University Press 2013) Chap 4.

91 Gleider I Hernández, 'The Responsibility of the International Legal Academic: Situating the Grammarian within the "Invisible College"' in Jean d'Aspremont, Tarcisio Gazzini, André Nollkaemper and Wouter Werner (eds), *International Law as a Profession* (Cambridge University Press 2017) 166–188, 170.

92 ibid.

across time and in multiple geographic locations'.[93] If we recognise the millions of different lives of international law created through their interactions with individual actors, as Hohmann argues, '[a]ttempting to write *the* life of international law would be both an impossible task as a matter of practice, and a monumental exercise of ego'.[94]

Since the phenomenological correlation was introduced to steer channel between Scylla and Charybdis, international legal intentionality requires us to pass the narrow cognitive channel between subjectivist psychologism and objectivist logicism. Scandinavian legal realists appear to absorb the will in the subjective emotions; i.e. the psyche in the body, for which everything is reducible to subjective emotions acquired through upbringing and rationalised as tradition and brute prejudice.[95] In contrast, as Anthony Carty notes, phenomenology envisaging an *intersubjective* human order restores the unitary movement of the voluntary and the involuntary in that 'the emotions only take on sense in relation to a will which they solicit, while the will takes on these senses even if only by its resignation'.[96] By rejecting the Hobbesian order oscillating between the fear and security in which the individual is comprehended inters of interests and alienation, international legal phenomenology explores the possibility of a theory of international law founded in a 'vocabulary of alterity' and a political community unified by a definitional association of the self and the other.[97]

4.2 *Intercorporeal Pairing of International Lawyers in Alterity*

The phenomenological concept of intentionality illuminates the universal correlation between lived bodies of the self and *others*. In this regard, the differentiation of a lived body (*Leib*) from a physical body (*Körper*), which Husserl introduced, was radicalised by himself to an in-between-body phenomenon in *Ideen II*: 'But by touching the left hand [by right hand], I find there a series of senses of touch which are localized there. [...] If I speak of physical thing "left hand", I ignore these senses. [...] If I add them to it, the physical thing doesn't

93 Jessie Hohmann, 'The Lives of Objects' in Jessie Hohmann and Daniel Joyce (eds), *International Law's Objects* (Oxford University Press 2018) 30–46, 34.

94 ibid.

95 For a comparison of Scandinavian realism with other strands of realism, see Peter G Staubach, *The Rule of Unwritten International Law: Customary Law, General Principles, and World Order* (Routledge 2018) 40–45.

96 Carty (n 39) 840.

97 Geoff Gordon, 'Natural Law in International Legal Theory: Linear and Dialectical Presentations' in Anne Orford, Florian Hoffmann and Martin Clark (eds), *The Oxford Handbook of the Theory of International Law* (Oxford University Press, 2016) 279–305.

get rich, but *it becomes a lived body, it senses*'.[98] In a later stage, Husserl developed the concept of *pairing* (*Paarung*) of *my* lived body and *other* lived body in the *Cartesian Meditations*. Pairing has the character of *association*, a primal form of passive synthesis, in that 'we find essentially present here an intentional overreaching, coming about *genetically* (and by essential necessity) as soon as the data that undergo pairing have become prominent and simultaneously intended. More particularly, we find a living mutual awakening and an overlaying of each with the objective sense of the other'.[99]

Husserl's account on the passive synthesis of corporeal intentionality was inherited by a great French phenomenologist, Maurice Merleau-Ponty. The fact that the above-cited passage in *Ideen II* was caught by the eyes of Merleau-Ponty when he visited Husserl-Archives at Louvain is a famous story. In his essay, titled *Le philosophe et son ombre*, Merleau-Ponty literally follows the shadow of Husserl: 'My two hands "coexist" or are "compresent" because they are one single body's hands. The other person appears through an extension of that compresence; he and I are like organs of one single *intercorporeality*'.[100] In his Sorbonne lecture, *Les relations avec autrui chez l'enfant*, Merleau-Ponty translates the Husserlian *Paarung* into *phénomène d'accouplement*: 'It is this transfer of my intentions to the other's body and of his intentions to my own, my alienation of the other and his alienation of me, that makes possible the perception of others'.[101] Merleau-Ponty's *intercorporéité* leads Thomas Fuchs to develop the notion of *embodied interaffectivity*: 'in every face-to-face encounter, the partners' subject-bodies are intertwined in a process of bodily resonance, coordinated interaction and "mutual incorporation", which provides the basis for an intuitive empathic understanding'.[102]

98 Hua IV 145 [emphasis added].

99 Translation 112–113 [emphasis added].

100 Maurice Merleau-Ponty, 'Le philosophe et son ombre' in *Signes* (Gallimard 1960) 201–228, 212–213; 'The Philosopher and His Shadow' in Maurice Merleau-Ponty (translated by Richard McCleary), *Sign* (Northwestern University Press 1964) 159–181, 168 [emphasis added]. See also, Scott L. Marratto, *The Intercorporeal Self: Merleau-Ponty on Subjectivity* (SUNY Press 2012).

101 Maurice Merleau-Ponty, 'The Child's Relations with Others' (translated by William Cobb), in Maurice Merleau-Ponty (edited by James M Edie), *The Primacy of Perception and Other Essays on Phenomenological Psychology, the Philosophy of Art, History and Politics* (Northwestern University Press 1964), 96–155, 118. «C'est ce transfert de mes intentions dans le corps d'autrui et des intentions d'autrui dans mon propre corps, cette aliénation d'autrui par moi et de moi par autrui qui rend possible la perception d'autrui».

102 Thomas Fuchs, 'Intercorporeality and Interaffectivity' in Christian Meyer, Jürgen Streeck and J Scott Jordan (eds), *Intercorporeality: Emerging Socialities in Interaction* (Oxford University Press 2017) 3–24, 4. See also, Shogo Tanaka, 'Intercorporeality and Aida: Developing an Interaction Theory of Social Cognition' (2017) 25 *Theory & Psychology*

These phenomenological insights of intercorporeality shed light on the *intersubjective* correlation of bodily sensibilities among international lawyers facing others. Referring to Koskenniemi's focus on the professional sensibilities of international lawyers, Andrew Lang and Susan Marks explain that such a sensibility is not just a subjective characteristic of particular individuals; instead, it evokes the practical consciousness of agents in dynamic interactions with others.[103] Put differently, the professional sensibilities of international lawyers are fostered through 'the complicated relationship between the projects of individuals and their simultaneous participation in the dynamic, multiple, and contested collective endeavor'.[104]

The phenomenological intercorporeality of international lawyers is particularly influenced by their *visual sensibility* or, in Professor Mogami's words, 'The Gaze to the Beauty of the World'.[105] It is interesting to note that Merleau-Ponty borrows a reflection by an artist named André Marchand to grasp the inevitable phenomenon of roles switching between the painter and the visible: '[t]here really is inspiration and expiration of Being, respiration in Being, action and passion so slightly discernible that it becomes impossible to distinguish between who sees and who is seen, who paints and what is painted'.[106] Moreover, international law is often visualised by international actors 'with a strong interest in controlling how it is portrayed worldwide and in reaching out to both people and (i.e. print, broadcasting, online, etc.) journalists'.[107] Movies

455–472 (referring to what Bin Kimura, Japanese phenomenological psychiatrist, calls '*aida*' (and '*ma*' as its auto-productive function, both of which are interestingly spelled by the same Chinese character '間')).

103 Andrew Lang and Susan Marks, 'People with Projects: Writing the Lives of International Lawyers' (2013) 27 *Temple International & Comparative Law Journal* 437–453; Andrew Lang and Susan Marks, 'Even the Dead Will Not Be Safe International Law and the Struggle over Tradition' in Wouter Werner, Marieke de Hoon and Alexis Galán (eds), *The Law of International Lawyers: Reading Martti Koskenniemi* (Cambridge University Press 2017) 321–339.

104 ibid [emphasis in the original text].

105 Costas Douzinas, 'A Legal Phenomenology of Images' in Oren Ben-Dor (ed), *Law and Art: Justice, Ethics and Aesthetics* (Routledge 2011) 247–258. For a critical position on phenomenological approach to aesthetics, see Andreas Philippopoulos-Mihalopoulos, 'Law Is a Stage: From Aesthetics to Affective Aestheses' in Emilios Christodoulidis, Ruth Dukes and Marco Goldoni (eds), *Research Handbook on Critical Legal Theory* (Edward Elgar 2019) 201–222.

106 Merleau-Ponty, *L'Œil et l'Esprit* (Gallimard 1964) 31–32; 'Eye and Mind' in Maurice Merleau-Ponty (ed. with an introduction by James M. Edie), The Primacy of Perception. Evanston (Northwestern University Press 1964) 159–190, 167.

107 Carlo Focarelli, *International Law as Social Construct: The Struggle for Global Justice* (Oxford University Press 2012) 138–139.

and photos reawaken the clichés of international legal publishing by literalising them and inviting attention to the material realities behind them.[108] To give an example of visual sensibility, the power of image in the context of international criminal justice not only relates to private and individual emotions but also to public and collective emotions, thus forming affective landscapes that shift with changing social and political conditions.[109] NGOs and other human rights collectives have sought to develop best practices and standards for visual documentation and investigation to facilitate a better interaction with institutional organisations where visual information is acquiring new levels of legitimacy.[110]

To invigorate the sensibilities of international lawyers, aesthetical imagination beyond reality should be cultivated in their phenomenological lives. In this respect, Gerry Simpson warns against melodramatic or operatic international law that is associated with sentimental failures such as sentimental excess, moral simplicity, solipsism and de-politicisation.[111] Simpson instead proposes *poetic* international law that might 'involve an attentiveness to the unseen and unheard or, seemingly, insubstantial or a commitment to an international law of style, love and smallness and an attentiveness to the everyday informalities of power'.[112] Likewise, Isobel Roele, while acknowledging how difficult it is for international lawyers to swallow unprofessional and unintellectual emotion, demands the imaginary room for their maturational process.[113] More precisely, international law as 'a beleaguered discipline that suffers constant defeat in

108 Karen Knop and Susan Marks, 'The War against Cliché: Dispatches from the International Legal Front' in Christine Chinkin and Freya Baetens (eds), *Sovereignty, Statehood and State Responsibiilty: Essays in Honour of James Crawford* (Cambridge University Press 2015) 3–22, 20–21 [emphasis added].

109 Immi Tallgren, 'Come and See? The Power of Images and International Criminal Justice' (2017) 17 *International Criminal Law Review* 259–280. See also, Carsten Stahn, *Justice As Message: Expressivist Foundations of International Criminal Justice* (Oxford University Press, 2020); Kamari Maxine Clarke, *Affective Justice: The International Criminal Court and the Pan-Africanist Pushback* (Duke University Press 2019).

110 See the examples examined in the Special issue: The Visual Politics of the Human (2019) 18 *Visual Communication.* See also, Robin Adele Greeley and Michael R Orwicz, 'An aesthetics of the human: Peru's Ojo que Llora memorial; Maria Elander, 'Visualizing Law and Justice at the Extraordinary Chambers in the Courts of Cambodia' (2020) 114 *AJIL Unbound* 128–132.

111 Gerry Simpson, 'The Sentimental Life of International Law' (2015) 3 *London Review of International Law* 3–29, 16–25.

112 ibid 28.

113 Isobel Roele, 'The Making of International Lawyers: Winnicott's Transitional Objects' in Jessie Hohmann and Daniel Joyce (eds), *International Law's Objects* (Oxford University Press 2018) 72–91, 83–85.

the outside world' can function as a transitional, *revelatory space* for international lawyers swaying between their private fantasies and the public space in the real world.[114]

From the oscillation between fantasy and reality, it is clear that international lawyers are never abstractly rationalised individuals who are covered with a 'garb of ideas'; instead, they are anytime and anywhere persons in the process of *becoming* international lawyers who are compresent with others in intercorpoeral lives. In developing a phenomenological account of law and lawyering, Julian Webb points out that the 'encounter' between lawyers and clients does not begin with a written legal text, but rather an unwritten, face-to-face 'conversation' in which the emerging relationship has a set of affective components.[115] Webb argues that if we reflect on the complex pattern of encounters, we may be struck by how much is going on and how far the representations of law and lawyering tend to fall short of capuring the thickness of that reality.[116] In a similar vein, Sahib Singh discerns from Koskenniemi's thesis of phenomenological lives – that there is a universal correlation in which an individual international lawyer is shaped and constituted in the 'face-to-face' level by the discipline's *background,* including historical practices, attitudes, habits and emotional dispositions (or *horizon* in the phenomenological term); more importantly, this is his means of entering into the world of international law as a shared enterprise.[117] Instead, he draws an interpretation that international lawyers are always in the *process of becoming* because their images are shaped through their interaction with the multiple other images of the international lawyers within the discipline.[118]

5 Conclusion

This chapter drew an inspiration from Professor Mogami's phenomenological intuition of international law as described in his essay *In This Corner of the*

114 ibid.

115 Julian Webb, 'On Encountering Life and Learning With/out the Text: Reflections on Bańkowski and Del Mar' in Zenon Bańkowski and Maksymilian Del Mar (eds), *The Moral Imagination and the Legal Life: Beyond Text in Legal Education* (Ashgate 2016) 65–84. See also, James R. Elkins, 'Becoming a Lawyer: The Transformation of Self During Legal Education' (1983) 66 *Soundings: An Interdisciplinary Journal* 450–468.

116 ibid.

117 Sahib Singh, 'Koskenniemi's Images of the International Lawyer' (2016) 29 *Leiden Journal of International Law* 699–726, 717–718.

118 ibid.

Beautiful World. The first section introduced the concept of phenomenological reduction as an attempt to heighten sensibility to the lives of people '*behind academic paradigms and objective concepts*' and invite international lawyers to their lifeworld upon which the scientific field rests (2). The second section then gave a phenomenological account that international lawyers situated in their lifeworld cast – '*the gaze to <the beauty of the world>*' – as a kinaesthetic perception in the passive sphere of aesthesis as the foundational for logical activities (3). The third section finally demonstrated the embodied intentionality, namely, the intercorporeality of international lawyers with the lived bodies of others through which the aesthetic sensibilities of international lawyers are correlated '*beyond <the beauty of the world for me>*' (4). Through this phenomenological lens, international lawyers tear off the rational garb of ideas and regain their lived bodies whose aesthetical sensibility is passively synthesised with those of others. Professor Mogami's yet-to-be-completed thesis, *A Social Science Sensibility Based on Empathy with Others*, is left to the coming generation to be accomplished.

> As the poetry of Hiroshi Osada spouts: *'Are on earth the daily debris called news like our history?' The reality is filled with barrenness to say the least.* (I) But as such, other way round, following the poet, *'Let's say beautiful things are beautiful'. 'There is nothing forever, and someday everything is turned into dust, so the world is beautiful'.* (II)
>
> By saying so, however, we have no need to step backward to the denial of universality. *There still remains the task to elevate <the beauty for each and every person> to <the beauty of the world>.*(III) It would be assuredly difficult to weave society in a harmonious way. But as a social scientist we cannot stay depressed.[119]

119 Mogami (n 4) 27.

CHAPTER 2

For Belated Justice in International Law: Righting Historical Wrongs in East Asia

Kohki Abe

1 Introduction: Setting the Scene

The issue of reparation for past injustices has gained momentum since the 1980s as if it is an underground stem stretching throughout the world. Brought into the public arena are people's memories forcibly silenced by the dominant legal and political discourse. The initial driving force behind the momentum was an institutional response to grave human rights violations in the immediate past in the name of 'transnational justice'. It is widely known that a comprehensive framework for truth, justice, reparation and non-recurrence has been rapidly developed after the model pioneered in Latin American countries in their transitions away from authoritarian rules.[1]

The emerging endeavor, however, extends far beyond the range of immediate past of transitional justice and attempts to go back several decades even to the colonial and imperial period of time. It is no more an exception in the international relations to hear a call demanding that grave historical wrongs falling upon individuals and groups in the remote past should be legally rectified.[2] Claims for historical injustices may be rephrased as a demand for 'belated justice' as opposed to transitional justice.[3] What comes to the foreground in

1 Report of the Special Rapporteur on the promotion of truth, justice, reparation and guarantees of non-recurrence on his global study on transitional justice, A/HRC/36/50/Add.1, 7 August 2017, para 5.

2 For an overview of reparation schemes, Eric A Posner and Adrian Vermeule, 'Reparations for Slavery and Other Historical Injustices' (2003) 103 *Colombia Law Review* 689–747, 696–697. Shelton classifies historical injustice claims into five categories (wartime violations, discrimination against minorities, colonialism, indigenous peoples, and slave reparations). Dinah Shelton, *Remedies in International Human Rights Law* (2nd ed, Oxford University Press 2005) 428–446.

3 The phrase 'belated justice' is employed in this essay to distinguish the context of historical injustice from that of transitional justice wherein the expression 'post-transitional justice' is occasionally used. Stiina Löytömaki, *Law and the Politics of Memory: Confronting the Past* (Routledge 2014) 8.

 | DOI:10.1163/9789004681477_004

this connection is the United Nations (UN) World Conference against Racism, Racial Discrimination, Xenophobia and Related Intolerance that took place in August of 2001 in Durban, South Africa.[4] Particularly noteworthy are the outcome documents of its African and Asian preparatory regional meetings wherein States were urged to assume responsibilities and to provide reparations for slavery and alien domination regardless of when they were committed.[5] While due to the strong opposition mainly by the Western States the final declaration of the Durban Conference was not so formulated as to reproduce the critical call for belated justice of the two regional documents,[6] Andreas Buster reminds us that: '[S]everal additional statements were issued by and in the name of more than 50 States which kept with the *opinion juris* that slavery, the slave trade and certain aspects of colonialism were crimes against humanity',[7] an indication that historical injustices would remain a keen issue to be addressed in international society.[8]

John Torpy suggests that the contemporary discussion on reparation politics has been ignited since the collapse of communism and the erosion of the nation-states. The frontiers for forward-looking vision of human coexistence

4 A/CONF.189/12, available at http://wwwun.org/WCAR/. For further details, Marc Bossuyt and Stef Vandeginste, 'The Issue of Reparation for Slavery and Colonialism and the Durban World Conference against Racism' (2001) 22 *Human Rights Law Journal* 341–350; Jose Augusto Lindgren Alves, 'The Durban Conference Against Racism and Everyone's Responsibility' (2003) 21 *Netherlands Quarterly of Human Rights* 361–384. See also, Special Issue: Roundtable on Reparations, *African Studies Quarterly*, Vol. 2, Issue 4 (1999), available at http://www.un.org/WCAR/.

5 A/CONF.189/PC.2/8, para.20; A/CONF.189/PC.2/9, para 50.

6 The final declaration only refers to slavery and slave trade as something that "are a crime against humanity and should always have been so", implying that they were not illegal at the time they were conducted. The declaration, however, acknowledges the grave negative consequences of historical wrongs that have been inflicted upon the Global South. ibid paras 13, 158.

7 Andreas Buster, 'Colonial Injustices and the Law of State Responsibility: The CARICOM Claim to Compensate Slavery and the (Native) Genocide' (2017) 77 *Heidelberg Journal of International Law* 409–446, 413, available at https://www.zaoerv.de/77_2017/vol77.cfm.

8 Surely, this is not an invitation to replace the dominant Western historical narrative with a new post-colonial one as I do agree to the view that "no one today thinks that he or she could produce a new grand narrative of international law which would be objective, entirely neutral, absolute, and universal." Emmanuelle Tourme Jouannet and Anne Peters, 'The Journal of the History of International Law: A Forum for New Research' (2014) 16 *Journal of the History of International Law* 1–8, 5. On the complicated political reality of dealing with historical wrongs in international law, see Corrine Lennox, 'Reviewing Durban: Examining the Outputs and Review of the 2001 World Conference Against Racism' (2009) 27 *Netherlands Quarterly of Human Right* 191–235. Buster thoroughly analyzes the intractable difficulty of making a case in international law for the reparation of slavery and (native) genocide. Buster (n 7) 409–446.

are lost and newly focused is the past that continues to influence the present and establishes the precondition of our future.[9] This is not where to elaborate on Topy's provocative post-utopian arguments, but regardless of how it is reviewed, his work is a typical example which shows that the major intellectual initiative for discussing and hopefully righting the past wrongs has been furnished by such disciplines as sociology, history and politics. On the other hand, not much weight has been placed on international law perspectives in confronting historical wrongs apparently because there is a legal restraint hindering the retroactive application of contemporary standards to the incidents in the distant past as stressed by the Western States in the Durban Conference.[10] Yet, as the issue of reparation keeps popping up here and there and one fundamental function of international law is to change political attitudes of States for the stable future, it is inconceivable that it remains to be sidelined in regard to the issue of rectifying past injustices. As Richard Falk maintains that:

> Throughout the history of international society, the evolution of international law has been closely related to prevailing political currents, evolving moral standards, and dominant trends in religious thought. Such a linkage has been particularly evident in the war/peace context, international law essentially embodying the just war tradition as evolved by theologians, but it is also true with respect to the recent prominence of a global justice agenda in which redress and restitution play such a large part. In one sense the role of international law has been generally

9 John Torpy, *Making Whole What Has Been Smashed: On Reparations Politics* (Harvard University Press 2006).

10 See generally, Max Du Plessis, 'Historical Injustice and International Law: An Exploratory Discussion of Reparation for Slavery' (2003) 25 *Human Rights Quarterly* 624–659. Past injustices were regarded 'as morally problematic, but they did not seem to have any legal significance' (Jeremy Sarkin, *Colonial Genocide and Reparation claims in the 21st Century: The Socio-Legal Context of Claims under International Law by the Herero against Germany for Genocide in Namibia, 1904–1908* (Praeger Security International 2009) 1). The Italian Supreme Court's decision to deny Germany sovereign immunity for serious violations of human rights committed by the German occupying power during World War II was not endorsed by the International Court of Justice. *Jurisdictional Immunity of the State* (*Germany v. Italy: Greece intervening*), Judgment, ICJ Reports 2012, 99. But see Pierfrancesco Rossi, 'Italian courts and the evolution of the law of State Immunity: A reassessment of Judgment no 238/ 2014' (2022) 94 *QIL Zoom-in* 41-57, available at http://www.qil-qdi.org/wp-content/uploads/2022/08/04_Jurisdictional-Immunities-Again_ROSSI_FIN_2.pdf. On the most recent national courts' judgements denying immunity to foreign states for claims based on serious violations of international law, Vessera Terzieva, 'State Immunity and Victims' Rights to Access to Court, Reparation and the Truth' (2022) 22 *International Criminal Law Review* 780-804.

> one of codifying behavioral trends in state practice and shifting political attitudes on the part of governments with the intention of stabilizing and clarifying expectations about the future.[11]

It is encouraging in this context to see the current propensity to turn to history in the discipline of international law. The resurgence of interest for the history of international law has encouraged a renewed way of thinking about international law. As suggested by the editors of the specialist journal on the history of international law: '[T]his return to history, in a world which rejects pre-established truths, means precisely that historians of international law today no longer settle for the classical content of earlier accounts, but look instead to re-work a domain which they deem highly fertile – provided it is renewed. From this point of view, work on the history of international law must be understood as a contribution to international law itself'.[12]

East Asia is no exception to the emerging global calls for righting historical wrongs. Well known worldwide would be the issue of 'comfort women' that is yet to be resolved. Initiated by late Kim Hak Soon and two other Korean women who resolutely filed a civil action against the culpable State of Japan in 1991, a sequence of lawsuits of the same kind were presented to the Japanese domestic courts wherein national and international frontiers on the legality and legitimacy of the military sexual slavery were passionately explored.[13]

The issue of 'comfort women', however, just symbolises the beginning of the age of seeking belated justice in East Asia. Little known among others would be the issue of Ryukyu/Okinawa, a formerly distinctive political entity (now the southernmost prefecture of Japan) that was forcibly incorporated into the Japanese territory in the latter half of 19th Century and has been suffering from the blatant structural discrimination since then. Invoking international law, the local people increasingly urge the Japanese government to face up to the

---

11 Richard Falk, 'Reparations, International Law, and Global Justice: A New Frontier' in Pablo de Greiff (ed), *The Handbook of Reparations* (Oxford University Press 2006) 478–503, 480. Loytomaki also states that: '[H]uman rights law, a discourse of international law *par excellence*, gives voice to those that have been excluded from power'. Loytomaki (n 3) 22.

12 Jouannet and Peters (n 8) 3.

13 For further details on the 'comfort women' lawsuits, Kohki Abe, 'International Law as Memorial Sites: The "Comfort Women" Lawsuits Revisited' (2013) 1 *Korean Journal of International and Comparative Law* 166–187.

past wrongs and respect their right to self-determination, some even hinting at the possibility of a remedial secession.[14]

The purpose of this essay is to illuminate the contemporary development in East Asia as it is related to the global dynamics for belated justice. Particular references will be made to the international law implications of past injustices imposed on Ryukyu/Okinawa and Korea, two of territories colonially dominated by the Imperial Japan. It thus critically portrays the contemporary interplay of colonialism and international law in East Asia. In so doing, this essay builds on Professor Mogami's philosophical thinking on the notion of time in international law. For him, the trajectory of international law is not an ever-advancing process of progress and development. Critiquing the standard evolutionary account of international legal history, he states:

> Certainly there are cases in which it is necessary to recognise that an act determined to be illegal *now* was illegal *then too*. These are cases in which reconciliation among nations may not be obtained if otherwise. One may refer to it as an endeavor of time-reversing for future.[15]

He reminds us that international law has gone through a nebulous period when dominant states forcefully imposed their understanding of law upon others against their will. Elegantly depicting the whole body of that period's international law as *jus coactum*, he calls for its rectification by properly turning back time so as to celebrate the coming future of international law.[16] Hopefully, this essay responds to and further develops Mogami's inspiring messages and perceptions.

2 From Inter-temporal to Trans-temporal Perspectives

It is obvious that international law has an inseparable relation with the past. Without mentioning Torpy's above work, since the end of cold war and in the 21st century intellectual concerns of the discipline of international law have

14 See generally, Jun Shimabukuro and Kohki Abe (eds), *Okinawa ga Tou Nihon no Anzenhosho* [*Revisiting Japan's Security from Okinawa*] (Iwanami Shoten Publisher 2015) (in Japanese).

15 Toshiki Mogami, 'Marumero no Youko, Jisaihou, Yusu koakutumu [El Sol Del Membrillo, Inter-Temporal Law, and *Jus Coactum*] ' (2014) 43 *UP* (University of Tokyo) 28–33, 32 (in Japanese).

16 ibid 33.

been increasingly focused on the past. While this historiographical turn in international law seems to be propelled by the pervasive sense of uncertainty in the increasingly insecure world that urges scholars to inquire into fundamentals of this area of law,[17] Koskenniemi offers the view[18] that the developing interest in international law's history is explained by the possible resumption of the liberal internationalist project and an attempt to break with the outmoded diplomatic system that has hitherto obstructed progressive social transformation.[19] He adds as a reason for the historiographical turn the breakdown of the modernist frame of politics that is linked with progress and provides universalistically inclined interpretation of the international world.[20]

Indeed, the historiographical turn is predominantly characterised as challenging and negating the master-narrative of Eurocentric evolutionist view of the history of international law. And, as described by Jounannet and Peters, it enables 'a renewed use of the history of international law through the slant of its "bottom-up" and not "top-down" reappropriation'. They further state that: 'This is done by groups which had long been deprived of their ability to speak out on this subject, such as decolonised peoples initially, but also currently by indigenous peoples, subalterns, minorities and women. In this way,

17 Randall Lesaffer, 'International Law and its History: The Story of an Unrequited Love' in Matthew Craven, Malgosia Fitzmaurice, and Maria Vogiatzi (eds), *Time, History and International Law* (Martinus Nijhoff Publishers 2007) 27–41, 29.

18 Martti Koskenniemi, 'Why History of International Law Today?' (2004) 4 *Rechtsgeschiche* 61–66, 63, available at http://data.rg.mpg.de/rechtsgeschichte/rg04_debatte_koskenniemi.pdf. See also, Matt Craven, 'Introduction: International Law and its Histories' in Craven *et al* (n 17) 1–25, 4.

19 'Such histories seek to foreshadow the coming of an altogether different type of international law, perhaps one with greater attention to the needs and status of human beings. Works in this vein often highlight the close ties of modern international law with colonialism and associate its demise with the emergence of human rights law as the focal point of liberal legal reform in the international field'. Koskkenniemi (n 18) 63. As the period of post-cold war euphoria is gone and the unstable 21st century proceeds, however, an introspective analysis is being made regarding the liberal reform project in international law. Thus, one commentator even argues that the golden age of human rights is over and that the discourse of human rights appears to have made international law weaker, less likely to generate compliance, and more likely to produce interstate frictions and conflicts. Ingrid Wuerth, 'International Law in the Post Human Rights Era' (2017) 96 *Texas Law Journal* 279–349. See also, *Debating the Endtimes of Human Rights: Activism and Institutions in a Neo-Westphalian World* (Doutje Lettinga & Lars van Troost (eds), The Strategic Studies Project initiated by Amnesty International Netherlands, 2014), available at https://www.amnesty.nl/content/uploads/2016/12/debating_the_endtimes_of_human_rights.pdf#search=%27hopgood+stephen+ending+times+of+human+rights%27.

20 Koskkenniemi (n 18) 64.

the enquiries into the history of international law respond to a demand for understanding the past'.[21] The voices historically suppressed by the Western evolutionary discourse are now given a chance to be heard in the public sphere through the reappropriated language of international law. The 'objective' historical narrative that effaces the narrator and has the effect of putting the past behind is passionately replaced by the active remembrance by marginalised people, thus altering the historical outlook of international law. Clearly, this provides a blessed setting for bringing belated justice into international law.

There is no doubt that the idea of human rights actuates the demand for righting historical wrongs. As a powerful normative locomotive for addressing past injustices, human rights seem to extend the reach of application beyond time[22] so as to morally subordinate the past to the present. A question would be raised, however, whether it is valid to condemn a distant past according to the present-day norms. At least, to the extent that the issue of past injustices is presented in the language of positive international law, one may not anyhow escape a question regarding the inter-temporal principle that prohibits the application of current rules to the past.

In this regard, Loytomaki is suggestive in anatomizing the typical modernist understanding of time in which the past is separated from the present as reflected in the historiography of the 19th century. 'Western modernity created a break with the past and a forward thinking orientation towards future progress and historical change. Modernist history thus creates distance with regard to the present by dividing the past from the future, by distinguishing between the past and the memory of that past'. What propels the current politics of remembrance and memory, on the other hand, relies on renewing past experiences in the present and on 'the notion of an absence of separation between past and present'.[23] While this might seem like a case of applying current

---

21 Jounannet and Peters (n 8) 7.

22 The reparation discourse does not reject the normative foundation of the current international order but universalizes its reach in time and space. 'Not only are the principles of human rights and democracy accepted as valid in the present (prospectively), they are also asserted with regard to the past (retrospectively)'. George Ulrich, 'Introduction: Human Rights with a View to History' in Ulrich and Louise Krabbe Boserup (eds), *Human Rights in Development Yearbook 2001 Reparations: Redressing Past Wrongs* (Kluwer Law International 2003) 1–10, 5.

23 Loytomaki (n 3) 125. Yamamoto reminds us that: 'The past does not exist isolated, it exists because of the present and it is interpreted according to the present values, in the same way as the future'. Lilian Mitsuko Yamamoto, 'Past Violations and the Principle of Non-Retroactivity: The Practice of International Human Rights Bodies and the International Criminal Tribunals' Doctoral Thesis (Kanagawa University Graduate School of Law, Japan 2011) 9.

standards retroactively, it should rather be viewed in the words of Ulrich 'as a process of instituting or resorting, by ritualized means, a comprehensive normative order that encompasses all parties who join forces in condemning certain acts and events that are seen to epitomize the collapse of a legitimate rule of law, or of politics conducted within acceptable bounds'.[24] Addressing past injustices is a process of broadening the scope of international law to meaningfully integrate the historically alienated voices into the world order.[25]

Loytomaki's anatomy resonates with the notion of 'trans-temporal justice' I once proposed in relation to the issue of 'comfort women'.[26] The endeavor of the plaintiffs of the 'comfort women' lawsuits was to recall the past that had been invisible under the dominant evolutionary legal paradigm and to connect the past to the present in an attempt to deconstruct the context of justice. The present and the past are not regarded as distinctively bifurcated temporal dimensions as implied by the term 'inter-temporal', but they are perceived to be linked within a new 'trans-temporal' framework. The trans-temporal pursuit of justice was embodied in the courts as an attempt to revisit and refine legal rules from the perspective of the racially and sexually alienated 'Other' so that they may be made relevant for them in the past and at the present. Put differently, it was an endeavor to respond to the suppressed voices of the past and resuscitate potentialities of law that had been made dormant by the evolutionary historical master-narrative.

It was not a fabrication of the past; Nor was it a case of retroactive application of the present legal standards. Rather, it was a re-acknowledgement of the then existing legal realities from the trans-temporal perspective, an endeavor to transform the current paradigm that excludes the past from the scope of protection and to stretch the reach of justice to the past. Law is not something fixed at a particular time of history as a static monumental building. Law presents itself as memorial sites. Patrick Macklem eloquently states that: 'Law's memorial sites are comprised of principles, rules and procedures that invest moments in history with normative significance … Law may regard memory in evidentiary terms but law itself is a form of memory. Law as memory, as

24 Ulrich (n 22) 5–6.

25 The inquiries into past injustices for reparation may end 'in a genuine failure to understand the others' interpretations, which shows the limits of the exercise. On the other hand, these confrontations also help in conceiving a far more open history, a history of international law that can better track the way by which legal practice and discourse have contributed to the imposition of domination of all kinds, but also to the forging of connections between identities and cultures'. Jouannet and Peters (n 8) 7.

26 Abe (n 13) 174–175.

opposed to memory in law, is a social enterprise that is thoroughly dialogical-an active, ongoing engagement with the past'.[27]

As memorial sites, international law is open to dialogues with the past and which pasts merit remembering is a profound question directly affecting the present and the future world order. The trans-temporal perspective stimulates the international law's capacity to re/memorialise the past, thus laying the ground for addressing the past injustices. This is exactly how the former 'comfort women' mobilised legal arguments in the courts. To be more concrete, the contemporary framework of violence against women and human trafficking, and the use of the legal term 'sexual slavery' effectively activated the capacity of international law to re/memorialise the past, and enabled the issue of "comfort women" to be firmly located in the present context.

As exemplified in the 'comfort women' lawsuits, it is increasingly to memories of particular victims rather than the detached evolutionary history that international law attaches itself in addressing past injustices. Accordingly, the inter-temporal principle is being transformed, if not negated, to activate and memorialise the past. Indicative of its transformative process is the increasing use of the notion of 'continuing violation' in relation to wrongs that, initiated in the past, persist and directly affect the present. All the more so would be the innovative application in international human rights bodies of the independent requirement that a remedy be provided even for violations that took place prior to entry into force of a Convention.[28] Arguments are also made to justify

---

27 Patrick Macklem, 'Ryna 9, Praha 1: Restitution and Memory in International Human Rights Law' (2005) 16 *European Journal of International Law* 1–23, 14 (notes omitted). In analysing the relevant jurisprudence of the Human Rights Committee, the monitoring body of the International Covenant on Civil and Political Rights, Macklem cautiously adds that not all pasts are given international legal significance. 'Establishing that a past possesses legal significance in light of an international legal commitment to equality is contingent on a state's decision to recognize past injustices'. ibid 18–19.

28 Shelton (n 2) 460. Tokugawa details the recent jurisprudence of international human rights bodies wherein the notion of continuing violation and the independent right to remedy were invoked in regard to past injustices. Shinji Tokugawa, 'Kokusai Jinken Kikan no Houjissen — "Kako no Fuseigi" eno Torikumi [Addressing "Past Injustices": The Practice of International Human Rights Bodies]' (2015) 87 *Houritu Jihou* 40–45 (in Japanese). A sequence of recommendations issued by human rights treaty bodies that Japan should take responsibility for the issue of 'comfort women' are also reflective of and conducive to the transformation of the inter-temporal principle. Thus, the Committee on the Elimination of Discrimination against Women, the monitoring body of the Convention on the Elimination of All Forms of Discrimination against Women, expresses the view in its Concluding Observation on the most recent periodic reports of Japan that: '[T]he issue of "comfort women" gives rise to serious violations that have a continuing effect on the rights of victims/survivors of those violations that were perpetrated by the State party's

the rejection of strict application of the inter-temporal principle when it comes to grave injustices equivalent to the crime against humanity.[29] Admittedly, if historical injustices were committed in violation of international law or were not properly sanctioned by laws in force at the time, the question regarding the applicability of inter-temporal principle does not arise straightforwardly and the claim for reparation for past injustices should be duly warranted if other conditions are met.[30] Infused with the trans-temporal perspective of justice, positive international law may be effectively revisited for addressing historical wrongs as described below.

3 Ryukyu/Okinawa Now and Then

The dynamics for addressing historical wrongs in the present are keenly felt in East Asia as demonstrated by the case of Okinawa. In no other part than Okinawa have there been such intensive mass protests continued in contemporary Japan. The immediate target of the protests is the ongoing construction of another new US military base in Okinawa initiated in 2015 against the local people's repeatedly expressed will. While US military bases are located throughout the Japanese Archipelago (including the Metropolitan area) under the Japan-US Security Treaty of 1960,[31] Okinawa Prefecture, comprising only 0.6 % of Japan's total land area, is where more than 70 % of military facilities for the American exclusive use are already concentrated. The UN *Special Rapporteur* on Racism admits that the overwhelming presence of US military bases has affected the environment, indigenous culture, custom and fundamental human rights of Okinawan people and that it is a manifestation of racially discriminatory policy against them.[32]

military during the Second World War, given the continued lack of effective remedies for those victims. The Committee, therefore, considers that it is not precluded *ratione temporis* from addressing such violations'. CEDAW/C/JPN/CO/7–8, 10 March 2016, para 29.

29 Patricia M. Muhanmad, 'The Trans-Atlantic Slave Trade: A Legacy Establishing a Case for International Reparations' (2013) 3 *Colombia Journal of Race and Law* 147–202, 183–185; Antonius R Hippolyte, 'Unearthing the Legitimacy of CARICOM's Reparation Bid' (2014) 21, available at http://www.academia.edu.

30 Shelton (n 2) 462–463. As mentioned above, for Mogami, nebulous *jus coactum* is subject to rectification according to the present-day standard. See Mogami (n 15).

31 Treaty of Mutual Cooperation and Security between Japan and the United States of America, available at https://www.mofa.go.jp/region/n-america/us/q&a/ref/1.html.

32 Report of the *Special Rapporteur* on contemporary forms of racism, racial discrimination, xenophobia and related intolerance, Doudou Dene, Addendum: Mission to Japan, E/CN.4/2006/16/Add.2, 24 January 2006, paras 5, 69, 88.

Voices of Okinawan people go unheard of simply because they are the colonised 'Other' forcibly incorporated into the Modern State of Japan.[33] In a rare display of political urgency, the then Governor of Okinawa Prefecture flew to the UN Human Rights Council and called international attention to the ongoing injustices inflicted upon Okinawa. Notably he expressed his indignation at the construction of a new US base by stressing that: 'Okinawan's right to self-determination is being neglected'.[34] The invocation of the right to self-determination by Okinawan people is a recent phenomenon, driven by the enhanced sense that they have been colonially discriminated in its relations with 'Mainland' Japan. The modern origin of such unequal relations, *i.e.*, Japan's annexation of the Kingdom of Ryukyu (thereafter named Okinawa Prefecture) in 1879, is now subjected to critical review from the viewpoint not of Eurocentric evolutionary history of international law but of the collective memory of Okinawans, which increasingly facilitates the local population to identify themselves as a distinctive 'people'.[35]

In the Japanese dominant master-narrative, the annexation of the Kingdom of Ryukyu has been referred to as the '*Ryukyu Shobun* (Ryukyu Disposition)' the implication of which is that it was simply a domestic action taken by the central government against a local entity under its total control.[36] It is only

33 For a historical trajectory of Ryukyu up to the present, see Gavan MacCormack and Satoko Oka Norimatsu, 'Ryukyu/Okinawa: From Disposal to Resistance' (2012) 10 *Asia Pacific Journal* 1–13, available at https://apjjf.org/-Satoko-Oka-Norimatsu--Gavan-McCormack/3828/article.pdf.

34 Oral Statement at the United Nations Human Rights Council by the governor of Okinawa, September 21 2015, available at http://dc-office.org/post/574.

35 Legal dealing with past wrongs was accelerated if not initiated by an epoch-making local newspaper reporting that shed light on the absence of legitimate international law grounds for the annexation. See 'Disposal of Ryukyu Was Illegal under International Law: Demanding Restoration of Sovereignty Is Possible Even Now', *Ryukyu Shimpo* July 11, 2014, 1 (in Japanese). Among groundbreaking researches that delve into international law implications of the annexation is Hideaki Uemura, 'The Colonial Annexation of Okinawa and the Logic of International Law: The Formation of an "Indigenous People" in East Asia' (2003) 23 *Japanese Studies* 213–222, in which the author, an expert on indigenous people, argues that the annexation was a violation of customary international law and was *null and valid* as Ryukyu's consent to it was procured by the coercion of its representative through acts or threats against him. The author adds that Ryukyu people are duly categorized as an indigenous people as they were incorporated into a nation state unilaterally, forcibly and illegally.

36 The dominant narrative of Mainland Japan on the Ryukyu Disposition is succinctly presented in Masaharu Yanagihara, 'Some Thoughts on the Concept of Territory in the Late Edo and Early Meiji Periods' *The Japan Institute of International Affairs/Resource* 20–23, available at https://www.jiia-jic.jp/en/resourcelibrary/pdf/Yanagihara_Some_Thoughts_on_the_Concept_of_Territory_in_the_Late_Edo_and_Early_Meiji_Periods01.pdf.

recently that the collective memory of Okinawan people has been so rigorously brought to the public sphere as to encourage the replacement of the term 'disposition' with 'annexation' indicating that it was in fact an action taken on the international dimension.

When Ryukyu was incorporated into Japan, the international order of East Asia just began to be taken over by the European-led international law order. Japan was rapidly incorporated into the new international system through the conclusion of unequal treaties with the Western powers,[37] when the Kingdom of Ryukyu also concluded treaties of amity with the US, France and the Netherlands.[38] While the then foreign minister clearly stated to the Resident Minister of the US at Tokyo that Japan would abide by all the provisions of the US-Ryukyu treaty[39] prior to the forcible confiscation of the original copies of the three treaties in 1874,[40] the current official view is nebulous with regard to the status of these treaties and the Kingdom of Ryukyu. Thus, responding to questions as to whether Ryukyu satisfied the requirement for statehood, when Ryukyu became part of Japan and how these treaties were characterised in international law, the Japanese government simply maintains that: 'It is difficult to state anything definite'.[41]

On the other hand, in his voluminous masterpiece thoroughly delineating the historical realities of Ryukyu and the process of the Disposition, Tsuneo

---

37 For an incisive analysis of unequal treaties as colonizing mission, see Mathew Craven, 'What Happened to Unequal Treaties? The Continuities of Informal Empire' (2005) 74 *Nordic Journal of International Law* 335–382.

38 Masaharu Yanagihara, '"*Shioki* (Control)", "*Fuyo* (Dependency)", and Sovereignty' in Anthea Roberts, Paul B Stephan, Pierre-Hugues Verdier and Mila Versteeg (eds), *Comparative International Law* (Oxford University Press 2018) 141–157, 146–149. See also, Yanagihara, 'Treaties Concluded by the Kingdom of Ryukyu' *Oxford Public International Law*, available at https://opil.ouplaw.com/page/ryukyu-treaties/treaties-concluded-by-the-kingdom-of-ryukyu.

39 ibid.

40 Tsuyoshi Arakaki, 'Ryukyu's International Treaties Returns after 141 Years', *Ryukyu Shimpo* February 4, 2015, available at http://english.ryukyushimpo.jp/2015/02/15/17075/.

41 Eg, Government Reply No 560, House of Representatives, June 18, 2012, available at http://www.shugiin.go.jp/internet/itdb_shitsumon.nsf/html/shitsumon/b174560.htm. Regarding the status of the treaties, Yanagihara illustrates that: 'According to the official position of the Meiji Government after September of 1872, Ryukyu had been an integral part of the Tokugawa Government after 1609 and the Kingdom of Ryukyu was regarded not as an "independent State" having official power to conclude treaties with foreign countries. This position would lead to the conclusion that those treaties concluded by the Kingdom of Ryukyu without any official permission of the then-Tokugawa Government had to be by nature considered as null and void'. Yanagihara, *Oxford Public International Law* (n 38).

Namihira of Ryukyu University delivers his view on the international status of Ryukyu at the time that: 'Internationally, sustaining the tribute relationship with the Qing Dynasty, Ryukyu was still an independent Kingdom. While Ryukyu concluded treaties with foreign powers as an independent state, its subordination to Japan was not internationally recognized. With regard to the relationship with the Satsuma Domain [to which Ryukyu had another tributary relationship after being invaded by them in 1609], the reality of its control was consistently concealed and the Qing China did not officially recognize it'.[42]

As illustrated by a number of Okinawa-based academic researchers represented by Namihira, until the time of annexation the Kingdom of Ryukyu seems to have enjoyed the status of a distinctive political entity.[43] As it was integrated into a new international order (albeit still bound by the tributary relations in the emaciated East Asian order), Ryukyu showed a degree of government authority sufficient for the general maintenance of order that was considered 'the only necessary condition' for statehood in international law[44] to which not only Ryukyu but Japan were subject from the mid 1850's. The system of 'suzerainty' in which the tributary relationship was established did not imply in East Asia an effective control by the dominant state[45] and indeed the political status of the Kingdom of Ryukyu was not determined under the law of China, Satsuma Domain or Japan. Thus it is increasingly argued that the Ryukyu Disposition should be reformulated as an action beyond the jurisdiction of Japan.[46]

---

42 Tsuneo Namihira, *Kindaihigashiajiashi no nakano Ryukyuheigou* [*The Annexation of Ryukyu within the History of Modern East Asia*] (Iwanami Shoten Publisher 2014) 147 (in Japanese).

43 This was so notwithstanding the fact that in 1872 the king of Ryukyu was forcibly designated by the Japanese government *Ryukyu Han Ou* (Chief of the Ryukyu Clan), a political step to eventually incorporate the entire Kingdom into Japan. *Id.* The Meiji Government was of the view that foreign countries did not know that Ryukyu did not have any power to conclude treaties, and that the then Tokugawa Government had exercised a purely feudal power over Ryukyu. Yanagihara, however, puts the Meiji Government's exposition into perspective: 'Certainly this is a pathetically weak argument, taking in particular into consideration an interpretation of the Tokugawa government not to regard Ryukyu as being included in to the proper domain of Japan'. Yanagihara (n 38) 154.

44 James Crawford, *The Creation of States in International Law* (2nd ed, Oxford University Press 2006) 260.

45 Namihira (n 42) 168.

46 Yanagihara emphasizes that: '[I]t would be seriously misleading to apply directly, without any reservations, modern European ideas of sovereignty or territory to the East Asian World, including Ryukyu at that time'. (Yanagihara, *Oxford Public International Law* (n 38)) His warning is in line with that of a refined historian according to whom the past had its own viewpoint in its particular context and 'we may not be able to reach the viewpoint

The Ryukyu Disposition was enforced forcibly under military threat. It was a unilateral delivery of the central government's decision to incorporate Ryukyu into Japan as Okinawa Prefecture. The Ryukyu's Capital Castle was seized and the Kingdom of Ryukyu ceased to exist accordingly. Assuming that it was an annexation of an independent political entity, it is hard to find a legitimate international law ground for justifying it as revealed by Uemura, who insists that it was indeed against international law already applied in East Asia.[47] The annexation of Ryukyu by force instantly reminds us of the fate of Hawaii which was also annexed into the US territory five years after the military overthrow of the Kingdom of Hawaii in 1893. The US Congress adopted a historic joint resolution in 1993 apologizing to the Native Hawaiians for the overthrow and characterised its action as 'illegal', in violation of 'international law'. The resolution also acknowledged that this action denied the Native Hawaiian people their 'inherent sovereignty through self-government and … their right to self-determination, their lands, and their ocean resources'.[48] As shown, in no small number of cases the colonial acquisition of territories may not be explained away even in accordance with international law in force at the time.[49] The Ryukyu Disposal is one that may be duly added to the list of those cases awaiting the recognition of historical wrongs from the perspective of trans-temporal justice.

Okinawa was placed under the US administration after Japan was liberated from the Occupation of the Allied Powers in 1952. Only in 1972 did Okinawa return to Japan. Since then, however, the US military forces formerly stationing in mainland Japan stared to be relocated to Okinawa against the will of

---

of the past, in any case certainly not by looking at the past through the present, universal criteria'. Certainly so, but it should be noted that: 'This is not necessarily something that memory actors, victims in particular, want to hear. Legal norms, on the other hand, in particular human rights norms, have precisely this universal character: they are or at least should be applied at all times and in all places. That for example slavery is characterized as a crime against humanity through law implies that the universality of legal norms is even projected into the past'. Löytömaki (n 3) 129.

47 Uemura (n 35). For further analysis of the possible grounds for acquisition of the Ryukyu territory, see Kohki Abe, 'International Protection of Human Rights for Okinawa' in Shimabukuro and Abe (n 14) 262–263.

48 Joint Resolution to Acknowledge the 100th Anniversary of the January 17, 1893 Overthrow of the Kingdom of Hawaii, Pub. L. No.103–50, 107 Stat.1510 (1993), whereas paras. 8, 23. For further detail, see John Van Dyke, 'Reconciliation between Korea and Japan' (2006) 5 *Chinese Journal of International Law* 215–239, 223–225.

49 On the problematic acquisition of native territories of indigenous peoples, Jeremie Gilbert, *Indigenous Peoples' Land Rights under International Law: From Victims to Actors* (Transnational Publishers 2006) 13–20.

the local population, who would continue to be exposed to the excessive US military presence. As mentioned above, they keep on making intensive protests against the construction of another US military base. Every time a grave incident threatening their daily life (*e.g.*, sexual violence by the US soldiers against women and girls) happens, Okinawa's pasts are recalled, helping them form and share their collective memory. It is no coincidence that their active remembering is prompted by international law, which opens avenues for contestation of the past and ongoing wrongs in normative language.[50]

In the context of a demand for reparation, particularly focused is the right to self-determination, a right acknowledged as having been denied to the Native Hawaiian people when their kingdom was militarily overthrown. Indeed, Okinawans appeal to the international human rights mechanisms for the recognition of their status as a 'people', an 'indigenous people' in particular, who have a right to freely determine their political status and freely pursue their economic, social and cultural development, which they have achieved against the objection of the Japanese government in the UN and universal human rights treaty bodies. Thus, in its most recent Concluding Observations on the combined tenth and eleventh periodic reports of Japan, the Committee on the Elimination of Racial Discrimination expressed its concern that 'the Ryukyu/Okinawa are not recognised as indigenous peoples despite its previous recommendation (CERD/C/JPN/CO/7–9, para. 21) and recommendations from other human rights mechanisms', and went to recommend that Japan 'reconsider its position on recognizing the Ryukyu as indigenous peoples and step up measures to protect their rights'.[51] As is the case with Hawaii, the right to self-determination is a critical notion that connects the present and the past, and justifies addressing the historical wrongs in the language of international law.

Little mention is made of the annexation of Ryukyu in the dominant discourse of the evolutionary history of international law reproduced in Mainland Japan, because it has been considered an action initiated and completed exclusively within the domestic sphere of Japan, thus not a matter of international law. Stimulated by the voices of memory actors in Okinawa, however,

50 'ACSILs demands an apology for annexation of Ryukyu, calling it a violation of International Law', *Ryukyu Shimpo* February 4, 2015, available at http://english.ryukyushimpo.jp/2015/02/17/17114/. ACSILs stands for the Association of Comprehensive Studies for Independence of the Lew Chewans. For further information on the Association, see http://www.acsils.org/english.

51 CERD/C/JPN/CO/10–11, 26 September 2018, paras 17–18. See also Concluding Observations issued by the Human Rights Committee, HRC/C/JPN/CO/5, 18 December 2008, para 32; HRC/C/JPN/CO/6, 20 August 2014, para 26.

international law's capacity to memorialise the past is vigorously activated so that the problematic Disposition/Annexation is now being reformulated as an issue of international law, a historical wrong to be rectified in the present. It is the contemporary legal notion of the right to self-determination that effectively facilitates the re/memorialization process and helps stretch the reach of justice from the present to the past. Underpinned by the trans-temporal perspective of justice, the ongoing process in Okinawa essentially parallels the case of 'comfort women' as stated above.

4 Colonial Wrongs Revisited

The forcible annexation of Ryukyu presaged Japan's colonial expansion into Asia and Korea in particular, which eventually resulted in the Asia-Pacific War. While standard international law literature in Japan seldom if any elucidates the effects of colonial domination, the Japanese government has admitted its wrongs since 1990's. On the occasion of the 50th anniversary of the war's end, the Prime Minister remarked that: 'During a certain period in the not too distant past, Japan, following a mistaken national policy, advanced along the road to war, only to ensnare the Japanese people in a fateful crisis, and, through its colonial rule and aggression, caused tremendous damage and suffering to the people of many countries, particularly to those of Asian nations'.[52]

52 Statement by Prime Minister Tomiichi Murayama 'On the occasion of the 50th anniversary of the war's end' (15 August 1995), available at https://www.mofa.go.jp/announce/press/pm/murayama/9508.html. Prior to this, Prime Minister Moriteru Hosokawa had already expressed in 1993 "our profound remorse and apologies for the fact that past Japanese actions, including aggression and colonial rule, caused unbearable suffering and sorrow for so many people", Policy Speech to the 127th Session of the National Diet, available at http://japan.kantei.go.jp/127.html. Subsequent Prime Ministers of Japan followed suit, including Naoto Kan who remarked ahead of the Centennial of Japan's annexation of Korea that: 'In August precisely one hundred years ago, the Japan-Korea Annexation Treaty was concluded, making the beginning of the colonial rule of thirty six years. As demonstrated by strong resistance such as the *Samil* independence movement, the Korean people of that time was deprived of their country and culture, and their ethnic pride was deeply scarred by the colonial rule which was imposed against their will under the political and military circumstances', available at https://japan.kantei.go.jp/kan/statement/201008/10danwa_e.html. On the 70th anniversary of the end of the war, however, Shinzo Abe markedly shifted the course, simply confirming in general terms that: 'We shall never again resort to any form of the threat or use of force as a means of settling international disputes. We shall abandon colonial rule forever and respect the right of self-determination of all peoples throughout the world'. Statement by Prime Minister

The Japanese government, however, does not go so far as to say that its colonial rule was against international law. Prime Minister Murayama stated that: 'The Treaty on the Annexation of Korea [of 1910] was concluded and enforced validly under the prevailing circumstances of international relations at the time'.[53] Endorsed at least tacitly by the Japanese international law academy at large,[54] the government's view dovetails with the Eurocentric evolutionary narrative of international law: The colonial domination would be unjust in light of the current standard but it was legal at the time. The phrase employed in Article 2 of the Treaty on Basic Relations Between Japan and the Republic of Korea of 1951,[55] 'already *null and void*',[56] is interpreted to mean that all the relevant documents were valid initially.

Such being the case, the decisions rendered by the Supreme Court of the Republic of Korea gravely jolted the very foundation upon which all the legal understandings are constructed, among ruling elites of Japan, in regard to the relations with Korea. In its 2012 decision,[57] the Supreme Court overturned the lower court judgment to dismiss the case filed by plaintiffs who were forced to work by a Japanese company during the World War II and remanded it the Seoul High Court, after holding that the claims are not precluded by the Agreement on the Settlement of Problems Concerning Property and Claims and the Economic Cooperation Between the Republic of Korean and Japan[58] (hereinafter as the Claims Agreement) signed in 1965 with the above-mentioned

---

Shinzo Abe, 14 August, 2015, available at https://japan.kantei.go.jp/97_abe/statement/201508/0814statement.html.

53 134th House of Councilors Record No.4 (5 October 20 1995) 19.(5 October or 20 October 20?).

54 See Shigeki Sakamoto, 'Nikkanhogojoyaku no Kouryoku- Kyousei ni yoru Jouyaku no Kanten kara [Validity of the Japan-Korea Annexation Treaty: From the Viewpoint of Coerced Treaties]' (1995) 44 *Kansaidaigaku Hougakuronsyuu* [*The Law Review of Kansai University*] 869–932 (in Japanese).

55 583 UNTS 173, available at https://treaties.un.org/doc/Publication/UNTS/Volume%20583/v583.pdf. Annexed in 1910, Korea was liberated in 1945, and got/restored independence in 1948. The diplomatic relation with Japan was normalized in 1965.

56 Article 2 confirms that: '[A]ll treaties or agreements concluded between the Empire of Japan and the Empire of Korea on or before August 22, 1910 are already *null and void*'.

57 Supreme Court of Korea, 2009 Da 68620, Decided on May 24, 2012 (S Kor). The English translation of the judgment is available at *Korean Journal of International and Comparative Law*, Vol. 2 (2014) 93.

58 583 UNTS 33 (n 53). Article 2(1) provides: The Contracting Parties confirm that the problem concerning property, rights and interests of the two Contracting Parties and their nationals (including juridical persons) and concerning claims between the Contracting Parties and their nationals, including those provided for in Article IV, paragraph (a) of the Treaty of Peace with Japan signed at the city of San Francisco on September 8, 1951, is settled completely and finally.

Treaty on Basic Relations. It held that the Claims Agreement was not a result of negotiation about compensation for Japanese colonization, but rather was a political agreement the purpose of which was to resolve the financial and civil debt/credit relationship between Korea and Japan. Explaining that Japan's colonial rule of the Korean Peninsular was no more than an unlawful occupation contrary the spirit of the nation's Constitution, it decided that the compensation claims based on the illegality of colonial rule were not subject to the Claims Agreement and that a citizen's individual right to make a claim may not be extinguished without the individual citizen's consent even under the circumstances where the state waives diplomatic protection.

The remanded case was again appealed to the Supreme Court, which on October 30, 2018 ordered the defendant company to pay compensation to the plaintiffs.[59] In so ruling, it held that the plaintiffs' claims were based on the inhumane and wrongful acts of the Japanese corporation arising out of Japan's unlawful colonial rule and that therefore the plaintiffs were not simply making claims for unpaid wages but in fact brought suit to seek damages for their suffering because of Japan's colonial rule. The decisions of the Supreme Court of Korea are another indication that the Euro-centric evolutionary history of international law in which colonial rule is considered a thing of the past and the past wrongs are prone to oblivion is fundamentally challenged as the active remembering contributes to the construction of narratives that present the past as a series of injustices.[60] In East Asia, too, the current inclination promoted by memory of injustices is clearly toward remembering and righting past wrongs in the present.

In addition to the Korean Constitution, international law is being mobilised to shed light on the legal fragility on which Japan's annexation of Korea was

59 Supreme Court of Korea, 2013 Da 61381, Decided on Oct. 30, 2018 (S Kor). The English translation of the judgment is available at (2019) 2 *Korean Journal of International and Comparative Law* 88. For a succinct summary of the decision, see Seokwoo Lee and Seryon Lee, '*Yeo Woon Taek v New Nippon Steel Corporation*. 2013 Da 61381. Compensation for Damages (Others)' (2019) 113 *American Journal of International Law* 592–599.

60 Foreign Minister of Japan harshly criticizes the ruling rendered by the Supreme Court of Korea in October, 2018 as follows: 'This decision is extremely regrettable and totally unacceptable. This decision clearly violates Article II of the Agreement and inflicts unjustifiable damages and costs on the said Japanese company. Above all, the decision completely overthrows the legal foundation of the friendly and cooperative relationship that Japan and the Republic of Korea have developed since the normalization of diplomatic relations in 1965'. Regarding the Decision by the Supreme Court of the Republic of Korea, Confirming the Existing Judgments on the Japanese Company (Statement by Foreign Minister Taro Kono), October 30, 2018, available at https://www.mofa.go.jp/press/release/press4e_002204.html.

enforced. The issues of coercion upon the representative of Korea and of material procedural defects in concluding the relevant treaties are under thorough review by a number of experts on international law and history, which has resulted in casting a deep and long shadow over the validity of the annexation process.[61] The wrongs of forced labor and 'comfort women' are presented as symbolically representing grave injustices committed during Japan's colonial domination that have continuing effects on the survivors. As a former colonial power, Japan is being hard pressed to face up to those wrongs/crimes committed in contravention of international law under its colonial rule. As Lees states that: 'While a forward-looking approach may make an amicable settlement achieved through joint diplomatic efforts between the two governments possible, avoiding legal responsibility for war crimes committed during Japan's occupation will certainly not be a viable option so long as the victims of such war crimes are living. A resolution can only be reached through adequate compensation and a genuine apology to those victims who are living witnesses of this unjust history'.[62]

It should be stressed from the trans-temporal perspective that historical wrongs are required to be resolved in such a way as to be compatible with the current international law since they have become tangible at the present time. Thus, in the words of the International Court of Justice, the 1965 Claims Agreement over the interpretation of which serious disputes have emerged in regard to the issues of 'comfort women' and forced labor between Japan and South Korea 'has to be interpreted and applied within the framework of the entire legal system prevailing at the time of the interpretation'.[63] Put differently, colonial wrongs exemplified by these issues need to be dealt with in accordance with current international human rights and humanitarian treaties in particular. In this respect, Weeramantry's following explication also

---

61 An outcome of the most comprehensive research is Norikatsu Sasakawa and Yi Taejin (eds), *Kankokuheigou to Gendai: Rekishi to Kokusaihou karano Saikentou* [*The Annexation of Korea and the Present: A Review from History and International Law*] (Akashi Shoten Publishers 2008 (in Japanese). See also, Totsuka Etsuro, 'Japan's Colonization of Korea and International Law' (2011) 9 *Asia-Pacific Journal* 1–15, available at https://apjjf.org/2011/9/9/totsuka-etsuro/3493/article; Kim Young-koo, 'The Validity of Some Coerced Treaties in the Early 20th Century: A Reconsideration of Japanese Annexation of Korea in Legal Perspective' (2002) 33 *Korea Observer* 637–667, available at http://koreaobserver.or.kr/html/?pmode=subpage&smode=aim.

62 Lee and Lee (n 59) 598.

63 *Legal Consequences for States of the Continued Presence of South Africa in Namibia (South West Africa) Notwithstanding Security Council Resolution 276 (1970)*, Advisory Opinion of 21 June 1071, ICJ Reports 1971, 16, para 53.

deserves to be taken heed of: 'Treaties that affect human rights cannot be applied in such a manner as to constitute a denial of human rights as understood at the time of their application. A Court cannot endorse actions which are a violation of human rights by the standards of their time merely because they are taken under a treaty which dates back to a period when such action was not a violation of human rights'.[64] This judicial message is clearly oriented toward justice that transcends time.

The phenomena of intervening into the past through international law to rectify historical injustices are increasingly seen in many parts of the world. The most vigorous and organizational among them would be a project launched by Caribbean States organised in the Caribbean Community and Common Market (CARICOM). Its 34th Regular Meeting of the Conference of Heads of Government in 2013 established the CARICOM Reparations Commission with a mandate to 'establish the moral, ethical and legal case for the payment of Reparations by the Governments of all the former colonial powers … for the Crimes against Humanity of Native Genocide, the Trans-Atlantic Slave Trade and a racialised system of chattel Slavery'.[65] The Ten Point Action[66] was announced, calling for full apologies and reparations. The project is criticised for lack of firm international law grounds for reparations,[67] and the response of Western governments is to all appearances dismissive as implied by the languages used by them such as 'look ahead rather than peer into history' and 'move on'.[68] Yet, as reminded by Nicola Frith of the University Edinburgh, there is no sign that the work of social movements for reparations is stymied. 'Indeed, the concept of reparation, and the associated quest for repatriation, have been steadily gaining currency throughout the world. … As the process of reparative justice for other crimes against humanity has gained credibility, we are witnessing the re-emergence of a new global push for reparations'.[69]

64 *Case Concerning Gabcikovo-Nagymaros Project, (Hungary/Slovakia)*, Judgment of 25 September 1997, ICJ. Reports 1997, Separate Opinion of Vice-President Weeramantry, 111.

65 CARICOM Reparations Commission, "About Us", available at http://caricomreparations.org/about-us/.

66 Available at http://caricomreparations.org/caricom/caricoms-10-point-reparation-plan/.

67 See Buster (n 7).

68 But even in Europe the politics of memory concerning colonialism are gaining particular relevance as Germany apologized in 2004 for a colonial-era genocide in Namibia and Britain announced in 2013 that it would pay compensation to 5228 Kenyans who were subjected to torture and other abuse at the hands of the colonial administration. Loytomaki (n 3) 29.

69 Nicola Frith, 'The Global Push for Reparations' (8 February 2019), available at http://caricomreparations.org/global-push-reparations/.

In the UN, too, the Working Group of Experts on People of African Descent and the Special Rapporteur on contemporary forms of racism, racial discrimination, xenophobia and related intolerance jointly sent comments to the International Law Commission (ILC) on the draft Articles on crimes against humanity that contain a number of recommendations of direct relevance to reparations for historical wrongs. ILC was thus advised to express the right to reparations for crimes against humanity in language sufficient to include reparations for historical injustices; to explicitly recognise that those who are entitled to reparations include not only those who most directly suffer crimes against humanity but also subsequent generations who live with the consequences of those crimes; and to ensure that reparations include honoring the memory of the victims of these tragedies, regretting or expressing remorse or presenting apologies and taking appropriate and effective measures to halt and reverse the lasting consequences of those practices.[70]

It is understood that revisiting and rectifying historical wrongs is not simply about the past but about the future, a prerequisite for re/constructing a legal order in which human dignity is given the fullest respect. The relevance of that endeavor is no different in any part of the world including East Asia. At stake is the credibility of international law and international lawyers to respond to the demand for belated justice for historical wrongs that continue to inflict sufferings upon people. Before us is the age when the past is constantly summoned to the public sphere as an issue of law. While international law academy is urged to squarely take it upon them, historical injustices relating to Ryukyu/Okinawa and Korea present a momentous challenge to be confronted by international lawyers based in Japan, a country that expresses in its Constitution a desire to occupy an honored place in international society striving for the preservation of peace, and the banishment of slavery, oppression and intolerance *for all time* from the earth.[71]

---

70 Re: Comments on the Draft Articles on Crimes against Humanity, 1 April 2019, ARDS/WGEP AD/20190122/CS/jf, available at https://www.ohchr.org/Documents/Issues/Racism/WGEAPD/CommentsDraftArticlesCrimesAgainstHumanity.pdf. ILC once discussed a proposal to criminalize colonial domination in its work, which, however, was eventually rejected. See *Summaries of the work of ILC on the Draft code of crimes against the peace and security of mankind (Part II)—including the draft statute for an international criminal court*, available at https://legal.un.org/ilc/summaries/7_4.shtml.

71 Emphasis added.

PART 2

(Re-)Constructing Peace and Justice in International Law

CHAPTER 3

Gender-Based Violence against Women in International Law: Transformative Possibility of International Law

Miho Omi

1 Introduction

There have been tremendous efforts made to combat gender-based violence against women (hereinafter, GBVAW) worldwide, both practically and theoretically. In the field of feminist international law, many scholars have also devoted their efforts to the issue.[1] Violence against women is globally wide-spread and even when violence is not directly inflicted, it gives women undeserved fear that may limit their possibilities to develop their lives fully and freely and to participate in every aspect of life.

The developments in international law regarding violence against women is a result of advocacy from women's movements worldwide to get this issue recognized and solicit measures to eliminate such violence internationally and nationally. It is now recognized as a human rights violation and some regions have legally binding treaties attempting to eliminate violence against women.[2] However, to our great dismay, GBVAW has not been eliminated nor diminished yet.

1 Kate Ogg and Susan Harris Rimmer, 'Introduction to the Research Handbook on Feminist Engagement with International Law' in Susan Harris Rimmer and Kate Ogg (eds), *Research Handbook on Feminist Engagement with International Law* (Edward Elgar 2019) (hereinafter, *Research Handbook*) 9. They surveyed books, journal articles, textbooks on international law in English or French on the topics of women/gender/feminism and international law from January 1950 and July 2016 and empirically presented that violence against women was the most written topic in this field.

2 These treaties are: the Inter-American Convention on the Prevention, Punishment and Eradication of Violence against Women (Convention of Belém do Palá) [1994] OAS Multilateral Treaty A-61; the Protocol to the African Charter on Human and Peoples' Rights on the Rights of Women in Africa (Maputo Protocol) [2003]; and the Council of Europe Convention on preventing and combating violence against women and domestic violence (Istanbul Convention) [2011] CETS No.210.

 | DOI:10.1163/9789004681477_005

In this chapter, I would like to review the developments of related international human rights law to see if international law can rectify 'injustice' of GBVAW. In other words, this chapter tries to explore the transformative possibility of international law, especially international human rights law, in relation to violence against women. When there is a need to eliminate some sort of behavior, it may be usual to introduce a binding or stronger law. However, since violence against women is a matter of 'gender', to combat the problem also requires changing the social circumstances in which gender exists. Gender in this chapter refers to a set of social constructs, varying over time and place, which defines that masculinity and femininity are opposite to one another. Those qualities or traits deemed masculine, which are often associated with the public sphere, are assigned a superior value than those defined as feminine, associated with the private.[3] As a result, gender makes it look natural that women are placed as subordinate to men. It may not be a usual task for international law to transform society, but feminist international law has been trying to 'do international law differently' so that 'the theory and practice of international law might be done better'.[4]

Although Professor Toshiki Mogami has not explicitly discussed issues related to women or gender in his work, he recognizes violence against women as a form of human rights violation that should be rectified along with issues such as poverty, access to safe water, and lack of medical care for children.[5] He also states that if a person is discriminated, excluded, saddened or hurt because of a reason that she/he is not responsible for, her/his situation cannot be called peace, even in the absence of war or armed conflict. Peace in this sense is an issue of social justice caused by structural violence.[6] However, as he articulates, international law which is closely related to war and peace is not very clear about the human rights to live in peace.[7] In this chapter, I would like to challenge such structural silence of the system of international law on GBVAW which disturbs women's human rights to live in peace. I also would like to add that I was encouraged by Professor Mogami's following statement: 'if it is true that something existing in reality is absent in the world of international

---

3 See Hilary Charlesworth, 'Forward' in Rimmer and Ogg (n 1), xxv.

4 Loveday Hodson and Troy Lavers, 'Feminist Judgments in International Law: An Introduction' in Loveday Hodson and Troy Lavers (eds), *Feminist Judgments in International Law* (Hart Publishing 2019) (hereinafter, *Feminist Judgments in IL*) 2–21, 3.

5 Toshiki Mogami, 'Peace, Human Rights, and Citizens: Towards Globalization of Civil Society', *What is Peace Now? Nine Stories Around Human Rights and Humanity* (Iwanami Shoten 2006) 131–148, 135–136(in Japanese).

6 ibid 97.

7 ibid 105–106.

law, the academic challenge posed is to pursue how and to what extent such reality can legally exist'.[8] I believe feminist international law's quest for silence of international law resonates with his pursuit for the absent in international law because both are trying to rectify international injustice using international law.

In the next section, I will briefly overview the feminist approaches to international law and the developments regarding violence against women in international law. In Section 2, some issues of international law and international human rights law related to violence against women are examined from feminist perspectives. In Section 3, transformative approach to violence against women as well as human-centered reading of international law cases by the Feminist Judgment Project will be presented as a way of making international law more transformative before concluding the chapter in Section 4. Although the author is aware that violence can take diverse forms according to different contexts, in this chapter, violence against women or GBVAW is used as a general term unless otherwise indicated.

2 Feminist Approaches to International Law and the Violence against Women

2.1 *Feminist Approaches to International Law*

Feminist approaches to international law were inspired, at least partially, by the fight against GBVAW and has also contributed to it. In fact, the very article that first presented the approach was published at almost the same time as women organized around the globe to claim international attention on the issue of violence against women.[9] The feminist approach in international law is, as Hilary Charlesworth summarizes, 'a type of inquiry, a way of asking questions that draws attention to particular silences in the field of international law and that often relies on sex and gender as categories of analysis'.[10] Another important feature of feminist inquiry is that it is 'a specific political project, making women's lives visible, in the hope that such investigations will

---

8 Toshiki Mogami, 'Non-State Actors and International Law: A Tentative Theorization on the Conversion of the Principle of the Legal Order' (2009) 108, *Journal of International Law and Diplomacy*, 117–143, 118 (in Japanese).

9 See Hilary Charlesworth, Christine Chinkin and Shelley Wright, 'Feminist Approaches to International law' (1991) 85, *American Journal of International Law*, 613–645, especially 628–629.

10 Charlesworth (n 3) xxv.

shape the future'.[11] Violence against women is indeed an issue which has been kept silent in international law but affects women systemically and severely because of sex and gender. It is also 'a specific political project' because it requires changes in the power relationship between men and women which is deeply engrained in society as 'gender'.

Feminist international law criticizes international law that it is constructed upon a particular assumption taking 'man' to represent 'human'. International law has claimed to have authority because of its impartiality and objectivity and, thus, it is universally applicable.[12] However, from the feminist perspective, the fact that international law traditionally is almost entirely made by men is impinging upon its authority and universality.[13] Furthermore, it is also articulated that men, regardless of where they come from, have used the statist system to establish economic and nationalist priorities to serve male elites, even when basic human, social and economic needs are not met.[14] The abstract states have concealed the fact that it was based on the interests of men who had the privilege of presenting themselves in international arena. On the other hand, domestic terrain was left invisible from the international. It may have been even convenient for male leaders to put everything in a black box labelled 'domestic' so that they did not have to deal with uncomfortable issues such as violence against women in international negotiations.[15] The quests by feminist international law scholars have revealed that the international law is not autonomous but affected by deeply engrained gender in various aspects of the discipline.[16]

---

11 ibid xxvi.

12 Hilary Charlesworth and Christine Chinkin, *Boundaries of International Law: A Feminist Analysis* (Manchester University Press 2000) 17–18.

13 ibid.

14 Charlesworth, Chinkin and Wright (n 9) 615.

15 See Rosa Ehrenreich Brookes, 'Feminism and International Law: An Opportunity for Transformation' (2002) 14, *Yale Journal of Law and Feminism,* 345–361, 348.

16 See Charlesworth and Chinkin (n 12) for international law in general. Since then, there have been other works, for example, on peace and security, Diane Otto and Gina Heathcote(eds), *Rethinking Peacekeeping, Gender Equality and Collective Security* (Palgrave Macmillan 2014); on the state sovereignty, Karen Knop, 'Re/Statements: Feminism and State Sovereignty in International Law' (1993) 3 *Transnational Law and Contemporary Problems* 293–344; Gina Heathcote, *Feminist Dialogues of International Law: Successes, Tensions, Futures* (Oxford University Press 2019) 103–132; on the Law of the Sea, Irini Papanicolopulu, *Gender and the Law of the Sea* (Brill 2019); on international economic law, Anne Orford, 'Trade, Human Rights and the Economy of Sacrifice' in Anne Orford (ed), *International Law and its Others* (Cambridge University Press 2006) 156–196 and Miho Omi, 'Trade Liberalization and Women: A Feminist Analysis of the WTO System'

International human rights law is a venture to hold states accountable to the individuals living in their jurisdictions who are not necessarily visible in international law. Although sharing the need to pay attention to the individuals with international human rights law, the feminist analysis has shown that international human rights law does not always help women; it may even conceal vulnerability and discrimination women endure because international human rights law, as part of international law, also assumes men as the standard.[17]

2.2 *International Developments on Violence against Women: an Overview*

Violence against women was mentioned without being so named during the International Women's Year in 1975 and subsequent UN Decade for Women (1976–1985).[18] The Nairobi Forward-Looking Strategies for the Advancement of Women, adopted at the end of the Decade, stated '[G]ender-specific violence is increasing and Governments must affirm the dignity of women as a priority action'[19] and referred to the issue in several paragraphs.[20] However, it was the global campaign organized by women in preparation for the Second World Conference on Human Rights held in Vienna in 1993 that presented women's voices clearly and strongly in the international community. The campaign, claiming that 'women's rights are human rights', successfully challenged the invisibility of abuses in private contexts of family and intimate relationships.[21] It brought the recognition that the human rights of women and of the girl-child were an inalienable, integrated and indivisible part of universal human rights into the Vienna Declaration and Programme of Action.[22] In the rise of such momentum, the Committee on the Elimination of Discrimination against Women (hereinafter, CEDAW Committee) to monitor

in Jaya Segade, Vedna Jivan an Christine Forster (eds), *Feminism in the Subcontinent and Beyond: Challenging Laws, Changing Laws* (Eastern Book Company 2014) 283–307.

17 See Charlesworth and Chinkin (n 12) 231–244.

18 Christine Chinkin, 'Violence Against Women' in Marsha A Freeman, Christine Chinkin and Beate Rudolf (eds), *The UN Convention on the Elimination of All Forms of Discrimination against Women: A Commentary* (Oxford University Press 2012) 443–474, 444–445.

19 'Report of the World Conference to Review and Appraise the Achievements of the United Nations Decade for Women: Equality, Development and Peace, Nairobi, 15–26 July 1985', A/CONF.116/28/Rev.1 (1986) para 288.

20 ibid paras 231, 245, 258, 271 and 287.

21 Niamh Reilly, 'Women, Gender, and International Human Rights: Overview' in Niamh Reilly(ed), *International Human Rights of Women* (Springer 2019) 1–18, 4.

22 World Conference on Human Rights, Vienna, 14–25 June 1993 'Vienna Declaration and Programme of Action (25 June 1993)' A/Conf.157/23 (12 July 1993) para 18.

the implementation of the Convention on the Elimination of All Forms of Discrimination against Women (hereinafter, CEDAW Convention)[23] adopted General Recommendation No 19 in 1992. It defined GBVAW as 'violence that is directed against a woman because she is a woman or that affects women disproportionately including acts that inflict physical, mental or sexual harm or suffering, threats of such acts, coercion and other deprivations of liberty'.[24] It also stated that it is a form of sex discrimination as provided in Article 1 of the Convention.[25]

After the Vienna Conference, the UN General Assembly adopted the Declaration on the Elimination of Violence against Women (hereinafter, DEVAW)[26] and the Commission on Human Rights, the predecessor of the Human Rights Council, appointed the first Special Rapporteur on Violence against Women.[27] The Beijing Platform for Action adopted by the Fourth World Conference on Women in 1995 included violence against women as one of its twelve critical areas of concern.[28] The Beijing Platform urged the Governments and other domestic as well as international actors to take integrated measures to prevent and eliminate violence against women.[29] These international developments lead by women worldwide also encouraged national governments to work on domestic policies and legislation on the issue of violence against women.[30] Moreover, regions such as the Americas, Africa and Europe adopted legally binding treaties. These regional treaties also have their own monitoring mechanisms and can be used in respective regional human rights courts.[31]

---

23 UNTS, vol 1249, no 20378.

24 CEDAW, 'General Recommendation No 19 (1992) on violence against women (hereinafter, GR No 19)' in A/47/38 (1993) para 6.

25 ibid para 7 and CEDAW, 'General Recommendation No 35 on Gender-Based Violence against Women, Updating General Recommendation No 19 (hereinafter, GR No 35)', CEDAW/C/GC/35 (14 July 2017) para 1.

26 'UN Declaration on the Elimination of Violence against Women (hereinafter, DEVAW)', A/RES/48/104 (20 December 1993).

27 UN Commission on Human Rights, 'Special Rapporteur on Violence against Women, Its Causes and Consequences', E/CN.4/RES/1994/45 (4 March 1994).

28 Beijing Platform for Action in UN, 'Report of the Fourth World Conference on Women, Beijing, 4–15 September 1995', A/CONF.177/20/Rev.1 (1996) para 44.

29 See ibid Strategic Objective D1.

30 In Japan, for example, the Act on the Prevention of Spousal Violence and Protection of Victims was adopted in 2001 in the process inspired by and followed the Beijing Conference. See, for example, Taeko Kojima, *Domestic Violence no Hou* [*The Law of Domestic Violence*] (Shinzansha 2002) 61–70.

31 See (n 2).

3 International Law on Violence against Women from Feminist Perspectives

3.1 *Violence against Women and Women's Human Rights*

Despite the developments as described above, international law regarding GBVAW has some 'failures' in dealing with the issue. One is that the CEDAW Convention, the first internationally binding document to specifically guarantee women's human rights, does not have any reference to violence against women in its articles. There are several reasons to explain it. First, in the UN World Conferences on Women held by the UN from 1975 to 1985, the drafting process of the Convention and other meetings of the UN, violence against women was mentioned but was not perceived as an issue of gender or unequal power relationship between men and women until the Nairobi Forward-Looking Strategies referred to it as 'gender-specific violence'.[32] Even after the Nairobi Conference, UN General Assembly's first resolution on domestic violence[33] did not identify women as the main victims of such violence.[34] Second, it was widely considered that violence against women was a personal problem in the private sphere and, therefore, it was conceptually difficult to compress the harm of violence against women into the public frame of the Convention.[35] Third, violence against women in the private sphere did not fit directly into the equality model on which the CEDAW Convention was based.[36] The CEDAW Convention is mostly constructed on liberal feminist model whose central concern is to place women on the same footing as men in the public sphere.[37]

The equality model adopted by the CEDAW Convention involves a further problem in guaranteeing human rights for women. As Charlesworth and Christine Chinkin articulate, equal treatment only provides circumscribed protection to women if the existing law identifies sexual equality with equal treatment. 'Sexual equality' here means not only substantive equality but also 'a fuller set of rights in the international law on women's rights'.[38] In other words, substantive equality requires recognition of and appropriate responses to gender-specific harms that will not be addressed by gender-neutral or formal equality measures.[39] Therefore, equality construct of the international human

32 See (n 19).
33 UNGA, 'Domestic violence' A/Res/40/36 (29 November 1985).
34 See Chinkin (n 18) 444–445.
35 Charlesworth and Chinkin (n 12) 231.
36 ibid.
37 ibid 229.
38 ibid.
39 Chinkin (n 18) 463.

rights law including the CEDAW Convention has been criticized by feminist scholars because it does not take 'women's rights' into consideration. Charlotte Bunch wondered if these crimes were perpetrated against any group other than women, it 'would be recognized as a civil and political emergency as well as a gross violation of the victims' humanity'.[40] However, when it is inflicted on women, it is not considered as a human rights issue because women's rights and human rights have been viewed as distinct despite a clear record of death and demonstrable abuse against women.[41] Therefore, she claimed that 'the specific experiences of women must be added to traditional approaches to human rights in order to make women more visible and to transform the concept and practice of human rights in our culture so that it takes better account of women's lives'.[42] Violence against women is a touchstone that illustrates the limited concept of human rights and highlights the political nature of the abuse of women.[43] GBVAW is an issue which requires defining rights particular to women, that cannot be placed in the framework of equality with men because men are not in a comparative position to women in this regard. Defining specific women's rights is one way of moving beyond the limitations of the non-discrimination focus of women's international human rights law.[44]

Alice Edwards explored this critical view of the equality approach and shed light on the effect of formulating violence against women as a form of sex discrimination. She pointed out that violence was condemned in society to an extent that discriminatory treatment against women was not.[45] Edwards warns that utilizing sex discrimination law because it is the only available remedy almost covers up the violence that has occurred or diminishes the extent of the conduct. We need to be careful about calling violent conduct discrimination rather than violence itself because violence that disproportionately affects men is not burdened to prove an additional link to sex discrimination or any other additional factors.[46]

Gender-based violence is not limited to violence against women; it may include violence against men and sexual orientation and gender identity

---

40 Charlotte Bunch, 'Women's Rights as Human Rights: Toward a Re-Vision of Human Rights' (1990) 12, *Human Rights Quarterly*, 486–498, 486.

41 ibid.

42 ibid 487.

43 ibid 490.

44 Charlesworth and Chinkin (n 12) 249.

45 Alice Edwards, 'Violence against Women as Sex Discrimination: Judging the Jurisprudence of the UN Human Rights Treaty Bodies' (2008), 18 *Texas Journal of Women and the Law*, 1–60, 57.

46 ibid 57–58.

(SOGI) minorities. GBVAW also takes many different forms and expressions affected by various intersectional factors such as race, class, ethnicity, religion, language, and nationality, among others. However, GBVAW still is a major problem for women as a group because such violence is caused and exacerbated by the social, cultural, economic, and political inequality affected by gender.

3.2 *Violence against Women and International Injustice*

Feminists have claimed that violence against women is an international or global phenomenon to be recognized in international law. It is a grave and systemic violation of women's human rights worldwide and requires international measures to protect women 'universally'.[47] The Declaration on the Elimination of Violence against Women listed human rights of women to be enjoyed and protected especially in relations to violence against women:[48] the right to life;[49] the right to equality;[50] the right to liberty and security of person;[51] the right to equal protection under the law;[52] the right to the highest standard attainable of physical and mental health;[53] the right to just and favorable conditions of work;[54] and the right not to be subjected to torture, or other cruel, inhuman or degrading treatment or punishment.[55] General Recommendation No 19 by the CEDAW Committee also has a similar list.[56] These are human rights that have been guaranteed elsewhere in international human rights law such as the Universal Declaration of Human Rights and the International Covenants on Civil and Political Rights and on Economic, Social and Cultural Rights. Chinkin states, that since General Recommendation No 19 presented violence against women as a form of discrimination which is a violation of women's human rights, the Convention recognizes that 'women are entitled to be free from violence and the fear of violence and State parties have

47 See Bunch (n 40) 486.
48 DEVAW (n 26) art 3.
49 See UNGA, 'Universal Declaration of Human Rights (UDHR)', A/Res/217(III) (10 December 1948) art 3.
50 See ibid art 1.
51 See ibid art 3.
52 See ibid art 7.
53 See ibid art 25 and International Covenant on Economic, Social and Cultural Rights (hereinafter, ICESCR), UNTS, vol 993, no 14531, art 12(1).
54 See UDHR art 23(1) and ICESCR art 7.
55 See UDHR art 5 and International Covenant on Civil and Political Rights (hereinafter, ICCPR), UNTS, vol 999, no 14668, art 7.
56 CEDAW, GR No 19 (n 24) para 7 which also mentions equal protection according to humanitarian norms in time of international or internal armed conflict and equality in the family.

a legal obligation to ensure this right'. This rights-based approach shows that violence against women is not 'natural' or 'inevitable' but a failure of States parties' obligations.[57] The CEDAW Committee's General Recommendation No 35 also elaborates on state party's obligation that '[F]or more than 25 years, in their practice, States parties have endorsed the Committee's interpretation. The *opinio juris* and State practice suggest that the prohibition of GBVAW has evolved into a principle of customary international law'.[58] It seems appropriate to blame the failure of states in meeting their obligation on protecting women's rights to be free from violence.

In the construct of international justice, states are held responsible if they break the rule and cause harm to 'other states' as they invoke international responsibility. International justice in this regard is a form of justice between equals operating on the horizontal plane of international law that emerges from the possibility of calling other states to account.[59] However, the promise of human rights is judged by whether the state prevents and protects human rights of individuals and not of 'other states'. Asking if the concept of international justice is applicable to the sphere of international human rights, Frédéric Mégret referred to the expansion of the human rights ideal, through the Universal Declaration of Human Rights and related treaties, beyond the domestic sphere. Such human rights ideal is adopted as a standard of common achievement for the international community. Nevertheless, as Mégret articulates, there is a tendency of international human rights law not to problematize the international legal system within which human rights operate.[60] This tendency has prevented international human rights law from actively questioning, for example, international economic justice and global redistribution which is closely related to the idea of economic and social rights.[61]

Another reason why it is difficult for violation of international human rights law to be considered as an international injustice may be, as Charlesworth states, that justice and the protection of human rights are not regarded as synonymous in international law because the monitoring institutions of international human rights law are based on processes of dialogue and pressure rather

---

57 Chinkin (n 18) 450–451.

58 CEDAW, GR No 35 (n 25) para 2.

59 Frédéric Mégret, 'Justice' in Jean d'Aspremont and Sahib Shingh (eds), *Concepts for International Law: Contributions to Disciplinary Thought* (Edward Elgar 2019) 585–606, 589.

60 ibid 590.

61 ibid.

than traditional adjudication.[62] This may be linked to the fact that human rights are traditionally considered as a domestic matter of state and, thus, realization of human rights are left in the hands of each state. Furthermore, since the State was supposed to have contact only with men in the public sphere, imagination of traditional international human rights law was limited to 'what men fear will happen to them'[63] and that rendered women invisible from international law.[64] As a result, the inside of each nation became a black box of which the world of international law could not or did not wish to see the inside.[65] Even after international human rights law set some limits on state sovereignty, international human rights law was expected to regulate the act of state agency in the public sphere only. Violence against women committed by non-State actors such as fathers and husbands in the private sphere was made invisible, because they were in another black box called the family or an intimate space.[66]

Since traditional international law is a discipline devoted to the study of positive rules,[67] the forms of justice envisaged in the international legal system is very limited and there is 'a dissonance between the promise and performance of international law'.[68] The issue of violence against women is clearly such a matter which has fallen in the gap between the promise and performance of international law.

3.3 *Claims for New Legally Binding Instruments*

If international law does not respond to the injustice many women endure because the current international norm on GBVAW is not 'positive' enough, the next imaginable step to take is to have clear rules prohibiting such acts. In fact, there have been claims for a new United Nations Convention on the Elimination of All Forms of Violence against Women or a new Optional Protocol on this

62 Hilary Charlesworth, 'International Law and International Justice' (hereinafter, International Justice) in Chris Brown and Robyn Eckersley (eds), *The Oxford Handbook of International Political Theory* (Oxford University Press 2018) (paperback 2020) 143–152, 148.

63 Hilary Charlesworth, 'What are Women's International Human Rights?' in Rebecca Cook (ed), *Human Rights of Women: National and International Perspectives* (University of Pennsylvania Press 1994) 71.

64 Brookes (n 15) 348.

65 ibid.

66 ibid.

67 Mégret (n 59) 585.

68 Charlesworth (n 62) 150.

matter to the CEDAW Convention.[69] Proponents of a new instrument assert that there is a 'normative gap' between the standard of human dignity widely agreed upon by states and the binding rules instituted to hold states accountable to this standard in laws and practice related to GBVAW.[70]

The reasons behind such claims include, first, the existing CEDAW Convention has a problem with state accountability. It does not directly require states to respond to and eradicate violence against women except Article 6 on trafficking in women and exploitation of the prostitution of women.[71] In addition, the state parties have numerous reservations to the Convention which constitute a substantial obstacle to the implementation of the Convention.[72] Under such circumstances, it is not easy to hold states accountable for their obligation to eliminate violence against women within their jurisdiction. Secondly, reliance on non-binding interpretation of the treaty limits the effectiveness of existing treaty body procedures in addressing violence against women.[73] In addition, Rashida Manjoo states, that the soft law developments within the UN system have not led to substantive change at the national level[74] and the difference between the soft law developments within the UN human rights system and the hard law developments within three regional human rights systems should not be ignored.[75] In binding treaty obligations at the regional level, as Manjoo states, violence against women has been addressed more specifically and comprehensively. Such obligations also produced important case law from the commissions and courts related to these systems, operating in parallel to the international system.[76] However, Asia, the Pacific, and the Middle East do not have such regional conventions yet.[77]

It is true that a 'soft law' approach which continues today may not have sufficient power to make states accountable to their normative obligation. However, it is also true that states have responded by reporting on the measures they

69 Aisha K Gill, 'Introduction: Violence Against women and the Need for International Law' in Jackie Jones and Rashida Manjoo (eds), *The Legal Protection of Women from Violence: Normative Gaps in International Law* (Routledge 2018) 1–8, 3.

70 David L Richards and Jillienne Haglund, 'Exploring the Consequences of the Normative Gap in Legal Protections Addressing Violence Against Women' in Jones and Manjoo (eds), ibid 40–72, 40–41.

71 Gill (n 69) 3.

72 ibid 4.

73 Rashida Manjoo, 'Normative Developments on Violence Against Women in the United Nations System' in Jones and Manjoo (n 69) 73–106, 94–95.

74 ibid 97.

75 ibid 95.

76 ibid.

77 Gill, (n 69) 5.

take on violence against women, revising their laws, or confirming responsibility of the states in their judiciary. On the other hand, it is possible that states place reservations on the new Convention or the Optional Protocol if they are allowed. The new instrument could limit the power of states to put reservations, but it may decrease the possibility of the instrument to be adopted or ratified. Although to have a legally binding international document specifically on GBVAW remains an option, it does not seem to be realized in the coming years.

3.4 *Criminal Law Approach*

There is another way to make states internationally accountable for their obligations on GBVAW, which is to recognize it as an international crime. International criminal law such as the Rome Statute of the International Criminal Court[78] and the Protocol to Prevent, Suppress and Punish Trafficking in Persons Especially Women and Children (Palermo Protocol)[79] include violence against women in their jurisdiction. However, reliance on international criminal justice remedies may have their own limitation because they cover only certain aspects of gender-based violence. As a result, the state response could be confined to articulating criminal remedies and not transformative remedies that potentially change the realities that women face.[80] On the other hand, since criminal law traditionally has been placed at the very heart of national laws and state sovereignty, only serious forms of international crimes such as terrorism, torture, trafficking in human beings, and the border-crossing sexual exploitation of children have been recognized as necessary to have harmonized rules within domestic rules.[81] Minni Leskinen, on this point, states that 'it should not be understated that the Istanbul Convention, with its obligations to criminalise certain crimes on a national level, places violence against women into a framework of serious criminality'.[82]

There are also concerns about strengthening domestic criminal law on violence against women. Ratna Kapur cautions us that stricter criminal law to punish violence against women can be adopted without consideration to the gender relationship in society. She criticizes the Indian criminal law reform in

78 Sexual violence is included in art 7 on crimes against humanity and art 8 on war crimes in the Rome Statue, UNTS, vol 2187, no 38544.

79 UNTS, vol 227, no 39574.

80 Manjoo (n 73) 95.

81 Minni Leskinen, 'The Istanbul Convention on Sexual Offences: A Duty to Reform the Wording of National Law or the Way We Think?' in Johanna Niemi, Lourdes Peroni and Vladislava Stoyanova (eds), *International Law and Violence Against Women: Europe and the Istanbul Convention* (Routledge 2020) (hereinafter, *Istanbul Convention*) 133–156, 134.

82 ibid.

2012, which took place as a response to the protests by women against the rape and murder of the 23-year-old woman on a moving bus in New Delhi. The government introduced a provision for the death penalty where rape resulted in the death or maiming of the victim, strengthened law enforcement machinery, and increased surveillance on public transportation.[83] However, Kapur points out that the protests represented a defiant demand by women 'for the recognition of women's rights not only concerning public safety, but also in relation to bodily integrity and sexual autonomy'.[84] The government, on the other hand, refused to remove the marital rape exemption from the criminal law and the colonial and Victorian provisions concerning the outraging of a woman's modesty and chastity.[85] Kapur summarizes the situation as follows:

> Women's rights advocacy is directed at the state to demand redress and protection, primarily in the form of carceral measures, which in turn translates into a general tightening of the sexual security regime in accordance with national and cultural imperatives. This carceral vision is also embedded within a neoliberal paradigm that view VAW as an obstruction of women's participation in the market, with the market epitomizing the desired coalescence of subjectivity, choice and economic agency – crucial variables in the calculus of liberal freedom.[86]

Concerns on reliance on criminal law is that it may leave the 'gender' part of the matter which is interwoven in many aspects of social fabric untouched. As Kapur cautions, such an approach may even strengthen the existing gender framework without recognizing women's agency.

4 Transformative Approach to Gender-Based Violence against Women

4.1 *Transformative Equality*

The issues that traditional international law has avoided facing as pointed out in the previous discussion, including GBVAW, are the ones which require transformative effort to change some aspects of the present order. Therefore,

83 Ratna Kapur, *Gender, Alterity and Human Rights: Freedom in a Fishbowl* (Edward Elgar 2018) 87.
84 ibid 86–87.
85 ibid 87.
86 ibid 89.

it is worth referring to the discussion about transformative equality in international human rights law. Discussing the principle of equality of opportunity irrespective of sex, Evelyn Ellis states that '[T]he non-discrimination principle is essentially the non-dynamic part of the equality package; it works only in conjunction with dynamic measures of social reorganization'.[87] The static nature of non-discrimination does not require adjustment of circumstances to guarantee equal treatment[88] and, thus, women's rights tend to be determined with reference to a male norm unless 'the non-discrimination principle is coupled with serious positive measures for the reordering of society so as to eliminate gender segregation and stereotyping'.[89] In other words, 'reordering of the society' is indispensable to overcome current gendered structure of the society.

The concept of such 'transformative equality' is already included in international human rights law. For example, Article 4 (1) of the CEDAW Convention stipulates temporary special measures to accelerate *de facto* equality between men and women shall not be considered discrimination. Explaining about the object and purposes of the Convention in relation to this clause, the General Recommendation No. 25 states '[T]he position of women will not be improved as long as the underlying causes of discrimination against women, and of their inequality, are not effectively addressed. The lives of women and men must be considered in a contextual way, and measures adopted towards a real transformation of opportunities, institutions and systems so that they are no longer grounded in historically determined male paradigms of power and life patterns'.[90] It also states 'to address prevailing gender relations and the persistence of gender-based stereotypes that affect women not only through individual acts by individuals but also in law, and legal and societal structures and institutions' is a States parties' obligation.[91]

4.2 *Transformative Approaches to Gender-Based Violence against Women*

Transformative measures are necessary not only for attaining gender equality in, for example, employment and political participation, but also to combat

87 Evelyn Ellis, 'The Principle of Equality of Opportunity Irrespective of Sex: Some Reflections on the Present State of European Community Law and the Future Development' in Alan Dashwood and Siofra O'Leary (eds), *The Principle of Equal Treatment in EC Law* (Sweet & Maxwell 1997) 172–188, 180.

88 ibid 173.

89 ibid 180.

90 CEDAW, 'General Recommendation No 25 on article 4, paragraph 1, of the Convention (Temporary Special Measures)' in A/59/38 (2004) para 10.

91 ibid para 7.

GBVAW. As we have seen above, it is true that there are problems arising from the formation of violence against women as a form of sex discrimination in responding to such violence. However, it is also true that GBVAW is an expression of inequality between men and women and tackling the issue necessarily involves fight for equality and non-discrimination.

Regarding what should be transformed to eliminate violence against women, the General Recommendation No 35 stressed that the term 'gender-based violence against women' is used to make explicit the gendered causes and impacts of the violence as well as to strengthen the understanding of the violence as a social rather than an individual problem.[92] The General Recommendation also regards GBVAW as being rooted in gender-related factors, such as the ideology of men's entitlement and privilege over women, social norms regarding masculinity and the need to assert male control or power, to enforce gender roles, and to prevent, discourage or punish what is considered unacceptable female behavior.[93]

Lourdes Peroni, discussing the measures included in the Istanbul Convention, articulated that the Istanbul Convention challenges the existing value patterns by addressing dominant societal attitudes, beliefs and behaviors that regard women as inferior to men and keep women in subordinate positions and roles in society.[94] Peroni classifies the measures contained in the Istanbul Convention into two groups: societal measures and institutional measures.[95] The first set of measures seeks to transform the negative view on women prevailing in society at large, including in schools and through the media, to promote 'changes in mentality and attitudes' to prevent violence against women from occurring.[96] The second group aims to address women's inferior status in state institutional contexts to ease, for example, the attitudinal barriers women victims of violence face in seeking justice in instances of sexual violence. The Convention prohibits States to use evidence related to victims' sexual conduct or history unless it is 'relevant and necessary' in Article 54 because this type of evidence 'may reinforce the perpetuation of damaging

92 ibid para 9.

93 ibid para 19.

94 Lourdes Peroni, 'Unleashing the Gender Equality Potential of the Istanbul Convention' in Niemi *et al* (n 81) 43–56, 45.

95 ibid.

96 ibid 46.

stereotypes of victims as being promiscuous and by extension immoral and not worthy of the protection provided by civil and criminal law'.[97]

In addition to these societal attitudes, Peroni claims, 'if the [Istanbul] Convention is to fully realise its substantive equality aspiration and to effectively combat violence against women, it needs to be interpreted so as to promote women's de facto equality political and socio-economically'.[98] Regarding these aspects, the General Recommendation No 35 of the CEDAW Committee refers to 'the neglect or denial of women's civil, political, economic, social and cultural rights' together with 'patriarchal attitudes and stereotypes' as the underlying causes of GBVAW and asks States to address these causes.[99] As the Explanatory Report on the Istanbul Convention states, '[A]ny measures taken to prevent and combat violence against women need to promote equality between women and men as only substantive equality will prevent such violence in the future',[100] it is indispensable to change societal and political circumstances for women to eliminate violence against women. 'Equality between women and men' should not be equality based on a male standard as was shown in the discussion on the necessity of 'women's human rights' based on the experience of women.

There are also references to transformative 'means' in existing international documents. For example, in the General Recommendation No 35, the CEDAW Committee recommends, as an obligation to prevent violence against women, States parties to adopt and implement effective legislative and other appropriate measures to address the underlying causes of GBVAW, including patriarchal attitudes and stereotypes, inequality in the family and the neglect or denial of women's civil, political, economic, social and cultural rights, and to promote the empowerment, agency and voices of women.[101] It also recommends developing and implementing effective measures to address and eradicate the stereotypes, prejudices, customs and practices set out in Article 5 of the Convention, which condone or promote GBVAW and underpin the structural inequality of women with men.[102] Such measures to transform these factors is heavily reliant on education of the general society, the younger generation,

97 ibid 47–48 and Council of Europe, 'Explanatory Report to the Council of Europe Convention on Preventing and Combating Violence against Women and Domestic Violence, Istanbul, 11.V. 2011, CETS no 210 (hereinafter, Explanatory Report)' para 277.

98 ibid 44. Peroni also expects the Convention's monitoring body (GREVIO) plays an important role to advance women's equality in political, social, and economic rights. ibid.

99 CEDAW, GR No 35 (n 25) para 34.

100 Council of Europe (n 97) para 49.

101 CEDAW, GR No 35 (n 25) para 30 (a).

102 ibid para 30 (b).

the judiciary, lawyers and law enforcement officers, the legislators, and healthcare professionals.[103] The Explanatory Report of the Istanbul Convention, regarding necessary measures of prevention that State parties should take, refers to the needs of specific programmes and activities for women's political and economic empowerment to increase women's agency and reducing their vulnerability to violence.[104] There are also cases of individual complaint and investigation procedures under the Optional Protocol to the CEDAW Convention on violence against women in which the Committee recommended the state parties concerned to take transformative action.[105] Although such soft-law approaches have been criticized as weak in holding the states accountable, these recommendations articulated the necessity to change the culture and general perception of women in the society and in legal procedures according to each concrete circumstances. Due diligence obligation recommended in the Committee's views[106] also requires reorganization of prevention, protection, investigation, prosecution, and support in existing practices. These elements tend to be left invisible in domestic legal systems but international human rights law including the soft-law approach can shed light on such aspects in guaranteeing women's rights.

---

103 See DEVAW (n 26) art 4 (j) and ibid para 30 (b) (i), (ii) and (e).

104 Council of Europe (n 97) para 90 on art 12 (6).

105 Individual complaint cases of gender-based violence against women with views of the CEDAW Committee that referred to some transformative or structural elements includes, for example, *Kell v Canada* Communication no 19/2008 [2012)], CEDAW/C/51/D/19/2008; *Jallow v Bulgaria* Communication no 32/2011[2012], CEDAW/C/52/D/32/2011; *RPB. v Philippines* Communication no 34/2011 [2014], CEDAW/C/57/D/34/2011; *Correño v Spain* Communication no 47/2012 [2014], CEDAW/C/58/D/47/2012; *X and Y v Georgia* Communication no 24/2009 [2015], CEDAW/C/61/D/24/2009; *Belousova v Kazakhstan* Communication no 45/2012 (2015), CEDAW/C/61/D/45/2012; *L R v. Moldova* Communication no 58/2013 [2017], CEDAW/C/66/D/58/2013; *JI v Finland* Communication no 103/2016 [2018], CEDAW/C/69/D/103/2016; *S T v Russia* Communication no 65/2014 [2019], CEDAW/C/72/D/65/2014; and *SL v Bulgaria* Communication no 99/016 [2019], CEDAW/C/73/D/99/2016. Inquiry cases related to violence against women based on art 8 of the Optional Protocol to the CEDAW Convention on which the Committee produced reports with transformative or structural views include: 'Report on Mexico', CEDAW/C/2005/OP.8/MEXICO (27 January 2005); 'Report of the inquiry concerning Canada', CEDAW/C/OP.8/CAN/1 (30 March 2015); 'Inquiry concerning Kyrgyzstan', CEDAW/C/OP.8/KGZ/1 (21 September 2018); 'Inquiry concerning Mali', CEDAW/C/IR/MLI/1 (24 December 2918); and 'Inquiry concerning South Africa', CEDAW/C/ZAF/IR/1 (14 May 2021).

106 See, for example, *Goekce v Austria* Communication 5/2005 [2007], CEDAW/C/39/D/5/2005 para 12.3(a); *Yildirim v Austria* Communication 6/2005 [2007], CEDAW/C/39/D/6/2005 para 12.3(a); *Correño v Spain*, ibid para 11(b)(ii); and *JI v Finland*, ibid para 10(b)(iii).

4.3 *Human-Centered Reading of International Law: Challenges by Feminist Judgments*

Feminist judgments in international law[107] is a notable recent development in feminist international law. Feminist judgments first started as a project called 'Women's Court of Canada' to rewrite the judgments made by the Supreme Court of Canada to show alternative practical and legal expressions of substantial quality from feminist perspectives.[108] It highlights law's silences through the use of contextual materials.[109] In the project to rewrite international law cases, although decision of the cases was left to each 'court' comprising of one to four 'judge(s)' who are mostly academics, it seems that most of the courts took contextual and human-centered approaches with attention to gender and intersectionality in rewriting cases.

Zoi Aliozi, Bérénice K. Schramm and Ekaterina Yahyaoui Krivenko, for example, drew five elements of feminist theorizing in rewriting an ICJ case: context specific analysis, attention to the individual and his/her suffering, intersectionality, deconstruction of binaries, and absence of hierarchies.[110] Focusing on the specific context questions the assumption that the law is always autonomous and distinct from the society it regulates. Attention to the individuals shows that abstract rationality on which international law is supposed to operate does not always pay enough attention to individual sufferings because it often prioritizes the benefit of an abstract state over the welfare of an actual human person who is in the center of the matter. Intersectionality is a tool to deconstruct the premise of universal applicability of international law because intersectional impact of race, culture, religion, class, gender among others makes each individual's suffering different.

Another project rewriting the *Opuz v Turkey*,[111] a domestic violence case decided by the European Human Rights Court, stresses intersectionality in order not to single out Turkey but to express that the 'phenomenon' of

107 See Hodson and Lavers (n 4) and Loveday Hodson, 'A feminist approach to *Alyne da Silva Pimentel Teixeira (deceased) v Brazil*' in Gonzalez-Salzberg and Hodson (eds), *Research Methods for International Human Rights Law: Beyond the Traditional Paradigm* (Routledge 2020) 42–68.

108 Rosemary Hunter, Clare McGlynn and Erika Rackley, 'Feminist Judgments: An Introduction' in Rosemary Hunter, Clare McGlynn and Erika Rackley (eds), *Feminist Judgments: From Theory to Practice* (Hart 2010) (hereinafter, *Feminist Judgments*) 1–29, 3.

109 Rosemary Hunter, 'An account of Feminist Judging' in ibid, 30–43, 35–40.

110 Zoi Aliozi, Bérénice K. Schramm and Ekaterina Yahyaoui Krivenko, '*Germany v Italy*', in Hodson and Lavers (n 4) 117–148, 123–124.

111 *Opuz v Turkey* APP no 33401/02 (ECtHR, 9 June 2009).

domestic violence is a global and culture-free issue,[112] Shazia Choudhry and Jonathan Herring also listed their own elements in rewriting the *Opuz* case in addition to intersectionality. Although the original judgment recognized violation of the European Human Rights Convention by Turkey in protecting the victim and her mother from domestic violence by the victim's husband, their elements mostly centered on the act of domestic violence itself. The original judgment did not provide a definition of domestic violence nor acknowledge the patriarchal social structures that enables an abusive man to control his female partner. In addition, it did not mention the prevalence of domestic violence or its impact on children.[113] The re-written judgment is constructed on the knowledge that women's and feminist movements have accumulated and showed the case in a wider context of gender inequality in society.

These feminist judgment cases show us that even without having a new instrument and mostly following the procedures that existing courts use, it is possible to reach more context-oriented and human-centered judgments. Rewriting cases is also a process for feminist international law to verify how binary oppositions determine the outcome of the case and deconstruction of such binaries as male/female, state/individual, and international/domestic together with hierarchies that underlie the reasoning of the existing judgments can change the way international law operates.[114] The challenges of feminist judgment may be able to make international law listen to the silences kept in the system for so long.

5 Conclusion

Feminist international law in the past 30 years has tried various ways to make a difference on the issue of GBVAW. Bringing the issue of violence against women into the arena of international law marked an ideological shift to make a private matter to a social problem, which has increased public awareness.[115] Despite the difficulties faced by the quest for a violence-free world for women, feminists generally believe that international law can be a weapon against systemic

112 Shazia Choudhry and Jonathan Herring, '*Opuz v Turkey*' in Hodson and Lavers (n 4) 253–278, 255.
113 ibid 254–255.
114 Aliozi *et al* (n 110) 124.
115 Aisha K Gill, Gina Heathcote and Emma Williamson, 'Introduction' (2016) 112 *Feminist Review*, 1–10, 2.

oppression[116] based on the promise of universal human rights. Strong equality guarantees in legal systems are also necessary for transformative approaches to be employed.[117] Therefore, international law and international human rights law still occupy an important position in the fight against GBVAW.

In this chapter, I tried to show that the issue of GBVAW should be considered in a wider context of gender inequality because, although it may sound tautological, it is a problem caused by gender inequality. Transformative equality stressed the need to reorganize the social structure where inequality is engrained. Charlesworth, Chinkin and Shelley Wright pointed out more than 30 years ago that it is necessary to focus on the context, be sensitive to the effect of gender as well as of intersectionality to overcome the state- and male-centric abstractness. Feminist judgments in international law presented us a way to correspond to that appeal of context-centered approach. Knowing that there are alternative ways of applying international law may transform the system that has kept silence on GBVAW. Furthermore, as Beth Goldblatt articulates, if we try to prevent violence against women by addressing the material causes of women's vulnerability using social and economic rights, it can also shift the emphasis away from protection and the consequent dangers of state control,[118] which may alleviate such concerns as indicated by Kapur.

Charlesworth states 'the law is one among many regulatory influences in international society and it gains strength from being woven with other strands to form a web of regulation that can be animated by networks of actors, but by itself cannot redress injustices based on oppression and domination'.[119] Bringing in more structural contexts including socio-economic factors into the fight against GBVAW through international law may 'unsettle its boundaries'[120] and eventually make a real difference in women's lives.

---

116 Jackie Jones, 'The Importance of International Law and Institutions' in Jones and Manjoo (n 69) 9–39, 10.

117 See Jarlath Clifford, 'Equality' in Dinah Shelton(ed), *The Oxford Handbook of International Human Rights Law* (Oxford University Press 2013) 420–445, 430.

118 Beth Goldblatt, 'Violence against Women and Social and Economic Rights: Deepening the Connections' in Ogg and Rimmer (n 1) 359–378, 365.

119 Charlesworth (n 62) 151.

120 Charlesworth (n 3) xxvi.

CHAPTER 4

The Right to Peace Revisited: beyond an Aspiring Norm

Yasue Mochizuki

1 Introduction

The pursuit of peace seeking has been the ideal of humankind. Devastating wars in the 20th century provoked the establishment of international organisations. The United Nations (UN) was founded to maintain international peace and security. To this end, it is empowered to take collective measures to prevent and remove threats to peace and to suppress acts of aggression. It can also resort to peaceful means. The desire for realising peace raised the idea of identifying and establishing a right to peace. Having adopted resolutions on the right since the 1970s, the UN regularly deliberates the issue. The debate on the right to peace continues in the 21st century, inducing the adoption of 'the Declaration of Right to Peace' at the General Assembly (GA) in 2016.

The ongoing discussion at the international level presents the debate on the legal character of the right to peace: whether it is a non-binding declaration, whether it is an evolving norm, or whether it has been developed as a legally-binding international norm.

At the regional level. the right can be situated in a variety of contexts. The right to peace is provided in treaties in Africa: the African Charter on Human and Peoples' Rights (ACHPR) and the Protocol to the African Charter on Human and Peoples' Rights on the Rights of Women in Africa (Maputo Protocol). In Asia, the Association of Southeast Asian Nations (ASEAN) adopted the ASEAN Human Rights Declaration, which incorporates the right to peace for every person.

Professor Mogami has argued that the right to peace has an inherent character as an aspiring norm as realising peace continues to be an unachievable goal for humans.[1] The right to peace is, by its very nature, a right that is always aspired to, and its realisation requires constant effort. Examining the

1 Toshiki Mogami, 'The Right to Peace' (1989) 40, *Freedom and Justice*, 33–39 (in Japanese).

 | DOI:10.1163/9789004681477_006

development of the right to peace, its varied discussions at global and regional levels, and who holds the right and obligations is imperative.

This study first overviews the debates at the UN on the right to peace and examines how the right to peace is identified and addressed. The deliberations made and resolutions adopted at the international organisation signify the progress of the right and the remaining challenges. It then looks at regional efforts in Africa and Southeast Asia to develop the right to peace through a critical analysis of their legal instruments.

It is submitted that global concerns about the right to peace at the global level induce varied discussions on the right to peace and contribute to the adoption of the resolutions at GA, whereas its legal character remains equivocal. At the regional level, it has been proven that the right to peace is established as a legal norm. This study further demonstrates the polemic on the right to peace and the ongoing challenges in identifying the relevance between the right holder and duty bearer in discerning the right itself or in determining how to realise the right as a human/people's right.

2 Debate on the Right to Peace at the International Forum

The issue of peace has been debated at the UN since the 1940s. The International Law Commission was mandated to codify crimes against the peace and security of mankind, but it failed due to the difficulties in defining acts of aggression, which presumes the crime against aggression.[2] The GA recognised 'the essentials of peace', which the UN Charter established the basic principles necessary for enduring peace and called upon its member states to 'settle international disputes by peaceful means and to co-operate in supporting the United Nations efforts to resolve outstanding problems'.[3]

The issue of peace has primarily been on the agenda of the GA. In the 21st century, it is placed on the agenda of the Economic and Social Council, with the reform of the UN, on the agenda of the Human Rights Council (HRC). The right to peace is being discussed in the context of human rights (Table 1). The change in the title of the resolution from 'life in peace' to 'the right to peace' shows a shift in emphasis to human rights, which requires further analysis in each period.

---

2 William A Schabas, *The International Criminal Court: A Commentary on the Rome Statute* (Oxford University Press 2010) 410.

3 UN Doc A/RES/4/290, 1 December 1949.

TABLE 1 Resolutions adopted at the UN General Assembly and Human Rights Council (as of 31 July 2023)

Year	Resolution number (main committee)	Title of resolution	Voting
1978	A/RES/33/73 (C.1)	Declaration on the Preparation of Societies for life in Peace	138-0-2
1981	A/RES/36/104 (C.1)	Implementation of the Declaration on the Preparation of Societies for Life in Peace	143-0-2
1984	A/RES/39/11 (Plenary)	Declaration of the Right of Peoples to Peace	92-0-34
	A/RES/39/157 (C.1)	Implementation of the Declaration on the Preparation of Societies for Life in Peace	119-0-28
1985	A/RES/40/11 (Plenary)	Right of peoples to peace	109-0-29
1986	A/RES/41/10 (Plenary)	Right of peoples to peace	104-0-33
1987	A/RES/42/91 (C.1)	Implementation of the Declaration on the Preparation of Societies for Life in Peace	128-0-24
1988	A/RES/43/22(Plenary)	Right of peoples to peace	118-0-29
1990	A/RES/45/14 (Plenary)	Implementation of the Declaration on the Right of Peoples to Peace	without vote
2001	E/CN.4/RES/2001/69	Promotion of the right of peoples to peace	29-16-7
2002	E/CN.4/RES/2002/71	Promotion of the Right of People to Peace	33-15-4
	A/RES/57/216 (C.3)	Promotion of the Right of People to Peace	116-53-14
2003	A/RES/58/192(C.3)	Promotion of peace as a vital requirement for the full enjoyment of all human rights by all	119-50-9
2004	E/CN.4/RES/2004/65	Promotion of peace as a vital requirement for the full enjoyment of all human rights by all	32-15-6

TABLE 1 Resolutions adopted at the UN General Assembly and Human Rights Council (as of 31 July 2023) (*cont.*)

Year	Resolution number (main committee)	Title of resolution	Voting
2005	E/CN.4/RES/2005/56 A/RES/60/163 (C.3)	Promotion of peace as a vital requirement for the full enjoyment of all human rights by all. Promotion of peace as a vital requirement for the full enjoyment of all human rights by all	32-15-6 116-53-8
2007	A/RES/62/163 (C.3)	Promotion of peace as a vital requirement for the full enjoyment of all human rights by all	126-54-6
2008	A/HRC/RES/8/9	Promotion on the right of people's right to peace	32-13-2
2009	A/HRC/RES/11/4	Promotion of the right of people's right to peace	32-13-1
2010	A/HRC/RES/14/3	Promotion of the right of people's right to peace	31-14-3
2010	A/RES/65/222 (C.3))	Promotion of peace as a vital requirement for the full enjoyment of all human rights by all	127-54-4
2011	A/HRC/RES/17/16	Promotion of the right of peoples to peace	32-14-0
2012	A/HRC/RES/20/15	Promotion of the right to peace[a]	34-1-12
2012	A/RES/67/173 (C.3)	Promotion of peace as a vital requirement for the full enjoyment of all human rights by all	127-54-6
2014	A/HRC/RES/27/17	Promotion of the right to peace	33-9-5
	A/RES/69/176 (C.3)	Promotion of peace as a vital requirement for the full enjoyment of all human rights by all	134-53-2
2015	A/HRC/RES/30/12	Promotion of the right to peace	33-12-2
2016	A/HRC/RES/32/28	Declaration on the Right to Peace	34-9-4
	A/RES/71/189 (C.3)	Declaration on the Right to Peace	131-34-19

TABLE 1 Resolutions adopted at the UN General Assembly and Human Rights Council (as of 31 July 2023) (*cont.*)

Year	Resolution number (main committee)	Title of resolution	Voting
2017	A/HRC/RES/35/4	Promotion of the right to peace	32-11-4
2018	A/RES/73/170 (C.3)	Promotion of peace as a vital requirement for the full enjoyment of all human rights by all	135-53-1
2019	A/HRC/RES/41/4	Promotion of the right to peace	32-13-2

a Since 2012, the word 'peoples' was deleted from the title of the relevant resolutions.

2.1 *1970s–1980s: Cold War Context*

It was in the 1970s that the GA began to discuss the right to peace in earnest. During this period, the issue of peace was discussed in the context of the right to self-determination, being suggested that '[e]very nation and every human being ... has the inherent right to life in peace' (A/RES/33/73, para.1). States had 'the duty to respect the right of all peoples to self-determination, independence, equality, sovereignty, the territorial integrity of States' (para.5). Peace was interpreted as the right to live in peace, and the duty of states to respect the sovereignty of independent countries.

Debates developed in the 1970s in the context of the Cold War, when the fear of nuclear weapons was global. With a dismal perspective of the nuclear war emergence, identifying the notion of peace and the right to peace under international law was critical, which was believed to enable people to demonstrate the danger of war and to prove the illegality of nuclear arms' existence.[4] The call for the right to peace was, in part, a demand for nuclear weapons' elimination to deter nuclear wars. It explained why the deliberation of the draft resolution 'Declaration on the Preparation of Societies for Life in Peace' was

4 Ved P Nanda, 'Nuclear Weapons and the Right under International Law' (1983) 9, *Brooklyn Journal of International Law*, 283–296, 283.

held at the First Committee (disarmament), not at the Third (human rights) or the Sixth (legal) Committees, which continued during the 20th century. The first resolution in 1978 as mentioned above, proposed by the representative of Poland, connected peace and disarmament.[5]

The 1970s debates indicated the efforts to 'create' a new right by positively introducing situations or actors into a legal framework and identifying them as the issue of right. 'To live in peace has been recognised by GA, which reflects the legal consciousness of the international community'.[6] This new right, however, was not fully elaborated at that time, 'right to peace … has been proclaimed in varying formulations by both the Commission and the Assembly, but neither its status as a human right nor its precise formulation, let alone its content, has ever been studied or formally debated'.[7]

Proclaiming the right to peace gained momentum in the 1980s. The resolution entitled 'Declaration on the Right of Peoples to Peace' was first adopted in 1984, which states:[8]

1. *Solemnly* proclaims that the peoples of our planet have a sacred right to peace;
2. *Solemnly* declares that the preservation of the right of peoples to peace and the promotion of its implementation constitute a fundamental obligation of each State;
3. *Emphasizes* that ensuring the exercise of the right of peoples to peace demands that the policies of States be directed towards the elimination of the threat of war, particularly nuclear war, the renunciation of the use of force in international relations and the settlement of international disputes by peaceful means on the basis of the Charter of the United Nations;
4. *Appeals* to all States and international organizations to do their utmost to assist in implementing the right of peoples to peace through the adoption of appropriate measures at both the national and the international level.

5 UN Doc A/C.1/33/PV.61, 4 December 1978, 27–40.

6 Mogami (n 1) 36.

7 Philip Alston, 'Conjuring Up New Human Rights: A Proposal for Quality Control' (1984) 78, *American Journal of International Law,* 607–621, 612.

8 UN Doc A/RES/39/11, Annex, 12 November 1984.

The process of adopting the resolution was unusual, as no prior reference to the relevant committees.[9] This resolution features, first, that it ascertains the right to peace is identified as the collective rights that the peoples enjoy, without referring to individuals. Second, it declares that the 'preservation' and 'promotion' of the execution of the right comprises a fundamental obligation; it does not identify the duty bearer responding to the rights holder. It argues that this resolution does not create a new type of right but merely reaffirms the existing principles of the UN Charter.[10]

The concept of the right to peace brought up various questions: whether peace may be considered a human right, if so, the right belongs to who and who is obliged to promote and protect the rights,[11] and under which situation is identified as peaceful so that the right to peace is achieved. As for the question of who enjoys the right, one argues that the right was categorised as 'solidarity rights',[12] as a concept to the protect collective rights of peoples and to counter developed countries. Another suggests that it belongs to individual rights in the realm of civil and political rights. Others maintain that the right to peace is both an individual and collective rights.[13] The fact that the concept was open to a wide range of interpretations and who could enjoy the right was one of the reasons why it was widely supported.

2.2 *1990s: Post-Cold War Context*

After the end of the Cold War, the topic of the right to peace became less popular. The proposition stipulated in the GA resolution 'Declaration on the Right of Peoples to Peace' (1984) was disregarded. The peoples' right to peace lacks a clear meaning and thus cannot be transformed into a meaningful action.[14]

---

9 Philip Alston, 'People's Rights: Their Rise and Fall' in Philip Alston (ed), *Peoples' Rights* (Oxford University Press 2001) 259–293, 265.

10 Mogami (n 1) 35.

11 Cecilia M Bailliet, 'Normative Foundation of the International Law of Peace' in Cecilia Marcela Bailliet and Kjetil Mujezinović Larsen (eds), *Promoting Peace Through International Law* (Oxford University Press 2015) 43–65, 55–57. It is suggested if one looks into the solidarity rights, i.e, the third generation of human rights, it is assumed that there is no contradiction among respective rights, as rights of solidarity 'can only be implemented by the combined efforts of everyone: individuals, states and other bodies, as well as public and private institutions'. Karel Vašák, 'A 30-Year Struggle: The Sustained Efforts to Give Force of Law to the Universal Declaration of Human Rights' (1977) 30 *UNESCO Courier* 29, 32.

12 Carl Wellman, 'Solidarity, the Individual and Human Rights' (2000) 22, *Human Rights Quarterly*, 639–657, 649–650.

13 Philip Alston, 'Peace as a Human Rights' (1980) 11, *Bulletin Peace Proposals*, 319–329, 329.

14 Alston (n 9) 279.

In the post-Cold War era, the issue of peace was closely associated with direct operations initiated by the UN. As the report of the Secretary General 'Agenda for Peace' demonstrated, this issue entailed concrete measures and actions following Chapters VI and VII of the UN Charter. Rather than advocating for the abstract right to peace, the central question was how peace could be secured under the UN Charter.[15]

While the debate at the GA was at a standstill, UNESCO took a positive approach in the area of the promotion of a 'culture of peace'. It resonated with the founding principle of UNESCO, whose Constitution provides 'the peace must … be founded … upon the intellectual and moral solidarity of mankind' (preamble), and '[t]he purpose of the Organization is to contribute to peace and security by promoting collaboration among the nations through education, science and culture to further universal respect for justice, for the rule of law and for human rights and fundamental freedoms' (Article 1). UNESCO adopted the Culture of Peace Action Programme in 1992, the Director General declared 'The Human Rights to Peace'[16] and drafted the 'Declaration on the Human Right to Peace as the Foundation of the Culture of Peace'.[17]

From the legal perspective, the UNESCO draft was criticised, as it was only for being 'platitudinous and vacuous'.[18] One opines that UNESCO's efforts were not successful in facilitating the development of the right to peace. 'Despite UNESCO's somewhat maverick efforts over a lengthy period to resuscitate it, the right to peace has proven to have virtually no support within the work of international organizations and neither its conceptual nor its legal foundations have been developed in a convincing manner'.[19]

Not successful in establishing a legal concept, the idea of a culture of peace was incorporated into the UN peacebuilding. The UNESCO proposal for the Culture of Peace Programme purported to complement peacekeeping operations[20] in post-conflict situations. It was recognised that 'the task of the United Nations to save future generations from the scourge of war requires transformation towards a culture of peace, which consists of values, attitudes and behaviours that reflect and inspire social interaction and sharing based on the principles of freedom, justice and democracy, all human rights, tolerance and solidarity'.[21] How to penetrate the culture of peace to overcome the culture

15 UNSG, An Agenda for Peace, UN Doc. A/47/277-S/24111, 17 June 1992, para 22.
16 SHS-97/WS/6 (1997).
17 UNESCO Doc154 EX/40(1998) Annex.
18 Alston (n 9) 280.
19 ibid 290.
20 UN Doc A/51/395, 23 September 1996, 3–4.
21 UN Doc A/RES/52/13, 15 January 1998.

of violence on the ground was greatly emphasised. The GA proclaimed 2000 as the 'International Year for the Culture of Peace',[22] it further declared 2001–2010 as the 'International Decade for a Culture of Peace and Non-Violence for the Children of the World'.[23] In the post-Cold War context, the debate centred on how to establish durable peace in post-conflict situations. It was also expected that peacekeeping forces would engender a culture of peace.[24]

2.3 *2000 Onward: the Right to Peace in a Global Context*

The movement towards campaigning for the right to peace re-emerged in the 21st century. The war in Iraq was launched without a clear legal basis, provoking considerable legal debate about the legality of the attack and the use of force in the absence of a SC resolution. There was no clear consensus among the states regarding the military attack against Iraq; the military operations by the coalition of willing caused a strong anti-war campaign worldwide. Against this background, it was argued that if the right to peace had been established, the war could have been evaded, and people's lives could have been saved. The civil society organisations initiated advancing the right to peace, the Spanish Society for International Human Rights Law (SSIHRL) led the global campaigns in particular.[25] The associations of the civil society organisations purported to facilitate codification and progressive development of the right to peace within the framework of human rights law. In regional conferences, declarations were adopted, including 'the Santiago Declaration on the Right to Peace' (2010), which outlined specific elements of the human rights to peace and the obligations of each state to fulfil these rights.

The civil society organisations attempted to ensure that the Santiago Declaration would be fully considered in the draft declaration on the right to peace prepared at the HRC. Owing to efforts by civil society, the draft declaration finally included 85% of the standard proposed by the Santiago

22 UN Doc A/RES/52/15, 15 January 1998.

23 UN Doc A/RES/53/24, 10 November 1998.

24 Christine Chinkin and Mary Kaldor, *International Law and New Wars* (Cambridge University Press 2017) 398.

25 Conferences regarding the right to peace were held in the following regions: La Plata, Argentina (November 2008), Yaoundé, Cameroon (February 2009), Bangkok, Thailand (April 2009), Johannesburg, South Africa (April 2009), Sarajevo, Bosnia and Herzegovina (October 2009), Alexandria, Egypt (December 2009), Havana, Cuba (January 2010), Morphou, Cyprus (October 2010), Caracas, Venezuela (November 2010), Nagoya, Tokyo, Japan (December 2010), Santiago de Compostela, Spain (December 2010), Slovenj Gradec, Slovenia (October 2012), San Jose, Costa Rica (February 2012, 2013), Oswiecim, Poland (May 2013), London, UK (May 2013), La Plata, Argentina (September 2013).

Declaration.[26] One appreciated the Santiago Declaration and the HRC draft declaration on the right to peace take a comprehensive approach to the right to peace, putting into human rights perspectives.[27] Others expressed uncertainty about the legal aspects of the documents: the Santiago Declaration only listed the elements that constitute peace, without addressing issues like the definition of peace or the identification of rights as human rights.[28] Furthermore, although the Security Council (SC) has primary responsibility for international peace and security, the document did not spell out the relevance of the right to the functioning of the SC.

The civil society organisations initially aimed to adopt the 'Universal Declaration of the Human Right to Peace' at the GA by 10 December 2014,[29] the same day the Universal Declaration of Human Rights was adopted. They took strategic approaches so that relevant resolutions were adopted yearly at the HRC, which would be deliberated and adopted at the GA to obtain global recognition. The Progress Report of the HRC Advisory Committee on the Right of Peoples to Peace was prepared and deliberated at the HRC since 2010, inducing the resolution adopted at the HRC in 2016. The resolution was then passed to the GA for further deliberation and adoption.

The 'Declaration on the Rights to Peace' was adopted in 2016 (A/RES/71/189, Annex). Negotiation and discussion at the meeting of the HRC and the GA produced a simple document with five main articles. First, it provides that '[e]veryone has the right to enjoy peace such that all human rights are promoted and protected and development is fully realized' (Article 1), which ascertains the right of every person, avoiding the term 'individual' or 'people(s)', which provokes ongoing legal arguments about who is the right holder of this right to peace and the definition and scope of peace. In addition, states 'should respect, implement and promote equality and non-discrimination, justice and the rule of law, and guarantee freedom from fear and want as a means to build peace within and between societies' (article 2). It reiterates the pre-existing obligation of states in general terms, avoiding imposing detailed duties. Article 3 states that 'State, the United Nations and specialized agencies

26 Carlos V Durán, 'Legal Foundations of the Human Right to Peace' (2013) 2, *Przegląd Strategiczy*, 123–146, 126.

27 Christin G Fernandez and David F Puyana, 'The Adoption of the Declaration on the Right to Peace by the United Nations: A Human Rights Landmark' (2017) 2, *Peace Human Rights Governance*, 275–297.

28 Shigeki Sakamoto, 'A Recent Activity of the Human Rights Council Advisory Committee-Focusing on the Draft Declaration on the Right to Peace' (2013) 24, *Human Rights International*, 118–125, 119 (in Japanese).

29 Durán (n 26) 126.

should take appropriate sustainable measures to implement the present Declaration', and '[i]nternational, regional, national and local organizations and civil society are encouraged to support and assist in the implementation of the present Declaration'. States and international organisations are requested to take appropriate measures to execute the declaration, while civil society ornigasations are exhorted to support its implementation. Overall, the declaration is a general statement of the right to peace. It does not enumerate specific rights. Nor does it explicitly mention legal obligations responding to the right to peace, leaving uncertain whether and how the right can be realised.

The reaction to the adopted declaration varied, widely divided among states and between states and civil society. The civil society organisations took a positive view in adopting the declaration. 'The Declaration has positively become an important landmark on the field of human rights and fundamental freedoms'.[30] They continued to address the issue at the HRC, aiming to codify a treaty or to develop customary international law. As for states, their opinions were mixed: developing countries supported the right; some regarded it as legally binding, while others asserted the necessity of the right. In contrast, developed countries were doubtful of the right, arguing that it remained undeveloped as an established right or that it remained a politically motivated term. Their particular concerns were no consensus on the existence of the right to peace among states, the lack of legal bases in international law, and the right could be invoked to justify the violation of established human rights.[31] Developed countries did not completely oppose the idea, as the rights signify 'a constructive path forward in affirming the relationship between human rights and peace' or '[t]he Declaration on the Right to Peace reinforced that commitment and reaffirmed that peace and security, development and human rights were the Pillars of the United Nations system and the foundations for collective security and well-being'.[32] It was suggested that the normative value of the right to peace has the merits of strengthening the interlinkage of peace and human rights, whereas its inherent broad concept of peace and the ways in which to realise the rights cause apprehension among states.

30 Fernandez and Puyana (n 27) 290.
31 UN Doc A/C.3/71/SR.52, 12 January 2017, 4–7.
32 ibid 4–5.

3 'Right to Peace' in Regional Contexts

The 2016 Declaration endorses that everyone has the right to enjoy peace. The right is non-discriminatory and applicable to all persons on the globe. The universality of the right and assumed obligations that respond to it have been suggested. 'The right to peace implies a whole set of duties and obligations for a range of entities from individuals to collectives such as State and the international community as a whole … The right implies both a negative … and positive obligation to take and to support measures at the local … and international levels.'[33]

In the 2000s, the right to peace was incorporated into regional instruments. In Africa, two human rights treaties stipulated the right to peace; the African Charter on Human and Peoples' Rights and the Protocol to the African Charter on Human and Peoples' Rights on the Rights of Women in Africa (Maputo Protocol). Each treaty is examined respectively by the African Commission on Human and Peoples' Rights (African Commission) and the African Court on Human and Peoples' Rights (ACtHPR). As for Southeast Asia, ASEAN adopted the ASEAN Human Rights Declaration, which provides the right to peace. It is pertinent to examine the content of the right, who holds the right, and whether and how that right is to be realised through these regional instruments.

3.1 *Right to Peace in Africa*

The Organisation of African Union (OAU)/African Union (AU)'s approach to human rights was guided by the right to self-determination and Apartheid in South Africa. The attention to self-determination in the decolonisation context prompted its later expansion of the concept: independence and self-determination were regarded as fundamental rights, which were owned by the state but not the individual. Self-determination seems to be regarded as a continuing matter and in the course of the OAU considering self-determination as an independence issue, it also prompted to touch upon human rights.[34] As for apartheid, the OAU condemned the situation as a serious threat to peace and international security. It employed human rights standards regarding what was seen as a liberation struggle in South Africa; it 'took the opportunity to condemn the events in South Africa and, in the process, linked human rights issues with what was happening'.[35] These historical experiences demonstrate

33 Philip Alston, 'The Legal Basis of a Right to Peace' (1991) 3, *Peace Review*, 23–27, 26–27.

34 Rachel Murray, *Human Rights in Africa: From the OAU to the African Union* (Cambridge University Press 2004) 17.

35 ibid 17–18.

the prioritisation of collectiveness in rights alongside ties with human rights and peace and security. In the African context, human rights were to be gained through a struggle against the former oppressive regime.

Whereas attention is paid to the particularity of Africa, such as African values or regionalism, one holds that legal instruments in African states reflect the Universal Declaration of Human Rights. 'Indeed, the African States which gained independence in the 1960s have incorporated into their constitutions provisions relating to human rights, with or without express reference to the Universal Declaration of Human Rights. This is not a case of mere imitation but … the fruit of a sincere conviction inherited from the anti-colonial struggle. The systematic human rights violations inherent in the colonial system had given birth, in nationalist African circles, to humanitarian aspirations and ideals; once independence had been gained, it was logical for them to be incorporated into legislation'.[36] In its communication procedures, discussed below, the African Commission refers to universal legal instruments, such as the UN Charter, rather than regional documents. The greater reliance on UN documents reflects its confidence in universal instruments and the development of its jurisprudence based on practices at the global level.

3.1.1 African Charter on Human and Peoples' Rights

As examined in the previous section, the right to peace has been discussed within the changing contexts: in the 1970s and 1980s during the Cold War, in the 1990s in the post-Cold War era, and the 21st century in a global context. In Africa, the right to peace was stipulated in the African Charter on Human and Peoples' Rights (ACHPR) 1981. It was suggested that Africa became a testing ground for the universal principles adopted by the UN,[37] and it took the initiative to develop its own regional standards. The ACHPR was the first multilateral convention on human rights to incorporate the rights of peoples and designate the people as their sole holder. Its principal importance lies in the fact that it apparently makes the people an international subject,[38] and the right to peace is classified as one of the solidarity rights. The ACHPR stipulates the right to peace as follows:

---

36 Fatsah Ouguergouz, *The African Charter on Human and Peoples' Rights: A Comprehensive Agenda for Human Dignity and Sustainable Democracy in Africa* (Martinus Nijhoff Publishers 2003) 6.

37 A Peter Mutharika, 'The Role of International Law in the Twenty-First Century: An African Perspective' (1995) 18, *Fordham International Law Journal*, 1706–1719.

38 Ouguergouz (n 36) 203.

Article 23:

1. All peoples shall have the right to national and international peace and security. The principles of solidarity and friendly relations implicitly affirmed by the Charter of the United Nations and reaffirmed by that of the Organization of African Unity shall govern relations between states.
2. For the purpose of strengthening peace, solidarity and friendly relations, States parties to the present Charter shall ensure that:
   (a) any individual enjoying the right of asylum under Article 12 of the present Charter shall not engage in subversive activities against his country of origin or any other State party to the present Charter;
   (b) their territories shall not be used as bases for subversive or terrorist activities against the people of any other State party to the present Charter.

The ACHPR unequivocally enshrines all peoples' rights to national and international peace and security. The following sentence, which sets out the principles of solidarity and friendly relations, indicates that the peoples' right is guaranteed both by the UN Charter and the OAU, thus testifying to its universal value.

The provision clarifies that the right to peace is a collective right for all peoples; it poses a question about the relationship between peoples, the right holder in the first paragraph and state parties, and the duty bearer in the second. It was suggested that confusion exists between the notions of 'peoples' and 'states' in the provision, as the term 'people' is assumed to be synonymous with the whole population of the state.[39] The scope of 'people' is potentially broad when examining communication by the African Commission. The duty bearer of this right is state parties, which should certify that any individual who enjoys the right to asylum shall not engage in subversive activities against any country and that their territories shall not be used as bases for subversive or terrorist activities. These provisions oblige state parties to strengthen their state sovereignty by preventing disruptive activities by individuals within the territory.

The reference to national and international peace indicates that it embraces both domestic and multinational issues. It also demonstrates the

39 James Crawford, 'The Rights of Peoples: Peoples or Government' (1985) 9, *Bulletin of the Australian Society of Legal Philosophy*, 136–147, 141.

right of negative peace – the absence of war of both an international and non-international character, alongside the positive peace on the national level – the protection of human rights.[40] Theoretically, this provision is innovative, as it unequivocally announces a collective right to international and national peace security.[41] Its potential merits attention; '[i]t holds out the possibility that peoples themselves, through the Commission, can hold to account both their own governments and the governments of other counties for the manner in which they protect or interfere with their peace and security'.[42] However, a question is raised as to whether this innovative peoples' rights provision in the ACHPR adds a significant dimension to the work of the African Commission.[43]

3.1.2 Protocol to the African Charter on Human and Peoples' Rights on the Rights of Women in Africa (Maputo Protocol)

The OAU/AU's approach to the status of women focused on the specific areas of conflict, participation and development, as the inclusion of women is necessary for peace and not to be achieved without them.[44] The motivation to adopt an additional protocol to women's rights was not driven by a clear vision of the rights already protected by existing international instruments but as a way to compel the ACHPR to be attentive to women's rights and to give women a sense of ownership over rights at this level.[45] In the preamble of the Maputo Protocol, state parties recognised 'the crucial role of women in the preservation of African values based on the principles of equality, peace, freedom, dignity, justice, solidarity and democracy' and determined 'to ensure that the rights of women are promoted, realised and protected in order to enable them to enjoy fully all their human rights'. The Protocol stipulates the following rights to peace:

---

40 Ola Engdahl, 'Protection of Human Rights and the Maintenance of International Peace and Security: Necessary Precondition or a Clash of Interests?' in Bailliet and Larsen (n 11) 109–131, 118.

41 Clive Baldwin and Cynthia Morel, 'Group Rights' in Malcolm Evans and Rachel Murray (eds), *The African Charter on Human and Peoples' Rights* (2nd edn, Cambridge University Press 2010) 282.

42 Ibid.

43 Alston (n 9) 266.

44 Murray (n 34) 140–152.

45 Rachel Murray, 'Women's Rights and the Organization of African Unity and African Union: The Protocol on the Rights of Women in Africa' in Doris Buss and Ambreena Manji (eds), *International Law: Modern Feminist Approaches* (Hart Publishing 2005) 253–255.

Article 10: Right to Peace

1. Women have the right to a peaceful existence and the right to participate in the promotion and maintenance of peace.
2. States Parties shall take all appropriate measures to ensure the increased participation of women:
   a) in programmes of education for peace and a culture of peace;
   b) in the structures and processes for conflict prevention, management and resolution at local, national, regional, continental and international levels;
   c) in the local, national, regional, continental and international decision making structures to ensure physical, psychological, social and legal protection of asylum seekers, refugees, returnees and displaced persons, in particular women;
   d) in all levels of the structures established for the management of camps and settlements for asylum seekers, refugees, returnees and displaced persons, in particular, women;
   e) in all aspects of planning, formulation and implementation of post-conflict reconstruction and rehabilitation.
3. States Parties shall take the necessary measures to reduce military expenditure significantly in favour of spending on social development in general, and the promotion of women in particular.

One pronounces the progressive value of the Protocol as it adopts a gender policy regarding peace participation rights and calls for the establishment of preconditions for peace through the reduction of military expenditure in favour of development, while others are more critical.[46] It is suggested that, in the drafting process, an ad hoc approach was taken; rather than exploiting the existing legal instrument, a new legal document was developed. The Protocol lacks a comprehensive vision by incorporating provisions from regional and international instruments, leaving controversial issues unanswered. The Protocol turned out to be an instrument without consistency. 'There is an underlying sense that the African organs and NGOs are trying to achieve an 'African' approach to women's rights; yet, what this 'African' vision is, has not been clearly developed'.[47]

It was suggested that the provisions in the Protocol were derived from the ACHPR,[48] the terms varied between the ACHPR and the Protocol, posing

46 Simon O'Connor and Cecilia M Bailliet, 'The Good Faith Obligation to Maintain International Peace and Security and the Pacific Settlement of Disputes' in Bailliet and Larsen (n 11) 66–85, 84.

47 Murray (n 45) 271.

48 ibid 265.

questions on differences between the two instruments. First, the scope of the right holder appears confusing. Article 23 of the ACHPR stipulates that all peoples 'shall have the right to national and international peace and security', whereas the Protocol states that 'women' have 'the right to a peaceful existence and the right to participate in the promotion and maintenance of peace'. One opines that an approach to earmarking women as people would have exacerbated the already existing confusion about the term 'people' in the ACHPR.[49] Besides, the difference in terms between 'international peace and security' in the ACHPR and 'the right to a peaceful existence and the right to participate in the promotion and maintenance of peace' in the Protocol are confusing, as one can read the latter proactively, rendering more rights to women than men.

Second, differences in the content of rights are pointed out. The Protocol obliges state parties to prioritise expenditure on social development over military spending. Article 26 (2) provides that 'States Parties undertake to adopt all necessary measures and in particular shall provide budgetary and other resources for the full and effective implementation of the rights herein recognised'. One suggests that the clause encompasses diverse approaches towards the domestic implementation of its provisions,[50] it is doubtful that there is any link between the realisation of women's right to peace and the priority of the budget for social development since the military expenditure itself is not directly linked to women's rights. Conversely, this provision could be used to legitimise the increase in military expenditure by states.

Concurrently, the ACHPR and the Protocol share the common objective of strengthening national sovereignty. The former obligates states to take measures to ensure that any individual shall not engage in disruptive activities and that their territories shall not be used as bases for subversive or terrorist activities. The latter provides the obligation of state parties to secure the increased participation of women in certain fields of activity and to reduce military expenditure. The ways in which these rights are sought therefore entail the fortification of state sovereignty. It rests with the idea that African states necessitate seeking self-determination externally, especially against developed countries. If African states remain internally weak, they will remain recipients of the development of international law. Reinforcing state sovereignty is considered imperative for African states, which resonates with seeking the right to peace.

---

49 Frans Viljoen, 'An Introduction to the Protocol to the African Charter on Human and Peoples' Rights on the Rights of Women in Africa' (2009) 16 Washington and Lee Journal of Civil Rights and Social Justice, 11–46, 20–21.

50 ibid 31.

Provisions of the above African treaties suggest the following features: one is an emphasis on the collective, and the other is on state sovereignty. These provisions were formulated against the background of African countries' departure from their historical experience of colonisation, with an emphasis on self-determination and territorial integrity. For them, the realisation of the right to peace is directly linked to the maintenance of a sovereign state in which peace is ensured.

These provisions in two treaties, in combination, entail both negative and positive peace. ACHPR focuses on interstate relationships, based upon solidarity and friendship among states, focusing on negative peace. On the contrary, the Maputo protocol provides women's rights in diverse structures and processes including post-conflict situations. These two documents thus complement each other to encompass both peace.

3.1.3 Elaborating on the Right to Peace through the Communication between the African Commission and the African Court on Human and Peoples' Rights (ACtHPR)

The African Commission and the ACtHPR have examined the right to peace in response to petitions. The following section analyses the interpretation of the right by these (quasi) judicial organs. This would provide insights into the right to peace within the African context.

3.1.3.1 *The African Commission*

The African Commission is mandated to interpret the provisions of the ACHPR relating to human rights (Article 45.3). It addressed Article 23 in two communications and has voluntarily referred to it in one case. It has no mandate to provide an authoritative interpretation of human rights issues,[51] an exploration of communications at the Commission would be helpful in examining the substance of the right to peace in Africa.

3.1.3.1.1 Democratic Republic of Congo/Burundi, Rwanda, Uganda 227/99

This case was the first interstate communication. The Democratic Republic of Congo (DRC) claimed that Burundi, Rwanda and Uganda perpetrated armed aggression, violating the fundamental principles between states as provided in the UN Charter and the OAU. It particularly accused the three countries that had committed violations of the provisions of Articles 2, 4, 6, 12, 16, 17, 19,

51 Murray (n 34) 66.

20, 21, 22 and 23 of the ACHPR, alongside the provisions of the International Covenant on Civil and Political Rights (1966), the Geneva Conventions (1949) and the Additional Protocol on the Protection of Victims of International Armed Conflicts (1977).

The Commission held that respondent states violated Article 23, which opines:

> The [African] Commission finds the conduct of the Respondent States inconsistent with the standard expected in them under *UN Declaration on Friendly Relations,* which is implicitly affirmed by the Charters of the UN and OAU, and which the [African] Commission is mandated by Article 23 of the African Charter to uphold. Any doubt that this provision has been violated by the Respondent States is resolved by recalling an injunction in the *UN Declaration on Friendly Relations:* 'No State or group of States has the right to intervene directly or indirectly, for any reason whatever [*sic*], in the internal or external affairs of any other States. Consequently, armed intervention and all other forms of interference or attempted threats against the personality of the State or against its political, economic and cultural elements are in violation of international law ... Also no State shall organise, assist, foment, finance, incite or tolerate subversive, terrorist or armed activities directed towards the violent overthrow of the regime of another State or interfere in civil strife in another States'. The substance of the complaint of the Democratic Republic of Congo against the Respondents is covered by the foregoing prohibition. The Respondent States have therefore violated Article 23 of the African Charter.[52]

The Commission found the respondent states in violation of Article 23 of the African Charter, arguing that the provision authorises the Commission to endorse the standard provided in the Declaration of Friendly Relations. It first examined the conduct by the respondent states by applying provisions of the Declaration of Friendly Relations, and then proceeded to that these clauses were materialised in Article 23; thus, the acts constituted a violation of the article. The communication referred to the Declaration of Friendly Relations to elaborate Article 23 on the principles of solidarity and friendly relations, which prohibit the threat or use of force by states in settling disputes (para.73).

52 AfCHPR, 227/99, Democratic Republic of Congo/Burundi, Rwanda, Uganda, para 68, May 2003.

Furthermore, it recommended that 'adequate reparation be paid, according to the appropriate ways to the Complainant State for and on behalf of the victims of the human rights by the armed forces of the Respondent States'.[53]

The Commission's explanation of Article 23 interpretation remained general and without further elaboration. It determined the violation of Article 23 by the respondent states and simply noted the provisions of the Declaration on Friendly Relations. The Commission did not take a detailed examination of Article 23 including the meaning of 'national and international peace and security' or 'peoples' in the context. Nor did it examine whether it signifies states or particular people, or which activities are considered to be 'subversive or terrorist activities against' people of any other state. It did not refer to the drafting process of the ACHPR or any other relevant African legal instruments.

Notably, in this communication, the African Commission stressed the binding nature of its decision. 'The African Commission would like to emphasise that the absence of reaction from Burundi does not absolve the latter from the decision the African Commission may arrive at in the consideration of the communication. Burundi by ratifying the African Charter indicated its commitment to cooperate with the [African] Commission and to abide by all decisions taken by the latter'.[54] It is equivocal whether the Commission indicated the legally binding nature of this specific communication in particular or whether it meant the binding nature of communication as a whole; it stressed the Burundian obligation to comply with the decision. One argues that the Commission found ways to stress the apparent binding nature of its decision through its communication to a member state that is unwilling to accept the binding character of the decision.[55] While the debate on the legally binding nature of the Communication continues, partly due to the Commission's ambiguous approach, the Communication at least emphasised the obligation of member states to implement the decision.

3.1.3.1.2 Association pour la sauvegarde de la paix au Burundi/Kenya, Uganda, Rwanda, Tanzania, Zaire (DRC), Zambia 157/96

The other communication that addressed Article 23 was submitted by the Belgian non-governmental organisation. It claimed that the embargo imposed

53 ibid, Holding.

54 ibid, para 53.

55 Rachel Murray and Debra Long, *the Implementation of the Findings of the African Commission on Human and Peoples' Rights* (Cambridge University Press 2015) 54.

on Burundi by its neighbouring nine countries violated several articles of the ACHPR, including Article 23.2(b).[56]

In its merits, the Commission held that the decision to impose an embargo was endorsed by the OAU and the UNSC based on the provisions of the UN Charter. It also suggested that the embargo endorsed by the SC's resolution was 'no longer the acts of a few neighbouring states but that it imposed obligations on all member states of the UN (para 73). It therefore decided that the respondent states were not guilty of violating alleged articles of the ACHPR.

The communication referred to the UN Charter and the Declaration of Friendly Relations in examining the alleged violation. It then associated the violation under these clauses with the violation of the ACHPR without any further explanation regarding the relation between these instruments.

While the complainant addressed the alleged violation of the ACHPR, the Commission nonetheless made references to the UN Charter provisions without elucidating the ACHPR provisions. It could be pertinent to apply the UN Charter as obligations under the Charter prevail over other obligations under other treaties following Article 103; the Commission missed the opportunity to examine the relevant provisions of an arms embargo, particularly whether the provisions of the ACHPR, including the right to peace, could apply directly to the arms embargo.

3.1.3.1.3 Malawi Africa Association et al / Mauritania 54/91 et al

The Commission referred to Article 23 voluntarily in a situation where no parties alleged the violation of the article. In this case, the complainant maintained a series of grave and massive violations of Articles 2, 3, 4, 6, 7, 16 and 26 of the ACHPR in regard to the prevailing situation in Mauritania in 1986 and 1992. The violation of Article 23 was not alleged, while the Commission spontaneously referred to Article 23 in its merit:

> 139. Article 23 of the Charter states: "All people shall have the right to national and international peace and security".

56 AfCHPR, 157/96, *Association pour la sauvegarde de la paix au Burundi/Kenya, Uganda, Rwanda, Tanzania, Zaire* (DRC), *Zambia*, 15 to 29 May 2003.

> 140. As advanced by the Mauritanian government, the conflict through which the country passed is the result of the actions of certain groups, for which it is not responsible. But in the case in question, it was indeed the Mauritanian public forces that attacked Mauritanian villages. And even if they were rebel forces, the responsibility for protection is incumbent on the Mauritanian State, which is a party to the Charter (cf. Commission's decision in communication 74/92). The unprovoked attacks on villages constitute a denial of the right to live in peace and security.[57]

It was decided that the military attacks on villages in its territory by the Mauritanian government contradicted Article 23 of the ACHPR. This statement implied that, even if rebel forces attacked villagers, which constituted a violation of the people's (villagers') right to peace, the government should assume its responsibility to protect inhabitants. This ascertained the role of the government to assure the right to peace of peoples, even if the government did not directly engage in a military attack. The Commission referred to Article 23 and announced the violation of the alleged articles; no detailed clarification of the article was sought in the communication.

3.1.3.2 *The African Court on Human and Peoples' Rights (ACtHPR)*

The ACtHPR was established by its Protocol. Its jurisdiction encompasses 'all cases and disputes submitted to it concerning the interpretation and application of the Charter, the Protocol and any other relevant Human Rights instrument ratified by the States concerned.' (Article 3) Those who are entitled to submit cases to the Court include: the African Commission, the state parties to the Protocol, who lodged a complaint to the African Commission, against which the complaint has been submitted to the Commission, and whose citizen is a victim of human rights violations. The Court may entitle nongovernmental organisations with observer status before the Commission and individuals to institute cases directly before it (Article 5 (3)).

The Court elaborated on the right to peace and national security on the merits of the matter of XYZ v Republic of Benin 2020. The case was instituted by a Beninese who brought a claim against the Republic of Benin. The applicant claimed to revise the Benin Constitution, which was adopted by the Benin Parliament and was found to conform with the Constitution by the

57 AfCHPR, 54/91-61/91-96/93-98/93-164/97_196/97-210/98, Malawi Africa Association, Amnesty International, Ms Sarr Diop, Union interafricaine des droits de l'Homme and RADDHO, Collectif des veuves et ayants-Droit, Association mauritanienne des droits de l'Homme/Mauritania, 11 May 2000.

Constitutional Court. The applicant maintained that the Constitutional Court was a biased institution, that the law to revise the Constitution was adopted in secret, and that 'the constitutional revision that was adopted outside the rules of democracy, the rule of law and the respect for human rights is a threat to the peace and security of the people of Benin.'[58] The applicant alleged Benin's violation of several provisions of the African Charter, one of which was the right to peace and security, Article 23 (1).

In its judgment, the Court held that Benin violated the right to peace and security. It first referred to the situation of peace in a general context: the absence of worry, turmoil, conflict or violence. It then highlighted the necessity to consider the full range of human rights, not only civil and political rights, regarding the right to peace. Observing that Benin had violated Article 10 (2) of the African Charter on Democracy, Elections and Good Governance,[59] the Court concluded that '[t]his context ... poses a threat to the peace and stability of Benin and the security of Benin citizens'.[60] It thus ordered Benin to take all measures to repeal the Law and amend its Constitution.

In this case, the Court highlighted the context of Benin in which the state had adopted a revision of the Constitution without a national consensus. As the Court held that discrimination and inequality could induce significant human rights violations and thus pose a direct threat to peace (para.134); it argued that the adoption of a law to amend the Constitution should conform with the rule of democracy. Then the Court articulated that the non-participation of the majority of Beninese in adopting the new revised law amounted to discrimination and inequality, which comprised economic, social and cultural rights, as the Court cited the Report of the UNHCR on 'Early warning and economic, social and cultural rights' in 2016.

Second, the procedure of the Court confirmed that the individual could institute the claim against the violation of the Charter by a state. The applicant claimed that Benin violated his fundamental rights, alleging violations of the African Charter. This procedure allowed any national or state party to institute an allegation against a state before ACtHPR, which could, as in this present case, conclude the violation of the right to peace of state.

---

58 AfCtHPR, *The Matter of XYZ v Republic of Benin*, App no 010/2020, Judgment 27 November 2020, para.6, Tresor M Makunya, 'Decisions of the African Court on Human and Peoples' Rights during 2020: Trends and Lessons' (2020) 21, *African Human Rights Law Journal*, 1230–1264.

59 'State Parties must ensure that the process of amending or revising their Constitution is based on national consensus including, where appropriate, recourse to a referendum'.

60 *The Matter of XYZ* (n 58) para136.

Third, the case made clear that the Court could require a state party to repeal its laws and amend its constitution on the basis of a violation of the right to peace. The right to peace has the potential to serve as a catalyst for change in a state's legal system.

3.2 *The Right to Peace in Southeast Asia*

The right to peace is stipulated in the ASEAN Human Rights Declaration (AHRD) adopted at the ASEAN Summit in 2012. As a non-binding, declaratory document, one argues that this human rights declaration precedes a future regional human rights treaty, as were cases of the American Declaration of the Rights and Duties of Man and the Universal Declaration of Human Rights, followed by the American Convention on Human Rights and the International Bill of Human Rights.[61] There is no clear position among ASEAN member states on whether to develop a human rights treaty in the region.

ASEAN's engagement with human rights dates back to 1993. After the World Conference on Human Rights in Vienna, ASEAN foreign ministers reaffirmed ASEAN's commitment to and respect for human rights and fundamental freedoms set out in the Vienna Declaration. The ASEAN states then agreed that '[they] should coordinate a common approach on human rights and actively participate and contribute to the application, promotion and protection of human rights' and agreed to consider the establishment of an appropriate regional mechanism on human rights.[62] The ASEAN Intergovernmental Commission on Human Rights (AICHR) was established in 2009 as an intergovernmental body based on consultation and consensus, with representatives nominated by member states.

The right to peace appeared initially in the five-year work plan of the AICHR 2010–2015, which 'aimed at realizing the aspiration of the people of ASEAN on human rights, strengthening AICHR, promoting awareness on human rights in ASEAN and enhancing cooperation with external partners, as well as to implement AICHR's overarching mandate on human rights, thereby contributing to the successful building of an ASEAN Community by 2015'.[63] It was scheduled

---

61 Catherine S Renshaw, 'The ASEAN Human Rights Declaration 2012' (2013) 13, *Human Rights Law Review,* 558. Gino J Naldi and Konstantinos D Magliveras, 'The ASEAN Human Rights Declaration' (2014) 3, *International Human Rights Law Review,* 185-186.

62 1993 Joint Communique of the 26th ASEAN Ministerial Meeting Issued in Singapore on 24 July 1993, https://cil.nus.edu.sg/wp-content/uploads/2019/02/1993-26th-AMMJC-1.pdf (accessed 30 July 2023).

63 https://aichr.org/wp-content/uploads/2018/10/AICHR_Five-Year_Work_Plan_2012-2015.pdf (accessed 24 June 2021).

to initiate thematic studies on human rights-related issues, one of which was the right to peace. The right to peace was again included in the following work plan 2016–2020, whose objectives included that peoples of ASEAN shall enjoy the right to live in peace, dignity and prosperity. Following the plan, the AICHR workshop on the thematic study on the right to peace was held in Lao, which opened a forum among representatives from AICHR and others to exchange views and share experiences on the right to peace.[64] The workshop aimed at information sharing and holding discussions among the member states on the topic of the right to peace.[65] The inclusion of the right to peace in the Commission's work plan signified its approach to human rights as a consultative body among the member states. Compared with other regional human rights mechanisms, its mandate was restricted, as it was not empowered to investigate alleged human rights violations, nor had it mechanisms to receive communications from member states or individuals.

The provision of the right to peace in AHRD is as follows:

> 38.Every person and the peoples of ASEAN have the right to enjoy peace within an ASEAN framework of security and stability, neutrality and freedom, such that the rights set forth in this Declaration can be fully realised. To this end, ASEAN Member States should continue to enhance friendship and cooperation in the furtherance of peace, harmony and stability in the region.

This provision has the following features. First of all, it resonates with the principles of the Charter of ASEAN, a founding document of ASEAN as a regional organisation. The term 'security and stability' is provided in Article 1.1 of the Charter, as the purpose of ASEAN is 'to maintain and enhance peace, security and stability and further strengthen peace-oriented values in the region'. It states that one of the purposes of ASEAN is '[t]o ensure that the peoples and Member States of ASEAN live in peace with the world at large in a just, democratic and harmonious environment' (Article 1. 4). Both provisions imply that member states affirm the right of their peoples to live in peace, which is one of the main objectives of ASEAN.

Secondly, both persons and peoples enjoy the right to peace within the framework of ASEAN's security and stability, neutrality and freedom. At the

---

64 Press Release: AICHR Workshop on the Thematic Study on the Right to Peace, 7 December 2018, LAO PDR, https://aichr.org/news/press-release-aichr-workshop-on-the-thematic-study-on-the-right-to-peace-7-december-2018-lao-pdr/ (accessed 15 April 2019).

65 The right to peace was not included in the Five-Year Work Plan 2021–2025.

global level, the right to peace has been categorised as a third-generation of human rights or solidarity rights, such as the right to development.[66] As it also refers to a right of every person and peoples, it is debatable whether this right could be categorised as a third generation right, i.e. a collective right.

Moreover, the Declaration speaks of the person's right, avoiding the term 'individual.' On the one hand, it is argued that the absence of the word individual reflects an antipathy to the putative Western ideas that emphasise individual rights.[67] On the other hand, it is alleged that the person is a legal concept, and the term suggests that the drafters' wish to give the subjects of the Declaration a legal status as a rights-holding subject.[68] It remains to be seen whether the provision with the term 'person' is merely a choice of words, without any significance in the content of the Declaration, or whether it may have some influence on the legal nature of an anticipated regional human rights convention.

Thirdly, it suggests that the right to enjoy peace by persons and peoples could be realised when member states could strengthen their friendship and cooperation. Accordingly, the article stresses the significance of good relations among member states. It focuses on the relationship among member states to achieve the right to peace of the citizens and peoples of member states. The article does not sufficiently elucidate the ways in which the right is realised and who bears the obligation to promote peace. As has been suggested, the right to peace implies a whole range of duties and obligations, both positive and negative, for different entities. The article provides the rights holder, i.e. persons and peoples, but does not speficy the bearers of the obligations. There is little connection between the enjoyment of the rights of persons or peoples and the friendly relations among member states. The suggestion that the member states should strengthen friendship and cooperation, with the aim of realising the right to peace, is a political statement. The article is silent on how the right can be realised, it does not explain to what extent the good relations among states serve the realisation of the right to peace of persons and peoples.

---

66 Naldi and Magliveras (n 61) 202–204, Renshaw (n 61) 574. Renshaw's analysis of the drafting process indicates different views among states in regard to the right to peace as an individual or a collective right. Gerald Clark, 'The Evolving ASEAN Human Rights System: The ASEAN Human Rights Declaration of 2012' (2012) 11, *Northwestern University Journal of International Human Rights*, 1–27, 23.

67 Clarke (n 66) 22.

68 Renshaw (n 61) 563, fn 44.

It is concluded that the right to peace in the AHRD is distinct and different from that in Africa and that endorsed by the UN. The emphasis on the relationship among states in the region to fulfil the end of the right to peace is in the context of ASEAN. This reminds us that the debate on 'Asian Values' dates back to the 1993 Bangkok Declaration, which referred to the universality of human rights and the 'significance of national and regional particularities and various historical, cultural and religious background' (para.8).[69] The reference to both universalism and relativism in human rights was reiterated in the AHRD (Article 7), indicating that the right to peace is also contextualised in the ASEAN framework. Compared to the right to peace at the African and international levels, it is more restricted in content and scope and does not envisage the concrete realisation of individual rights. Rather, it seems to be argued that the right to peace is achieved through the maintenance of good interstate relations.

4 Evolving the Right to Peace in Regional Contexts

The different practices in Africa and Southeast Asia regarding the right to peace demonstrate the breadth of the concept and the differences in the way in which the right is identified and conceptualised in each region. In Africa, legal instruments indicate that the right to peace is a collective right of peoples and/or that of women. The peoples' rights were initially encouraged by liberation movements, and the right to peace as a collective right is generally recognised in the African context.[70] It was once argued that 'it seems fair to say that [the right to peace] has definitively failed to capture the global imagination and that it has done little, if anything, to strengthen the concept of peoples' rights as a separate category of rights'.[71] The African experience suggests that the collective nature of the right to peace has been established through the ACHPR and the Maputo Protocol.

Article 23 of the ACHPR pronounces the positive duty on states to protect from domestic violence and external attack, and the right rests with the peoples who themselves have acclaim against the states acting in violation of it; the African Commission has not developed its own assessment.[72] The Commission often relies more on principles and standards developed by the

69 UN Doc A/CONF.157/ASRM/8A/CONF.157/PC/59 (7 April 1993) 5.
70 Ouguergouz (n 36) 10.
71 Alston (n 9) 281.
72 Baldwin and Morel (n 41) 279–282.

UN and other regional bodies rather than resorting to its own jurisprudence.[73] The communications referring to Article 23 have so far not elaborated on the right to peace. Its merits remain broad without detailed legal arguments about the provision itself. The ways in which the Commission has referred to the UN Charter and the Principle of Friendly Relationship may reinforce universal international norms but it does not provide a further discussion on the African context of the right to peace.

Furthermore, the African Commission follows a conventional process in interpreting the article, whereas the relevant article calls for a proactive approach to the realisation of the right. 'The African Charter on Human and Peoples' Rights has combined an impressive array of individual rights and duties, group rights, and state rights and duties. Some of these,...like the right to national and international peace and security, appear to be new additions to the list of internationally recognized rights. The possession of a right usually implies a duty for others to conform to a pattern of behavior. Even if it is accepted that there is a negative duty not to contravene these rights, a positive duty to support them, desirable as it may be, appears as yet to be futuristic, a *lex ferenda* rather than a *lex lata*. Whether these new rights have matured into principles of international law is still a matter of controversy'.[74] The jurisprudence of the African Commission is not equipped with the positive obligation of member states in interpreting the right to peace, but rather follows the traditional interpretation of international peace and security.

The judgment of the ACtHPR affirmed the feasibility of bringing a complaint by an individual against the member state, alleging its violation of the treaty in revising its Constitution. The decision indicated that individuals can challenge violations of the right to peace by a member state. The right can be used in Africa as a legal basis for alleging a breach of duty by states.

The right to peace as enshrined in the Human Rights Declaration in ASEAN illustrates the specificity of ASEAN, not in its content but in the ways in which the right is to be realised. While it is recognised that ASEAN has historically emphasised its regionalism, this may undermine the universal value of the right to peace, which applies to all persons or peoples. Moreover, the ASEAN framework, which stresses friendship and cooperation among member states to promote peace, harmony and stability in the region does not necessarily indicate the relevance between the relations of states and the realisation of persons and the peoples' right to peace.

73 Murray (n 45) 254–255.

74 U O Umozurike, 'The African Charter on Human and Peoples' Rights' (1983) 77, *American Journal of International Law*, 902–912, 911.

Finally, no direct connections exist between the UN debates on the right to peace and the regional initiatives to promote the right to peace. Notwithstanding the inclusion of provisions on the right to peace in regional documents, neither the AU nor the ASEAN has explicitly stated their position on the right to peace in the UN fora. The European Union has repeatedly made clear its cautious position on the right to peace as an established law;[75] African and Southeast Asian silence appears incoherent, given the fact that the regions have attempted to establish the right to peace.[76] It thus demonstrates that both African and Southeast Asian states are less interested in the global debate on the right to peace and more focus on the application of the right to peace within their regions.

5 Conclusion

This study has discussed the development of the right to peace in international law, both globally and regionally. First, the historical development of the right to peace was reviewed, focusing on the discussions at the UN. During the Cold War, the right to peace was asserted out of concern over the expanding nuclear weapons. In the Post-Cold War, a cultural aspect of peace was proposed at UNESCO, which was not well received from legal perspectives; in the 21st century, the war in Iraq led to a growing movement seeking the right to peace particularly by civil society. This movement resulted in the adoption of resolutions by the HRC and the GA. The overarching concept of the right to peace entailed inherent difficulty in being established as a legal right in the international community, which remains a non-binding instrument.

Secondly, the provision on the right to peace in the ACHPR and its legal interpretation by the African Commission and the ACtHPR supported the view that the right is no longer conditioned by African underdevelopment once suggested.[77] One can identify the jurisprudence by the African Human Rights mechanisms, taking a traditional approach to examining the right to peace by referring to the UN Charter. Such autonomy could, in the long run, contribute to the development of international law.

75 Bailliet (n 11) 59.

76 Some African countries make their position clear respectively, but there is no definite united position as Africa.

77 B Obinna Okere, 'The Protection of Human Rights in Africa and the African Charter on Human and Peoples' Rights: A Comparative Analysis with the European and American System' (1984) 6, *Human Rights Quarterly*, 141–158, 148.

It was once suggested:

> Internal forces within the African states, the dynamics of intra-African relations and the manner in which Africa interacts with the rest of the world will affect the role of international law in Africa as we enter the twenty-first century. Because of its marginalization, Africa has generally been a recipient of, rather than a contributor to, the development of international law ... In a legal system in which the principal actors are still nation-states, the fragile African states will continue to play a limited role in shaping new international legal norms so long as these internal weaknesses persist. African states must, therefore, address problems of political instability, economic stagnation, and cultural disunity.[78]

The present study demonstrated the established right to peace in Africa and the subsequent procedures and jurisprudence by the African Commission and the ACtHPR in applying Article 23. It also highlighted some perspectives about the African role in the development of international law.

As for Southeast Asia, the provision of the right to peace in the Declaration is partly a positive sign to identify the right of all persons and peoples. The Declaration is a political instrument that is not equipped with the mechanisms to realise the right. Emphasising the importance of friendship and cooperation among ASEAN member states suggests that the right to peace of persons and peoples would be achieved when states establish good relationships, which diverges from the argument at the global level.

These developments in regions seem to have no relevance to the movement on the right to peace globally; neither African nor Southeast Asian countries clarify their position on the right to peace. One recognises a gap between the efforts at the global level in elaborating and developing the Declaration on the Right to Peace and those of the African region in interpreting the treaty provisions of the right to peace. One can at least conclude that African achievements could facilitate the development of the right to peace within Africa, whereas the discussion at the UN or the ASEAN on the right remains unforeseeable. The relationship between the regional organisations and the UN should be examined to identify whether there is any contribution of regional legal efforts to the development of the right to peace at the global level, facilitating the development of international law.

78 Mutharika (n 37) 1719.

This study explored the legal development process of the right to peace through the adoption and interpretation of instruments. The adoption of the documents at the UN and the ASEAN attested consensus on the right to peace. In Africa, the right to peace was acknowledged as a special right for individuals, groups, and peoples, rather than just an aspirational norm. Achieving the right to peace is an ongoing pursuit, which this study proved.

PART 3

Constructive Resistance in International Law from Below

CHAPTER 5

Treaty on the Prohibition of Nuclear Weapons as Legal Correction of International Injustice

Issues of Normalization of 'Human Security' and Creation of World Law

Masashi Nakayama

1 Introduction

Human beings have been under threat and fear of the existence and use of nuclear weapons since atomic bombs were thrown upon Hiroshima and Nagasaki in August 1945. It has not been improved for more than three decades even after the end of the Cold War. There are still about 13,000 nuclear warheads around the world. Also, instability over nuclear weapons has been present such as nuclear development in North Korea and Iran, the lapse of the Intermediate-Range Nuclear Forces (INF) Treaty, unpredictability of nuclear terrorism, recent Russian suspension of the implementation of the New Strategic Arms Reduction Treaty (New START) and the countermeasures by the U.S., and the nuclear arms race between the U.S. and Russia. Furthermore, the war in Ukraine, triggered by Russia's military invasion of Ukraine on the 24th of February 2022, has made the crisis even more serious. The threat of nuclear war has become more real with Russia's threats to the use of nuclear weapons. Nuclear hegemony for national security represents international injustice and the 'culture of war and violence' because the governments acknowledge its destructive power and inhumanity.

However, the advisory opinion of the International Court of Justice (ICJ)[1] on the Legality of the Threat or Use of Nuclear Weapons, stating that the use of nuclear weapons violates international law in general, declared in 1996 led to establishing a treaty for the prohibition of nuclear weapons from humanitarian perspectives in the international society. Also, this international trend responded to the 'mainstreaming human rights' after the Cold War and to raising civil society. While these movements were seen, the United Nations (UN) adopted the Treaty on the Prohibition of Nuclear Weapons (TPNW)[2] on the

---

1 *Legality of the Threat or Use of Nuclear Weapons*, Advisory Opinion of 8 July 1996, ICJ Reports 1996, para 105.

2 *Treaty on the Prohibition of Nuclear Weapons*, A/CONF.229/2017/8, 7 July 2017 <http://www.undocs.org/A/CONF.229/2017/8> accessed 3 May 2021.

 | DOI:10.1163/9789004681477_007

7th of July 2017, then the Treaty came into effect on the 22nd of January 2021. The first meeting of the Conference of the Parties to the TPNW was also held in June 2022.

The purpose of this paper is to discuss the issues and outlook of constructing peace order in line with international justice through analysis and consideration of the TPNW. One of the reasons for selecting the TPNW as the theme for this paper is that the Treaty seems to represent and embrace Mogami's perspectives towards peace thoughts and that we will be able to envisage the meaning of Mogami's peace thoughts and the processes for the future by analyzing the current situation around the Treaty in international society.

I suggest these following three points can be raised as the characteristics of perspectives of Mogami's peace thoughts. These perspectives are significant and match with my arguments in order to consider new peace order from now onwards. Firstly, regulations as a role of means to resist violence. In Mogami's discussions, the importance of international regulations as peaceful means to fight against violence in international society is often emphasized.[3] However, it goes beyond the role as adjustment regulations of authority between nations, and it tends to seek 'rules of law' in international society, which suggests the vision of regulations so-called the 'world law'. In this context, violence means not only direct violence but also structural violence that includes social injustice. The issue of nuclear weapons that is a symbolic form of ultimate violence by nations is not only the matter of direct means of violence in a narrow sense in the existing issues for creating peace but it represents structural violence and international injustice in terms of the influence towards poverty and global environment brought by military budget, and placing ourselves in the social structure in the 'nuclear era'. Given that, the TPNW appears to try lawfully adjust international injustice.

Secondly, Mogami seems to perceive peace as the humanity point of view, attempting to reconstruct it.[4] In other words, a perspective to consider peace as human rights. This strand of thoughts was included the concepts of 'the right to live peacefully' or 'the Right to Live in Peace', that emerged in nuclear arms

3 These perspectives are seen in Mogami's arguments in his following works: Toshiki Mogami, 'Multilateralism and the Rule of Law: A Reflection on the Position of the Norm on the Prohibition of Use of Force' and 'The Legal Structure of Justice and Humanity: What Determines the Legal Justness?' in *An Era of International Constitutionalism* (Iwanami Shoten 2007) (in Japanese), which criticises unilateralism of the United States in the 'War on Terrorism' after the simultaneous terrorist attacks on 9.11.

4 Toshiki Mogami, 'Redefining Peace: Peace for Humanity' in *What is Peace Now? Nine Stories Around Human Rights and Humanity* (Iwanami Shoten 2006) (in Japanese).

race during the Second World War. Furthermore, it has a link to the thoughts of 'human security' that also emerged after the Cold War in order to redefine national security from a humanity point of view. Therefore, the TPNW echoes the principles of 'human security', and it tries to normalize 'human security' through a form of treaty as the preamble of the Treaty stated, 'Mindful of the risks posed by the continued existence of nuclear weapons [...] these risks concern the security of all humanity'. 'Treaty for human security'[5] can be another name for the treaty because it values human dignity as the highest priority, and spreads this new humanitarian norm has been playing an important role in building international constitutionalism[6] and the 'world law'. Furthermore, this trend has appeared in not only treaties but also goal-setting models without legal-binding agreement as a new norm such as Sustainable Development Goals (SDGs)[7] whose principle is 'no one will be left behind', which was adopted at the United Nations in 2015.

Thirdly, the perspective in relation to multilateralism and construction of order from the bottom. Mogami emphasizes the significance of emergence and its critical role of international organizations that are historically necessary to overcome the issues in international society. Mogami points out that its nature lies in multilateralism. He however argues that it is needed to redefine as a concept that can embrace NGOs, society of citizens and non-governmental bodies as well as multilateralism that tends to limit to nations.[8] In this sense, the key to the legal correction of international injustice can be a role of non-state actors such as the UN, non-profit organizations and civil society. It is widely known that the International Campaign to Abolish Nuclear Weapons (ICAN) and other non-profit organizations led to reach agreements on the TPNW. Trying to normalize human security at the United Nations through the cooperation of leading states and civil society can be a way to address international injustice and driving force to foster the 'rule of law' in the international society. As a result of this, treaties concerning inhumane weapons have been established such as the Convention on the Prohibition of Anti-Personnel Mines and the Convention on Cluster Munitions. It seems, however, that issuing the

5 Gerd Oberleitner, 'Human Security: A Challenge to International Law?' (2005) 11 *Global Governance* 185–203.

6 Mogami tried to clarify the principles of international constitutionalism, organising the discussions around it in 'What is International Constitutionalism?' in *The Era of International Constitutionalism* (n 3).

7 UN Doc A/RES/70/L.1, 18 September 2015.

8 Toshiki Mogami, *Lecture on the Theory of International Organization* (Iwanami Shoten 2016) 6–9.

TPNW will not abolish all nuclear weapons immediately. Criticism has been raised that adopting the treaty may form the deeper gap between the nuclear powers and the others and stagnate or even retrograde nuclear disarmament. These arguments over the TPNW themselves seem to reflect the reality of the international society over international injustice.

Given that, the TPNW can be seen as the integrated ideas and perspectives of Mogami. From this point of view, I would like to discuss the meaning of peace order, which was depicted by Mogami, and the prospects for the future. This paper will firstly review the background to the creation of 'culture of war' and transitions of perspectives on wars in the modern international society after the conclusion of the Peace of Westphalia. It will also consider the advent of Nuclear Age after the Second World War, the structure of the Treaty on the Non-Proliferation of Nuclear Weapons (NPT) that can be seen as hegemony system among five nuclear powers and international injustice in a security environment under nuclear threat from a viewpoint of the 'right to live in peace'. Secondly, the paper will examine the contents and the features of the TPNW along with the explanation of the process that humanitarian approaches against nuclear abolition have ended up the establishment of the TPNW. Then, the paper will discuss the arguments over the TPNW among the nuclear powers, states under the nuclear umbrella and other non-nuclear powers. It also will address the issues around normalizing human security and creating the world law. This paper will conclude with the prospects over the TPNW and some thoughts on the establishment of the 'culture of peace'.

2 'Culture of War' and Nuclear

2.1 *Issues around Nuclear as 'Justice That Cannot Cross the Border'*

First of all, I will argue the importance of perceiving the issues of nuclear weapons as a symbol of 'the culture of war and violence', resulting from historical, structural and ideological elements not as merely an issue of one single kind of weapon. Human beings entered the new era called, 'nuclear age' after 1945 when nuclear weapons emerged. Nuclear weapons are ultimately inhumane due to not only their great destructive power but their abusive nature that can lead to the extinction of all living things. Nonetheless, nuclear powers and states under the 'nuclear umbrella' cannot have extricated themselves from nuclear deterrence. These states argue that nuclear weapons are essential for the sake of national security, although admitting their inhumane nature. According to Inoue, however, this perspective that finds nuclear weapons 'necessary evil' is international injustice because it is a deception to regard them as 'justice that cannot cross the border' and oppression of 'hegemonic justice to cross the border willfully'.[9] In other words, in the world of the two different ideas, one is, 'justice that cannot cross the border' that justifies to ensure national security by possessing nuclear weapons, and the other one is, 'hegemonic justice to cross the border willfully' that believes nuclear deterrence among nuclear powers maintain peace in the international society, the question is for whom those ideas can be justified in the world. An ancient Roman proverb says 'If you want peace, prepare for war' advises that a nation should prepare the military force for maintaining peace and be even ready for war eventually. In this context, peace means protecting a nation from other outsiders. Although this idea should not be completely rejected from a perspective of state sovereignty which protects the safety of its lands and citizens, it should be remembered that wars were repeated in human history based on the idea justifying wars for peace and many people were sacrificed as a result. If this can be called 'culture of war and violence', Westphalian sovereignty strengthened this tendency started from Europe that sovereign states were appeared and monopolized great military forces after the middle of 17th century. However, issues in nuclear age are on entirely different wavelengths. Holding nuclear weapons to be prepared for wars for the sake of protecting a nation will not only threaten the peace of the nation but also the existence of humans and may have destructive consequences. There is a question of the nuclear issues from the perspectives of international justice or world justice. If world justice is defined as 'a principle of the critical regiment against any forms of oppression of powerful nations, not ideology of violently forcing their justice of gaining benefits to other countries across the border',[10] the TPNW applies the world justice.

2.2 *Westphalia System and 'Culture of War and Violence'*

Three points can be made when explaining the development of 'culture of war and violence' in the post-modern international society. The first point is a social structural factor. The beginning of the modern international society is generally known from when the conference of Peace of Westphalia was held after the Thirty Years' War in Europe (1618–1648). The medieval feudal society where the Holy Roman Emperor and the Pope were at the top of the society was destroyed after the Thirty Years' War, and sovereign states were established in Europe. The Westphalia system that was consisted of the sovereign states

9 Tatsuo Inoue, *The Theory of World Justice* (Chikumashobo 2012) 20 (in Japanese).
10 ibid 20.

kept the conflictive situation in its structure due to decentralization. To regulate the sovereign nations international law was established. However, international law as agreement rule lacked reinforcement of legal implementation and application, and the international society of anarchy structurally involved conflicts between nations. Therefore, nations eventually attempted to solve issues of authorial regulations between them by arms and wars when they did not by the law. Until the beginning of the 20th-century wars were legal based on so-called Just War Theory and the indiscriminate view of war. In this time 'peace' meant maintaining stability and order between nations,[11] so international law adjusted authorial regulations between states and played a role as conflict resolution norm. As a result, international justice was prioritized over national justice, and human rights were treated as national issues above all.[12]

Another factor of 'culture of war and violence' is cultural imperialism and Eurocentrism. Despite decentralization, international society did not involve all the countries at first. At the time international society referred to European society, and then it spread to North America, Latin America, Asia and Africa. This generalized European norm and value in the world and international society had been Eurocentrism from modern to post-modern time.[13] European countries regarded themselves as civilized nations and did other countries such as China and Japan as semi-civilized ones. In modern time imperialism fostered colonization in Asian and African countries as they were treated as uncivilized nations and taken over their sovereignty. Indeed, international law functioned as an ideology to justify the actions taken by the European nations. Regulating international law was a condition of participating in international society as a civilized state. The history of international society starting from European nations created the culture that the stronger prey on the weaker with the development of a capitalist economy that will be covered in the next paragraph.

Scientism and materialism can be raised as the third factor. The modern time that developed technology and capitalism was the era for pursuing material and economical wealth. Technological and industrial revolutions in Europe and spreading them were providing wealth in human society while growing unlimited human desire that variously sacrificed human beings and nature. Global

---

11 Joseph S Nye Jr and David A Welch, *Understanding Global Conflict and Cooperation: An Introduction to Theory and History* (10th ed, Pearson College Div 2016).

12 Hiroki Abe, 'Actualizing 'Value of Human Beings': Meaning of International Human Rights Law' in *Iwanami Lecture Series, Law in Modern Times vol 2: International Society and Law* (Iwanami Shoten 1997) 156 (in Japanese).

13 Yasuaki Onuma, *International Law* (Chikumashobo 2018) 30–50 (in Japanese).

environmental issues representing global warming symbolizes evil practices of bloated desire for mass production, a lifestyle of mass consumption and environmental destruction. The development of science and technology led to evolving weapons, and wars became crueler and larger scale alongside the nation's monopolistic system. As an extreme example of this, nuclear weapons are the symbolistic product of the 'culture of war and violence'.

The reason that nuclear weapons symbolize not only 'culture of war' but 'violence' is they involve direct violence and structural violence. Nuclear weapons are humanitarian and human rights issues due to their inhumane and non-discriminatory nature. Based on these qualities, the advisory opinion of the ICJ determined the use of nuclear weapons illegal according to the regulation of armed conflict in international law, especially principles of humanitarian law. Moreover, nuclear weapons are issues of poverty. Enormous costs for developing nuclear weapons resulted in reducing expenses for social security and education in Northern developing countries and for solving poverty in the South. The environment is also affected by using nuclear weapons, for example, disruption of ecosystem, radioactive contamination, and extreme weather which is known as 'nuclear winter'.

In the international society that was based on the indiscriminate view of war and system of power balance from 19th century to the beginning of 20th century, the arms race had been fierce and led to the First World War. It was a consequence of 'culture of war' and Westphalia system developed after modern times. Later the League of Nations was established as a universal organization with its mission of 'solving issues of Westphalia system such as disputes between nations and arbitrary division of human lives'.[14] Finally, the establishment of the League of Nations advanced illegal of wars and international security system but did not prevent from the Second World War.

3 Justice or Injustice around Nuclear Weapons

3.1 *NPT Regime as Nuclear Hegemony System*[15]

Ending the Second World War that is generally understood as wars between totalitarianism and liberal democracy fostered establishment of the United Nations whose highest priority in mission is 'to maintain international peace and security'. However, it consisted of only victorious countries, the League

14 Mogami (n 8) 341.

15 See Nobumasa Akiyama, 'Background to the NPT', Nobumasa Akiyama (ed), *NPT-Global Governance of Nuclear* (Iwanami Shoten 2015).

of Nations, and aimed to keep 'peace' as post-war management. The name of 'the United Nations' summarizes its characteristics of gathered nations, but it held hegemony system of five countries – the United States of America, Great Britain, France, the former Soviet Union and China – as Permanent member of UN Security Council (P5). Only the P5 is allowed to have a huge power of veto and restriction in the decision-making process. Also, the end of the Second World War involving the development and usage of nuclear weapons opened the era of nuclear. The P5 held nuclear hegemony where the five countries occupied nuclear weapons,[16] and the NPT was issued in 1970. UN Security Council that P5 is centered and the NPT are the two pillars of international order in post-war times and are characterized as 'power system' consisted of 'security and diplomatic order'.[17]

The NPT was one of the core nuclear-related treaties and aimed at prevention of nuclear proliferation, the peaceful use of nuclear energy and promotion of nuclear disarmament. In the treaty, Article 1 stated the nuclear haves' responsibility for non-proliferation. Also, non-nuclear powers were responsible for non-proliferation in Article 2. Article 3 stipulated a safeguard for this. The right and cooperation for the peaceful use of nuclear energy were assured in Article 4. In fact, Article 6 promised conscientious negotiation about nuclear disarmament for signatory states, especially the nuclear powers. Overall, the NPT was not a fair treaty as it allowed only the five nations to possess nuclear. The background to the formulation of the treaty, however, included a sense of crisis towards the proliferation of nuclear weapons in the international society. Starting with the United States, the five states possessed nuclear weapons having succeeded their nuclear tests one after another, the former Soviet Union (1949), the United Kingdom (1952), France (1960), and China (1964). A fierce competition of developing the means of transport for intercontinental ballistic missiles (ICBM) among the states also intensified. Further, based on the growing tension of the Cold War, the 'Cuban Missile Crisis' suddenly occurred in 1962, where the volatile climate between the United States and the former Soviet Union created a critical moment of an outbreak of a nuclear war. Having had such a situation, concerns about the proliferation of nuclear weapons and the recognition of preventing it were widely shared in the international society.

After the year of 1952, comprehensive disarmament was being discussed about all kinds of armaments including nuclear weapons in the UN, and the

---

16 Toshiki Mogami 'Though of Nuclear and Devastation: Destroying Peace as Oblivion of Humanity' in *What Is Peace Now?* (n 4), in which Mogami criticizes severely inhumanity of nuclear weapons and nuclear-centred systems.

17 As of May 2023, 191 state parties.

necessity of an international agreement on non-proliferation of nuclear weapons began to be discussed in the late 1950s. In doing so, Poland, Ireland and Sweden submitted the resolutions to the UN, which required non-proliferation of nuclear weapons. The reason that these non-nuclear powers submitted the resolutions was an intensified competition of nuclear development between the United States and the former Soviet Union in Europe. The Irish Resolution[18] was adopted at the UN General Assembly in December 1961, which drew an attention to have proper negotiations for formulating a treaty of non-proliferation of nuclear weapons. The Resolution normalized the form of the international society in terms of non-proliferation of nuclear weapons and nuclear disarmament for the following three points. Firstly, establishing fundamental principles of a treaty on non-proliferation of nuclear weapons. Secondly, establishing initiative of nuclear nations in the negotiations. Thirdly, since national security in relation to non-nuclear proliferation was entrusted to nuclear states, international security orders came to be considered on the assumption of the values of nuclear weapons in international security since then. As a result, non-proliferation of nuclear weapons structurally fixed authority, prestige and power in international politics.[19] Then, the United States and the former Soviet Union submitted identical treaty drafts separately to the 18 States Committee on Disarmament in August 1967, and based on the first amended treaty draft in January 1968, the fundamental parts of the treaty were decided, which were the obligation of nuclear non-proliferation stated in Articles 1 and 2, security measurement of the fulfillment of obligations by non-nuclear powers stated in Article 3.

It drew an attention that there were several political negotiations (Grand Bargain) from January to the date of adoption, 1st of July in the same year among nuclear states and non-nuclear states.[20] Among the negotiations, the obligation of nuclear disarmament stated in Article 6 was regarded to be the most important, which was inserted in the article as a mean to compensate for the loss of profit that was caused by the obligation of non-proliferation by non-nuclear states. Although the obligation that was promised in the Article was 'to negotiate sincerely', and it did not include the obligation to reach an agreement,[21] there was no doubt that the treaty was an important regulation

18 UN Doc A/RES/1665(16), December 1961.

19 Akiyama (n 15) 13–14.

20 ibid 21–32.

21 *Legality of the Threat or Use of Nuclear Weapons* (n 1) para 105. The ICJ's advisory opinion on the 'Legality of the Threat or Use of Nuclear Weapons' in 1996 stated in its final 105th paragraph F as, 'There exists an obligation to pursue in good faith and bring negotiations to a conclusion leading to nuclear disarmament in all its aspects under strict and effective

in order to support the unfairness of the NPT and to take balance of it. It can also be said that Article 6 was a resistance regulation to seek nuclear disarmament or even abolish of nuclear weapons against the hegemony and the international security order by the five states on assumption of the possession of nuclear weapons. Growing frustration towards the nuclear states that did not fulfill the obligation satisfactory led to the formulation of the Treaty on the Prohibition of Nuclear Weapons, which will be discussed below.

3.2 *Peace as Human Rights*

The Second World War was a significant turning point in terms of 'human rights' as well as issues of 'peace'. As discussed above, until then, the meaning of 'peace' had been understood in the way that it maintained and stabilized orders between states. Therefore, under passive peace that prioritized orders between states, peace and human rights were considered as different concepts, and human rights was treated as a national issue. However, the Holocaust toward against the Jews by the Nazis provoked the discussions that peace and human rights were inseparable and human rights was the foundation for creating peace. This suggested that actualization of justice (international justice) such as human rights, liberation of colonies, and protecting global environment was a critical element in peace.[22] The Charter of the United Nations stated, 'to achieve international co-operation in solving international problems of an economic, social, cultural, or humanitarian character, and in promoting and encouraging respect for human rights and for fundamental freedoms for all without distinction as to race, sex, language, or religion' along with its aim of maintaining international peace and security. This suggested that constructing orders for justice was the sufficient condition for peace. Then, as it is widely known, once the Universal Declaration of Human Rights was adopted, international security of human rights was employed by concluding and implementing of various treaties on human rights including the International Covenants on Human Rights.

If the Second World War was regarded as an event that had people recognize that human rights were an essential foundation for creating peace, the

---

international control'. The NPT Treaty Article 6 regulated to 'conduct negotiations sincerely', which did not include the obligation to reach a conclusion; however, most recent perception is that it includes the obligation to conclude the negotiations as in the advisory opinion.

22 See, Hideaki Shinoda 'Consideration of International Regulations and Theory: Order, Justice and State Sovereignty' (2001) 26 *Peace Research* 86–96 (in Japanese) in relation to how order and justice have been regarded in the international society.

emergence of nuclear weapons was in fact a turning point to transform the recognition to an idea that peace itself equals human rights. Mogami pointed out in relation to its background that, after the nuclear era began, the whole world was once placed in a middle-of-the-way situation neither peace nor war, that is, peace was always absent.[23] In such a situation of absence of peace or normalization of quasi-war time, the concept of the 'rights to peace' or the 'rights to live in peace' emerged. In which, a requirement of more positive acquisition of the right for peace was implied. Peace as reflective benefits, which was brought from a situation that states were not in war, is not enough in the normalization of the quasi-war situation with a sense of fear for nuclear war.[24] Then, the 'rights to peace' or the 'rights to live in peace' became normalized through the discussions at the UN. In 1978, the UN General Assembly adopted the Declaration on the Preparation of Societies for Life in Peace, and assured that the 'rights to live in peace' was a common concept in the international society.[25] The Declaration stated, 'Every nation and every human being, regardless of race, conscience, language or sex, has the inherent right to life in peace'. In 1984, the UN General Assembly also adopted the Declaration on the Right of Peoples to Peace,[26] where the Declaration regulated as, 'Solemnly proclaims that the peoples of our planet have a sacred right to peace'.[27] As more recent example, as the growing movements of a Spanish civic organization for actualizing the 'rights to peace' as International Law, the UN General Assembly adopted the Declaration on the Rights to Peace in November 2016.[28]

23 Toshiki Mogami, 'The Right to Peace' (1989) 40 *Freedom and Justice* 33–39, included in *The Era of International Constitutionalism* (n 3) 259 (in Japanese).

24 ibid 260.

25 UN Doc A/RES/33/73, 15 December 1978.

26 UN Doc A/RES/39/11, 15 November 1984.

27 The 'Right to Peace' was supposed to be included along with the 'Right to Develop' in the concept of 'Third Generation Human Rights', which was proposed by Director of the UNESCO Division of Human Rights and Peace, Karel Vasak in 1977. As a local treaty of human rights, African Charter on Human and Peoples' Rights (the Banjul Charter) that was adopted in 1981 first regulated the Third Generation Human Rights at treaty level, and Article 3 states that 'All peoples shall have the right to national and international peace and security'.

28 'Declaration on the Right to Peace' originated in the movements since 2005 by a Spanish civil organization (the Spanish Society for International Human Rights Law) in which they tried to have the 'rights to peace' been recognized as international human rights when the Iraq War provoked. The movements involved the NGOs around the world, and in Spain, the 'Declaration of Luarca' was adopted in 2006, followed by the adoptions of the 'Declaration of Bilbo' and the 'Declaration of Barcelona'. In December 2010, the 'Declaration of Santiago' that reflected the ideas for peace from a number of specialists and each NGO as human rights was adopted, where 900 NGOs gathered world-widely.

Having had the process above, a viewpoint that tried to perceive peace as human rights came to be recognized in the international society. However, because of the lawful nature of the declarations at the UN General Assemblies in general, it is difficult to say that the 'rights to peace' or the 'rights to life in peace' have been actualized. Mogami said that the concept of rights reflected people's longing requirement, therefore, the 'rights to peace' were normalized enough although it was not yet actualized.[29] It needs to be highlighted that if peace is people's desire and it is regarded as human rights, individual human being is the recipient of peace. Providing that under the NPT regime that allowed states to possess nuclear weapons, the hegemony order prevented to receive the benefits of peace as human rights, the 'rights to live in peace' was the concept of resistance against structural violence or the 'culture of war and violence', which underpinned the fundamental nuclear system, and also, it was the concept to seek liberation of human beings from the threat of nuclear weapons, which was the absence of peace. Mogami called the concept as 'structural rights'.[30]

4 The Treaty on the Prohibition of Nuclear Weapons as Lawful Rectification of International Injustice

4.1 *Background to the Formulation of the Treaty and Its Humanistic Approaches*

On the 7th of July 2017, the Treaty on the Prohibition of Nuclear Weapons was adopted for 122, against 1 (the Netherlands), and abstention 1 (Singapore) at the UN General Assembly.[31] The Treaty was a lawful rectification aimed to transform the situation with the existence of nuclear weapons that reflected international injustice by formulating lawful measures such as international

---

The Declaration denied not only wars and military actions but also structural violence that produced poverty and cultural violence that caused discrimination or prejudice. The 'Declaration of Santiago' was officially submitted to the UN in 2011, and the venue of negotiations was moved to the UN. On the 1st July 2016, the 'Declaration on the Rights to Peace' was officially adopted at the 32nd UN Human Rights Council, and 'Rights to Peace' was adopted as an international declaration at the 31st UN General Assembly in November 2016.

29 Mogami (n 23) 267–268.

30 ibid 269.

31 See Mitsuru Kurosawa 'Meaning and Issues of the Treaty on the Prohibition of Nuclear Weapons', (2017) 14 *Journal of Osaka Jogakuin University* 15–32; Tetsu Kawasaki 'New Dynamism around 'Inhumane of Nuclear' in Akiyama (n 15) 163–194.

treaty, and the Treaty can be perceived as structural resistance in terms of its purpose for structuring a new order. There were the following three points for the background to the Treaty. Firstly, after the end of the Cold War, although there were movements of nuclear disarmament including the Prague Speech by Barack Obama, the then President of the United States, the negotiations on nuclear disarmament between the United States, the former Soviet Union, and other states stagnated and did not make any progress. Also, nuclear states including the United States promoted and increased the number of nuclear weapons, which became more obvious in Trump administration, and because of the Intermediate-Range Nuclear Forces Treaty lost its effect. These aspects around the movements made frustration in the non-nuclear states reach its peak. Secondly, since 2010s, humanistic approaches for prohibiting and abolishing nuclear weapons had a momentum. And thirdly, international NGOs including ICAN co-operated the non-nuclear states and proceeded the negotiations of the Treaty at the UN.

Regarding humanistic approaches, the NPT Review Conference held in 2010 was a turning point of the movements, however, the trend of the prohibition of nuclear weapons began with the end of the Cold War. The most significant event among them, the advisory opinion on the 'Legality of the Threat or Use of Nuclear Weapons' published by the International Court of Justice (ICJ) in 1996, which was based on the civil movements that aimed to reveal the illegality of nuclear weapons at the 'world court'. In the advisory opinion, the ICJ expressed their viewpoint as 'a threat or use of nuclear weapons should also be compatible with the requirements of the international law applicable in armed conflict, particularly those of the principles and rules of international humanitarian law'.[32] Given the advisory opinion, NGOs such as the International Association of Lawyers against Nuclear Arms (IALANA) produced a draft of the 'Model Nuclear Weapons Convention', which Costa Rica submitted as a UN Document in the following year of 1997.[33] At the UN General Assembly, Malaysia submitted a series of resolutions that required to commence negotiations of the treaty on the prohibition of nuclear weapon every year since 1996, which had been adopted by the majority.

In such situations, the NPT Review Conference stated in the final document in 2010 as, 'the Conference expresses its deep concern at the catastrophic humanitarian consequences of any use of nuclear weapons and reaffirms the need for all States at all times to comply with applicable international law,

32 *Legality of the Threat or Use of Nuclear Weapons* (n 1) para 105.

33 UN Doc A/C.1/52/7, 17 November 1997.

including international law'[34] as well as 'the Conference notes the five-point proposal for nuclear disarmament of the Secretary-General of the United Nations, which proposes, inter alia, consideration of negotiations on a nuclear weapons convention or agreement on a framework of separate mutually reinforcing instrument, backed by a strong system of verification'.[35] It was the very first time that the TPNW was mentioned in the final document of the NPT review process, which was ground-breaking. In which, the idea that aimed to promote the discussions on nuclear disarmament from humanistic perspectives was expressed because of the concern about the possible catastrophic outcome caused by the use of nuclear weapons, and this was the starting point of humanistic approaches towards nuclear disarmament. Efforts made by the International Red Cross and the Swiss government influenced the movements behind-the-scenes, and the influence of the Red Cross whose standpoint was the middle-of-the-road in terms of politics was significant because it brought the idea of 'humanism' into the discussions of nuclear disarmament, which often fell into the military balance between the major states.[36]

After the event, a number of joint statements on the inhumane nature of nuclear weapons were submitted by each state to the NPT Preparatory Committee, which was held towards the NPT Review Conference in 2015, and to the UN General Assembly.[37] Alongside with these movements, a new process such as the international conferences on the 'humanitarian impact' of nuclear weapons began. Specifically, the first conference was held in Norway in March 2013, the second conference was held in Mexico in February 2014, and the third conference was held in Austria in December in the same year. At the first conference, Norway emphasized that the purpose of the conference was to

34 Final Document, 2010 Review Conference of the Parties to the Treaty on the Non-Proliferation of Nuclear Weapons, NPT/CONF.2010/50 (Vol.1) V of A Principles and Objectives. <https://www.nonproliferation.org/wp-content/uploads/2015/04/2010_fd_part_i.pdf> accessed 21 May 2024.

35 Final Document, III of B Disarmament of Nuclear Weapons.

36 Tetsu Kawasaki, *New Edition Prohibiting Nuclear Weapons: Treaty Changes the World* (Iwanami Shoten 2018) 30.

37 Joint statement had been submitted 6 times in total between 2012 and 2015. It was submitted first time at the NPT Review Conference in May 2012, then, it was announced second time at the UN General Assembly First Committee in Switzerland in October in the same year. For the third time, it was announced by South Africa at the NPT preparatory meeting in Geneva in April 2013, and then it was announced for the fourth time by New Zealand at the UN General Assembly First Committee in October the same year. Japan signed for the first time at the fourth joint statement.

examine the impact of the use of nuclear weapons scientifically.[38] Towards the end of the third conference, Austria announced a document of declaration on the pledge of acting for the abolition of nuclear weapons, which was known as, 'the pledge of Austria', and required each state's signature. Then, Austria submitted 'the pledge of humanity', which renamed as the pledge of Austria, to the NPT Review Conference in May 2015.[39] Although the negotiations at the NPT Review Conference broke down and the final document was not adopted, the legal prohibition of nuclear weapons as the 'effective measures' of nuclear disarmament in the final document became an official agenda. In December 2015, at the UN General Assembly, a resolution was adopted, which decided to hold a working group to discuss lawful measures for nuclear abolition in Geneva.[40] The working group, which was mentioned in the resolution, adopted the report in August 2016 that recommended to have negotiations in 2017 on a 'legally binding instrument to prohibit nuclear weapons, leading towards their total elimination', and the resolution was adopted at the UN General Assembly on the 23rd of December in the same year. In line with the UN General Assembly resolution, the first session was held from the 27th to 31st of March 2017, and the second session was held from the 15th of June, and finally, the Treaty on the Prohibition of Nuclear Weapons was adopted on the 7th of July.

4.2 *Contents and Characteristics of the Treaty*

The Treaty on the Prohibition of Nuclear Weapons consists of a 24-paragraph preamble and 20 articles. In this section, the contents and the characteristics of the Treaty will be discussed drawing on the relevant paragraphs in relation to the awareness of issues. One of the most outstanding characteristics of the preamble was: firstly, the Treaty stated that it prohibited nuclear weapons from humanistic point of view; secondly, the rationale of the Treaty stemmed from international law, especially international humanitarian law and international human rights law; and thirdly, the Treaty mentioned the background to the progress of the negotiation for formulating the Treaty as the deadlock of the

38 Summary by the Chair included: (1) Any states or international organizations are unable to fully respond to humanistic emergency that immediately brought by explosion of nuclear weapons and to conduct sufficient rescue operations for victims; (2) Experiences gained through the use and experiments of nuclear weapons in the history so far proved that it would bring immediate and long-term catastrophic outcomes; (3) Regardless of reasons, the results of the explosion of nuclear weapons would cause critical influence on states and citizens locally and globally beyond the borders of states. <http://www.mofa.go.jp/mofaj/gaiko/kaku/pdfs/hinw_201303_3.pdf> accessed 3 May 2021.

39 Japan did not agree to any of them.

40 UN Doc A/RES/70/33, 7 December 2015.

negotiations for nuclear disarmament, and there had been enhancement and modernization of nuclear weapons.[41]

Regarding the first point, the Treaty stated in the second paragraph as, 'deeply concerned about the catastrophic humanitarian consequences that would result from any use of nuclear weapons' and 'recognizing the consequent need to completely eliminate such weapons, which remains the only way to guarantee that nuclear weapons are never used again under any circumstances'. In the third paragraph, it highlighted, 'mindful of the risks posed by the continued existence of nuclear weapons [...] and emphasizing that these risks concern the security of all humanity'. In the fourth paragraph, it stated that if nuclear weapons were used, the impact does not limit to the risk of the existence of all human beings, economics, and environment but also it would unable humans to deal with the aftermaths, saying as, 'cognizant that the catastrophic consequences of nuclear weapons cannot be adequately addressed, transcend national borders, pose grave implications for human survival, the environment, socioeconomic development, the global economy, food security and the health of current and future generations, and have a disproportionate impact on women and girls, including as a result of ionizing radiation'. Then, in the sixth paragraph, it showed awareness to agony of the victims or *hibakusha* who have suffered from nuclear experiments. Regarding the second point raised above, in the eights paragraph, it stated, 'reaffirming the need for all states at all times to comply with applicable international law, including international humanitarian law and international human rights law', and in the tenth paragraph, it mentioned, 'considering that any use of nuclear weapons would be contrary to the rules of international law applicable in armed conflict, in particular the principles and rules of international humanitarian law'. Regarding the third point, in the twelfth paragraph, it referred as, 'concerned by the slow pace of nuclear disarmament, the continued reliance on nuclear weapons in military and security concepts, doctrines and policies, and the waste of economic and human resources on programs for the production, maintenance and modernization of nuclear weapons'. In which, the Treaty expressed concern and frustration that reverse movement had been seen against nuclear disarmament and that the obligation of negotiating for disarmament, which was stated in Article 6 of the NPT Treaty had not been fulfilled.

About the body of the Treaty, 'prohibition' that was stated in Article 1 was considerably important. Article 1 prohibited: (a) Develop, test, produce, manufacture, otherwise acquire, possess or stockpile nuclear weapons or other

41 Kurosawa (n 31) 21.

nuclear explosive devices; (b) Transfer nuclear weapons to any recipient; (c) Receive the transfer of or control over nuclear weapons; (d) Use or threaten to use nuclear weapons; (e) Assist, encourage or induce, in any way, anyone to engage in any activity prohibited; (f) Seek or receive any assistance, in any way, from anyone to engage in any activity prohibited; (g) Allow any stationing, installation or deployment of any nuclear weapons. That is, any activity in relation to nuclear weapons was comprehensively prohibited without exceptions, and envisaged the path to complete abolition of nuclear weapons. About 'experiment', while the Comprehensive Nuclear Test Ban Treaty (CTBT) only prohibited experiments with explosion, the Treaty did not limit experiments to prohibit. This can be interpreted that experiments not only with explosion but also subcritical experiments and computer simulations were prohibited. In particular, the Treaty prohibited the use or threaten to use nuclear weapons, which surpassed the advisory opinion by ICJ in 1996 that stated, 'the Court cannot conclude definitively whether the threat or use of nuclear weapons would be lawful or unlawful in an extreme circumstance of self-defense, in which the very survival of a state would be at risk',[42] and it was also beyond the NPT Treaty without mentioning the 'use or threaten to use nuclear weapons' in terms of denying nuclear deterrence theory.

Another characteristic of the Treaty was that Article 6 regulated, 'victim assistance and environmental remediation'. In the first paragraph the Treaty stated as, 'each state party shall, with respect to individuals under its jurisdiction who are affected by the use or testing of nuclear weapons, in accordance with applicable international humanitarian and human rights law, adequately provide age-and-gender-sensitive assistance, without discrimination, including medical care, rehabilitation and psychological support, as well as provide for their social and economic inclusion'. In the second paragraph, it explained as 'each state party, with respect to areas under its jurisdiction or control contaminated as a result of activities related to the testing or use of nuclear weapons or other nuclear explosive devices, shall take necessary and appropriate measures towards the environmental remediation of areas so contaminated'. In order to do so, the Treaty also regulated international co-operation and aid in Article 7. Since the Treaty shed a light on victims of nuclear weapons, it has the nature of humanitarian and human rights treaty as well as disarmament treaty.

In order to envisage a road map for the world with no nuclear weapons, a number of optional ideas had been discussed in the process of treaty

42 *Legality of the Threat or Use of Nuclear Weapons* (n 1) para 105.

negotiations. There was 'comprehensive' model such as the Nuclear Weapons Convention, which expansively regulated throughout from disposal to review of nuclear weapons; 'prohibition-first' model that regulated the prohibition of nuclear weapons first and foremost; 'framework' model that decided the whole framework by formulating a treaty, then discuss in detail through protocols such as the UN Framework Convention on Climate Change or the Kyoto Protocol. The Treaty took a 'prohibition-first' model, and it aimed to state that nuclear weapons were illegal, as well as label nuclear weapons as evil. However, Articles 2 to 4 of the Treaty were about 'declarations', 'safeguards', and 'towards the total elimination of nuclear weapons', and these articles regulated the measures to lead elimination of nuclear weapons, presuming nuclear states would accede to the Treaty. In this sense, the Treaty possesses the possibility of developing into a 'comprehensive' model in the future.

5 National and Human Security around the Treaty on the Prohibition of Nuclear Weapons

5.1 *Confrontation of Opinions around the Treaty*

The Treaty regulated in Article 13 about signatures as, 'this Treaty shall be open for signature to all states at United Nations Headquarters in New York as from 20 September 2017', and in Article 14, it stated, 'this Treaty shall be subject to ratification, acceptance or approval by signatory states. The Treaty shall be open for accession'. And, the Treaty entered into force 90 days after the fiftieth instrument of ratification, acceptance, approval or accession had been deposited (Article 15). According to these statements, signature and ratification were processed, and Honduras became the fiftieth nation that ratified the Treaty on the 24th October 2020. As a result, the Treaty came into force on the 22nd of January 2021. Because of the nature of the Treaty that is optional regulation, a state will not be restricted unless the state accedes to the Treaty.

Nuclear states and the states under 'the nuclear umbrella' strongly criticized the Treaty and they have been against it since the treaty negotiations even after the Treaty was adopted and it came into force. Five nuclear states, the United States, Russia, the UK, France, and China were against the Treaty in their joint statement announced on the 15th September, 2016 as below:[43]

43 US Department of State, 'Joint Statement from the Nuclear-Weapon States at the 2016 Washington D.C. P5 Conference', September 15, 2016. <https://2009-2017.state.gov/r/pa/prs/ps/2016/09/261994.htm> accessed 21 May 2024.

> The P5 expressed their deep concern with efforts to pursue approaches to nuclear disarmament that disregard the global strategic context. Such efforts will threaten the consensus-based approach that has served for decades to strengthen the NPT regime and enhance the Treaty's contribution to international security and may negatively affect the prospects for consensus at future NPT Review Conferences. The P5 reiterated a call upon all members of the international community to engage in an open and constructive dialogue on nuclear disarmament, international security, and stability issues that is inclusive of all states and focused on practical measures leading to a world without nuclear weapons and other weapons of mass destruction.

The United States raised the following four points to against the Treaty at the UN General Assembly in 2016:[44]

(1) A treaty banning nuclear weapons will not lead to any further reductions because it will not include the states that possess nuclear weapons;
(2) A ban treaty would undermine existing non-proliferation and disarmament regimes. It risks creating an unbridgeable divide between states, polarizing the political environment on nuclear disarmament, and effectively limiting any future prospect for achieving consensus;
(3) Verification regimes are one of the key components of successful nuclear disarmament and non-proliferation agreements; however, the Treaty does not include this;
(4) A ban treaty runs the risk of undermining regional security. We cannot deny the reality that nuclear weapons continue to play a role in maintaining peace and stability in some parts of the world.[45]

The non-nuclear states of the North Atlantic Treaty Organization (NATO) and 26 states including Japan, Korea and Australia also criticized the Treaty saying that nuclear disarmament cannot be accomplished without consideration of local and global security because it is critical to respond to relevant politics,

44 Statement by Ambassador Robert A Wood, 'Delegation of the United States of America', 71st UNGA First Committee October 14, 2016. <https://s3.amazonaws.com/unoda-web/wp-content/uploads/2016/10/14-Oct-USA.pdf> accessed 21 May 2024.

45 Kurosawa (n 31) 25.

security, and humanity.[46] Then, on the 7th of July 2017, the day that the Treaty was adopted at the UN conference, the United States, the United Kingdom, and France announced a joint statement as:

> France, the United Kingdom and the United States have not taken part in the negotiation of the treaty on the prohibition of nuclear weapons. We do not intend to sign, ratify or ever become party to it. Therefore, there will be no change in the legal obligations on our countries with respect to nuclear weapons [...] This initiative clearly disregards the realities of the international security environment. Accession to the ban treaty is incompatible with the policy of nuclear deterrence, which has been essential to keeping the peace in Europe and North Asia for over 70 years.[47]

These statements showed clear and strong intention to against the Treaty. Now there is a question as to what the difference between these nuclear states including the states under the 'nuclear umbrella' and the states in favor of the Treaty was. One is the difference of their approaches to nuclear abolition. That is, states against the Treaty, whose approach is 'step-by-step', insist that nuclear abolition should be progressed by consensus included nuclear states in a phased manner and that it must have examination. However, despite of the regulation of NPT Treaty Article 6, there was little progress for nuclear disarmament under the approach, therefore, states in favor of the Treaty took a position that prohibition of nuclear weapons should come first. In fact, even prohibition was most prioritized, nuclear abolition needs to be conducted step-by-step, so in this sense, there was no significant difference in terms of approaches between them. If so, the fundamental difference would be their perspectives towards security. In short, whilst the states against the Treaty conceived that abolition was possible once security was established, the states in favor took a position to illegalize nuclear weapons first from a humanistic point of view and proceed to abolish them promptly because the existence of nuclear weapons itself threatens security, and also, once nuclear weapons were used, it obviously leads to a catastrophic outcome. This is a question to

46 General Statement, Germany on behalf of 26 states, 17 October 2016. <https://2017-2021-translations.state.gov/2017/07/07/joint-press-statement-from-th-permanent-representatives-to-the-united-nations-of-the-united-states-united-kingdo-and-france-following-the-adoption-of-a-treaty-banning-nuclear-weapons/> accessed 21 May 2024.

47 United States Mission to the United Nations, 'Joint Press Statement from the Permanent Representatives to the United Nations of the United States, United Kingdom, and France Following the Adoption of a Treaty Banning Nuclear Weapons', New York City, 7 July 2017. <https://2017-2021-translations.state.gov/2017/07/07/joint-press-statement-from-the-permanent-representatives-to-the-united-nations-of-the-united-states-united-kingdom-and-france-following-the-adoption-of-a-treaty-banning-nuclear-weapons/> accessed 21 May 2024.

ask once again what security means, and it can be said that it is a confrontation between thoughts as to what they value fundamentally. Broadly speaking, this is also an issue of how to perceive security and human beings in constructing world orders.

5.2 *Issues of Regulating 'Human Security' and Formulating the World Law*

When considering the issues of states and humanity, it is an undeniable fact that orders and culture in the international society after Westphalia have been structured focusing on states because of its structural nature of the framework based on the sovereign states. In which, international law have played an important role to structure the orders as the law of the international society. However, because of its nature, which is to regulate relationships between states, humans have often been hidden behind the states.[48] Regarding security, under the Just War Theory or non-discriminatory concept of war, it developed from individual security, which insisted to guard each state using their own military power, to collective security system through the world wars, however, collective security still have not exceeded national security in terms of security that was based on the deterrence by military power with a view to conflicts between states.

In fact, international law has never been indifference regarding humanity. It can be said that international law was being negative from humanistic justice point of view in the modern international law until 19th century, which perceived 'peace' as stability of 'order' between states, and did not recognize eternally or coherent unique value in the international society, and also it considered that only international law contributed to stabilizing relationships between states.[49] However, it was true that tragic lessons of the wars in the 20th century that brought enormous human sacrifice led to illegalizing of wars in 'jus ad bellum', and wars and conflicts were regulated from humanistic perspectives as law of war and law of armed conflict in 'jus in bello'. Further, 'human beings that conventionally hid behind states came forward in international law'[50] through the promotion of international security of human rights, which was provoked by the Second World War and the development of new concepts of human rights such as rights to self-determination or rights to

48 Kentaro Serita 'Human Beings in International Law' in *Iwanami Lecture on Basic Law 5: Responsibility* (Iwanami Shoten 1984) 395.

49 Akira Onodera, Yuji Iwasawa and Akio Morita, *Lecture on International Law* (Yuhikaku 2004) 9.

50 Serita (n 48) 429.

develop in relation to independence of colonies. Whilst human beings especially people, whose minimum standard of life and living were at risk, gained an attention in the international society, the concept of 'human security' emerged based on the following reasons: international economic elements, such as increasing economic gaps due to the progress of globalization led by the end of the Cold War, and losing strategic interest in aiding by the donor states; international politics elements, such as various aspects of threats, frequent domestic conflicts, inhumane acts and refugees produced in the process of the threats or conflicts, emergence of failed states; and the concept of human security emerged in transformation of mainstreaming of human rights as the value for the Western states.[51]

In general, security has been considered in the international society to secure the maintenance of the territorial integrity and independence of a state in order not to be threaten by foreign militarily forces.[52] In this sense, security that the nuclear states and the states under the 'nuclear umbrella' insisted can be understood as the concept raised above. Indeed, the concepts of security of 'states' and security of 'humans' are not contradicted because national security is actually essential for human security, so, the concepts can be regarded as complemental to each other.[53] However, it is a fact that the use of military power for states sacrifices humanity, it is also obvious that it causes retaliation once nuclear weapons are used in the first place, and inhumane outcomes that would be brought by the use of nuclear power was already discussed above. For this point, the use of nuclear weapons for national security and human security are incompatible whatsoever the reason is. This is the reason why transforming perspectives based on the concept of human security and structuring orders are urgent.

---

51 UNDP, *Human Development Report 1994* (Oxford University Press 1994).

52 International Law Association (ed.), *Encyclopedia of International Relations,* (Sanseido 1995) 18. After the First World War, since the multilateral alliance policy as anti-Germany encirclement by France was the policy to the common thread, it was called 'security' policy distinguished from 'national defense'. Seizaburo Sato 'How come 'National Defense' came to be called 'Security' – Basic Issues of Security of Japan', *Diplomacy Forum 1999 Special Issue Security in the 21st Century – Japanese Diplomacy at its Turning Point* (Toshi Press Inc. 1999) 5–6.

53 Report of Human Security Committee also stated about their relationship that it was necessary to pay attention that 'human security' and national security were compensating and depending on each other, therefore, there was no national security without 'human security' and vice versa. Commission on Human Security, *Human Security Now* (New York 2003) 6.

Further, the word 'security' is originated from 'securitas' in Latin, and its original meaning was broader than now as in 'condition without worries' or 'means to secure such condition'. However, the word 'security' replaced the conceptual word 'national defense' that meant to secure the maintenance of the territorial integrity and independence of a state in order not to be threaten by foreign armed forces, therefore, security and national security started to be considered as the same meaning. Given that, security needs to be redefined returning to its original meaning. In this sense, the TPNW, that seeks elimination of nuclear weapons from humanity point of view, beyond authorities between states and arrangements of benefits for states is attempting to regulate 'human security' in the current trend of international society such as mainstreaming human rights and the emergence of civil society. That is, the Treaty is an archetype of 'the treaty of human security'.[54,55] And, it is transforming nuclear weapons from a 'necessary evil' to an 'absolute evil' by regulating nuclear weapons. Further, human security has the three pillars: 'freedom from fear'; 'freedom from shortage'; and 'dignity of humanity'.[56] The true nature of the issues of nuclear weapons is not only about passive peace in relation to 'freedom from fear' but it is also the issues of human rights, poverty, environment that stem from structural violence, which is the rationale for treating the issue of nuclear weapons as human security issue. Paragraph 3 in the preamble to the Treaty states, the danger of the continuous existence of nuclear weapons affects safety of all human beings, which summarizes the point above.

The concept of human security first appeared in the State of the Union Message by the then President of the United States, Franklin Roosevelt in 1941, in which he mentioned 'four freedom'. After the creation of the Atlantic Charter,[57] the concept was included in the purpose of founding the United Nations in the post-war. The preamble to the Constitution of Japan that was

---

54 Treaties on human security is used here as the treaties that were formulated from humans' point of view, who often become victims of inhumane behavior or events, for example, the conventions on the prohibition of anti-personnel mines, the statues of the International Criminal Court (ICC) or the Optional Protocol to the Convention on the Rights of the Child on the Involvement of Children in Armed Conflict. Oberleitner (n 4).

55 Although it is not a treaty, 'The 2030 Agenda for Sustainable Development' (SDGs) that was adopted at the UN in September 2015 can be perceived as 'regulating' human security in terms of its principle that aimed to actualize the society, 'No one will be left behind'.

56 UNDP (n 51); Kofi A Annan, *We the Peoples: The Role of the United Nations in the 21st Century* (2000); Commission on Human Security, *Human Security Now* (2003).

57 The Atlantic Charter declared: 'Sixth, after the final destruction of the Nazi tyranny, they hope to see established a peace which will afford to all nations the means of dwelling in safety within their own boundaries, and which will afford assurance that all the men in all the lands may live out their lives in freedom from fear and want'.

formulated around the same time stated, 'We recognize that all people of the world have the right to live in peace, free from fear and want'. In which, human security was regarded in a context of rights to live in peace. In this sense, the significance of regulating human security is to actualize the right to live in the peaceful world based on dignity of life. If the regulations that seek to establish 'rule of law' in the international society from a perspective of benefits for humans and humanity are called the 'world law', its process would be a touchstone that testes as to whether international law can be the regulations that contributes to the actualization of international justice as well as playing a role to adjust benefits between states.[58]

Also, the process of formulating the TPNW appeared to suggest the possibility of creating the world law because the Treaty was formulated: (1) through the discussions at the United Nations; (2) in the form of co-ordination between coalition states of non-nuclear and NGOs; and (3) actualized as a treaty. Especially, while the NPT regime has been maintained as a system as 'nuclear-haves control', the TPNW is led by 'non-nuclear-haves', and an agreement was achieved as NGOs and civil society strongly supported it, which reflected that

58 After the Second World War, the movements of the world government spread in the international society, but the actual starting point of the wide development of the movements was the emergence of atomic bombs. The characteristics of the common ways of thinking of the people who supported the world government was the crisis in the modern times, especially they accused state sovereignty of the cause of wars, and insisted that it was necessary for states to waive their sovereignty and to cooperate for the higher unit of the world government in order to accomplish world peace. Based on the movements, the Preliminary Draft of a World Constitution was announced by the Committee to Frame a World Constitution that had Provost of Chicago University, Dr Robert Hutchins in March 1948. Especially, the way of thinking in relation to human rights drew an attention, which was its position as liberal democracy, that is that the world government not only merely avoided wars but it would also assure freedom of humans and actualize democracy. This suggested to consider the concept of 'rule of law' in the international society if the world law was compared with the world constitution (Masashi Nakayama 'Current Situation of the "Preliminary Draft of a World Constitution" and Human Rights Security: Through "Idea of World Government" by Shigejiro Tabata' (2010) 40 *The Soka Law Review* 63–88). Also, Shinoda's critique to 'Responsibility of Protect' that has recently emerged is worth to mention. Shinoda argued that it was an attempt to place the concept of 'responsibility' in the task of reviewing 'state sovereignty'. He also said that there was a way of thinking, 'sovereignty as responsibility' behind it, and that it tried to urge positively to reassess as to how sovereignty should be (Hideaki Shinoda, *Thoughts of 'State Sovereignty': A Path to International Constitutionalism* (Keiso Shobo 2012) 306). It needs to be highlighted that the idea, which state sovereignty included the responsibility to protect humans, was recognized once again in the process of forming 'Responsibility to Protect'. This is suggestive for discussions to consider whether or not possessing or using nuclear weapons for national security can lead to fulfilment of the responsibility to protect humans.

the Treaty was not limited as a treaty of disarmament but also it was a treaty of human rights and humanity. Although this process of formulating the Treaty was also seen in the treaties created after the Cold War such as the Treaty on the Prohibition of the Use of Anti-personnel Mines, the Cluster Munitions, and the International Criminal Court (ICC) regulations, it showed that citizens and NGOs that were recipients of human rights and also potential victims coordinated with coalition states through their networks. And they enacted their influence on the formulation of the treaty, evoking general opinions internationally and exceeding the limitation of states that were obsessed with benefits only for them and can often be abusers of human rights. Also, it was important that the conferences of treaty negotiations were conducted at the United Nations Head Quarters based on the UN General Assembly resolutions. The negotiations for the Arms Trade Treaty (ATT) that was adopted at the UN General Assembly in 2013 had a similar process to that of the TPNW, and the role played by the UN for formulating the Treaty was connecting states and citizens as well as between states, which implied a form of multilateralism.[59]

6 Concluding Remarks: 'Culture of Peace' and Dignity of Humans

The establishment of the TPNW had a significance in terms of illegalization of nuclear weapons comprehensively through a form of treaty, which opened a path to the elimination of nuclear weapons. However, it also revealed that the path to nuclear abolishment would not be easy at all by showing the fierce conflicts between the states in favor of the Treaty and the states against. Although the Treaty has come into force effect, the process to the elimination of nuclear weapons, where nuclear haves and nuclear-dependent states accede to the Treaty, would not be realistic enough. Even though, if 'the purpose of the Treaty is long-term, and it proceed the movements of nuclear abolition by labelling nuclear weapons as evil, un-justifying them, and decreasing or distinguishing the value of existence of nuclear weapons',[60] it can be said that, the intentional purpose of the Treaty has been accomplished to some extent.

There appears to be the following issues from now onwards. In a short term, having held the first Conference of Parties in June, 2022, Japan should participate in the second Conference of the Parties (COP) that is scheduled to be held in the late November, 2023 so that as many as non-parties

59 Mogami (n 8) 115–117.

60 Kurosawa (n 31) 30.

can participate in the COP as observers. Although the nuclear haves and the nuclear-dependent states did not attend the negotiation conferences, Article 12 that is entitled 'Universality' regulated as, '[e]ach state party shall encourage states not party to this Treaty to sign, ratify, accept, approve or accede to the Treaty, with the goal of universal adherence of all states to the Treaty', as well as Article 8 stated that states not party to the Treaty should be invited to the meetings of state parties or review conferences of the Treaty after the entry into force of the Treaty, which showed consideration to these states. It is also expected to actively utilize the International Group of Eminent Persons for a World without Nuclear Weapons (IGEP), where the world political leaders and experts discuss a road map towards a nuclear-free world, in order to seek the resolutions.

In a mid-term view, the states in favor of the Treaty and the supportive NGOs should continue to proceed and take actions steadily in order to actualize the process of un-justification and elimination of nuclear weapons and accession of the states against the Treaty. In these processes, the relationship between the TPNW and the NPT would be another issue. The states against the Treaty have insisted that the TPNW and the NPT contradict to each other, and it deteriorates the NPT regime. However, the NPT that has 191 state parties is a significant treaty, which will be a foundation of nuclear non-proliferation and disarmament, and the TPNW is regarded as a mean for nuclear disarmament that has been regulated in the NPT, which was formulated based on the discussions at the NPT Review Conferences. In this sense, the treaties are not contradicted or confronted to each other, it rather, 'reinforces the weaknesses that the current NPT regime possesses, and has an effect to enhance nuclear disarmament and non-proliferation'.[61] The preamble to the TPNW also stated, 'the full and effective implementation of the Treaty on the non-proliferation of nuclear weapons, which serves as the cornerstone of the nuclear disarmament and non-proliferation regime, has a vital role to play in promoting international peace and security', and Article 18 indicated without using the expression of the NPT as, 'the implementation of the Treaty shall not prejudice obligations undertaken by states parties with regard to existing international agreements, to which they are party, where those obligations are consistent with the Treaty'. Unfortunately, the NPT Review Conference held in August 2022 ended in a breakdown as the document was not adopted due to Russia's opposition to the draft 'final document' as the conflict over the situation in Ukraine could not be resolved. Against this situation, the IGEP mentioned

61 Kawasaki (n 36) 65.

above issued a proposal calling for the maintenance and strengthening of the NPT regime in a view to the first Preparatory Committee for the NPT Review Conference to be held in Vienna, Austria, in the summer of 2023. Finally, as an important and essential issue in a long-term would be as to how to transform 'culture of war and violence' that was symbolized by nuclear weapons into 'culture of peace and non-violence'. There is no doubt that the elimination of nuclear weapons is the ultimate issue. However, as long as there are thoughts to have nuclear weapons, they would emerge once again even if they were once abolished. Since human beings' desire is unlimited, the history tells us that the progress of technology or knowledge can be a double-edged sword. The emergence of the Lethal Autonomous Weapons Systems (LAWS) that is operated by Artificial Intelligence (AI) implies that regulations are urgent because it can be a threat that could possibly bring a drastic change, which is equivalent to 'invention of the gun' and 'development of nuclear weapons', in the field of military. Thus, the existence of human beings and our future depend on as to how to settle 'culture of peace and non-violence' and spread it as the basis of culture of society. When structuring 'culture of peace', the core values should be human rights and humanity, which is underpinned by the ideological foundation – dignity of humans.

What is 'culture of peace' in the first place? The Declaration and Program of Action on a Culture of Peace[62] was adopted at the UN General Assembly in September, 1999. The Resolution stated, '[a] culture of peace is a set of values, attitudes, traditions and modes of behavior and ways of life based on', and the Resolution defined it as:

(a) Respect for life, ending of violence and promotion and practice of non-violence through education, dialogue and cooperation;
(b) Full respect for the principles of sovereignty, territorial integrity and political independence of States and non-intervention in matters which are essentially within the domestic jurisdiction of any State, in accordance with the Charter of the United Nations and international law;
(c) Full respect for and promotion of all human rights and fundamental freedoms;
(d) Commitment to peaceful settlement of conflicts;

62 UN Doc A/RES/53/243, 6 October 1999.

(e) Efforts to meet the developmental and environmental needs of present and future generations;
(f) Respect for and promotion of the right to development;
(g) Respect for and promotion of equal rights and opportunities for women and men;
(h) Respect for and promotion of the right of everyone to freedom of expression, opinion and information;
(i) Adherence to the principles of freedom, justice, democracy, tolerance, solidarity, cooperation, pluralism, cultural diversity, dialogue and understanding at all levels of society and among nations; and fostered by an enabling national and international environment conducive to peace.

In short, it is internalizing the thoughts of 'peace and non-violence', and having it everyday occurrences and ethos of society.

The end of the Cold War contributed to the background to the establishment of 'culture of peace'. That is, in the international society where the Cold War was no longer continuing, the concept of 'culture of peace' emerged as there was a growing recognition that human beings must revolutionize their values and actions in order to have peace be sustainable, and then 'culture of peace' started to be featured at the international conferences in the UN Educational, Scientific, and Cultural Organization (UNESCO).

The preamble to the Constitution of the UNESCO that is the prospectus of the UNESCO has promoted 'culture of peace', and there is a very famous sentence, '[s]ince wars begin in the mind of men, it is in the minds of men that the defenses of peace must be constructed'. In which, an idea was expressed, which was 'culture of war' and 'culture of peace' both originate from the mind of human beings. The preamble to the TPNW also refers to education around peace and disarmament and the importance of raising awareness of danger of nuclear weapons and the outcome nuclear weapons would bring for the current and the future generations. If there is a lack of compassion and respect for humanity underneath the thoughts that tolerate nuclear weapons, that is often called 'culture of war', the long-term issue that we must resolve is as to how to transform the situation, and settle 'culture of peace' in society. Needless to say, it would be an extremely difficult task. At the same time, the process towards peace that has been depicted by Mogami would never be simple or easy. However, the present systems have been established in the history of long battles around establishing justice, for instance, illegalization of wars, international security of human rights, and punishment of war crimes. In this sense, nuclear abolishment will not be an impossible path at all. The establishment of the TPNW as legal correction of international injustice appears to be a milestone that raises a question once again regarding what the 'rule of law' is in the international society towards transformation from 'the culture of war' into 'the culture of peace'.

CHAPTER 6

Enemy or Disobedience? Paradigm Crisis on the Use of Lethal Force in Occupied Territory

Kyo Arai

1 Introduction

Professor Toshiki Mogami, in his 2010 speech at Doshisha University, Kyoto, raised a fundamental question for students of International Humanitarian Law:[1] how should/could the law of occupation, which has been structured without any substantial legal protection for resistance movements, be reconceptualised, given the modern international law that underpins respect for human dignity?[2] His distrust of the law of occupation is unsurprising when we consider the fate of the occupied population that is routinely exposed to the harsh policies of the occupying forces and that their resistance can therefore arise spontaneously, as the Russian-Ukrainian war, which began on 24 February 2022, highlights.

The oppressiveness and arbitrariness of occupation rule are most dangerously materialised when the occupying forces turn their weapons against the occupied population. The laws of occupation indeed assume responsibility for maintaining order in the occupied territory to the occupying forces and apparently incorporate the authority of using force for that purpose, but how could this be reconciled with the *legitimacy* of such *spontaneous* resistance? The possibility of regulating the use of such force does matter not only in terms of the success or failure of the resistance but also because it concerns their very lives.

A legal suit against the Israeli Chief of Staff on the Rules of Engagement (ROEs) in the Gaza Strip clearly illustrates the difficulty in finding a balanced paradigm to regulate the use of force and the unacceptable consequence of poorly regulated overuse of force from which the territory's population suffers. In *Yesh Din v. Israel Defense Forces* (IDF) *Chief of Staff*,[3] the Israeli Supreme

1 As the manuscript was originally submitted in June 2020, this Chapter has not been able to address the events since then.

2 Professor Mogami referred to Patrick Capps, *Human Dignity and the Foundations of International Law* (Hart 2010), for this point.

3 *Yesh Din v IDF Chief of Staff* HCJ 3003/18, Israel Supreme Court sitting as the High Court of Justice, 24 May 2018, opinion of Deputy President Hanan Melcer.

 | DOI:10.1163/9789004681477_008

Court faced this difficult issue of how the ROEs for the Occupying Power – which Israel has denied to exist in the Gaza Strip since its 'disengagement' in 2005 – should be drafted for its campaign to disperse mass demonstrations by the Palestinian people in May 2018. The IDF was widely criticised for the overuse of lethal weapons against mass demonstrations near the 'border' fence between Gaza and Israeli territory, and some human rights organisations quickly filed petitions asking the Court to invalidate the ROEs of the IDF, allowing such means of the use of force. The Court was asked which paradigm for the use of force, the Law Enforcement or Conduct of Hostilities paradigm, applies when the IDF responds to a mass demonstration. The Court held that both paradigms apply in parallel in such situations. Relying on the Interpretive Guidance issued by the International Committee of the Red Cross (ICRC),[4] the Court held that those participants had been directly participating in hostilities (DPH) with a nexus to military operations by Hamas or other terrorist organisations, and thus could be legally targeted. This conclusion is at odds with some established case law or international documents on the human rights obligation of states to control such riots.[5] Deciding the targetability of civilians based on the concept of DPH is clearly grounded in the Conduct of Hostilities paradigm, which is more permissive for using lethal force than Human Rights Law. It may be noteworthy that while Israel has formally denied that human rights obligations apply extraterritorially to the occupied Territory of Palestine (oTP),[6] the Court did not deny that the Law Enforcement paradigm as such, which, in the Israeli Government's understanding, stems from the Law of Armed Conflict, not from Human Rights Law, can apply to IDF's conduct in the oTP. Nevertheless, the Court left more questions unanswered than it answered: what are the exact contours of both paradigms; how different is the Law Enforcement paradigm originating in the Law of Armed Conflict from that grounded in Human Rights Law; and how do those two paradigms apply in parallel and interplay with each other? These issues are related not only to how far the Occupying Force is allowed to go in using lethal force to counter violent resistance but also to a more fundamental question: under the

4 Nils Melzer (ed), *Interpretive Guidance on the Notion of Direct Participation in Hostilities under International Humanitarian Law* (ICRC 2009).

5 *Güleç v Turkey* App no 21593/93 (ECtHR, 27 July 1998); *Simsek et al v Turkey* App nos 35072/97 and 37194/97 (ECtHR, 26 July 2005). Basic Principles on the Use of Force and Firearms by Law Enforcement Officials, adopted by the Eighth United Nations Congress on the Prevention of Crime and the Treatment of Offenders, Havana, Cuba, 27 August to 7 September 1990, principles 12, 13, 14.

6 Human Rights Committee (HRC), Concluding Observations: Israel (CCPR/C/79/Add.93), 18 August 1998, para 10.

law of occupation, how is civilian resistance in the occupied territory to be legally regulated, protected, or privileged?

2 Elements of the Belligerent Occupation Regime

2.1 *Uncertain and Tentative Nature*

At the outset, to clarify the significance of regulating the use of lethal force against people resisting occupation, fundamental characteristics of the belligerent occupation, namely, uncertainty and tentativeness, should be noted.

2.1.1 Uncertainty

'Belligerent occupation' is defined under the Hague Regulations of 1899/1907 as a party to the conflict actually placing under its authority (effective control) a part or whole of the territory of the enemy country during armed conflict.[7] This definition represents the uncertain and ambivalent nature of belligerent occupation: ambivalence between war and peace, violence and order, and situational stability and instability. It is rightly because of this uncertainty that the law of occupation is essentially expected to function in balancing conflicting elements, the military necessity of the Occupying Power, retaining the sovereignty of the ousted party, and humanitarian protection of the population of the territory.[8]

However, the legal framework of occupation and its relevance assumes further uncertainty, especially when the Occupying Power finds itself in a situation where it recourses to lethal force beyond the regular exercise of police power in the occupied territory. This is not only because such a robust reaction might indicate that the situation is factually unstable but also because the Occupying Power's recourse to force on a significant scale could result in contradictory consequences. On the one hand, it can be seen merely as a security operation against resistance to the occupation; on the other hand, such a situation sometimes may lead to the end of the belligerent occupation as such, since the occupying power loses effective control over the territory.[9] Thus, for

---

7 Regulations concerning the Laws and Customs of War on Land, 1907 (the Hague Regulations of 1907), art 42.

8 Eyal Benvenisti, *The International Law of Occupation* (2nd ed, Oxford University Press 2012) 69.

9 As a case in which the Occupying Power lost such status through armed activities by partisans, see *United States of America v Otto Ohlendorf et al* ('The Einsatzgruppen Case'), *Trials of War Criminals before the Nuremberg Military Tribunals under Control Council Law No. 10*, vol 4, 492–493. In contrast, as a case in which the Occupying Power retains the status even though

the Occupying Power to retain that status, a clear distinction between two possible results of the use of force has to be presented, and rules and principles under two possible paradigms for the use of force that could result in contradictory consequences must be identified. At the same time, as the situation of belligerent occupation is fluid, varying day by day or probably area to area, in order to secure the integrity of the law of occupation or its conformity with reality, the relationship between the two paradigms must be clarified as well.

2.1.2 Tentative Nature

Second, in modern international law, the belligerent occupation has been regarded as a tentative or transitional situation between a *de facto* takeover by one party of the other's territory and the formal acquisition (or return) of sovereignty over the territory. In that sense, in the belligerent occupation situation, any attempt to regain control of the occupied area by the ousted party should be treated as an ordinary act of armed conflict. This is also the case even if the ousted power remotely mobilises civilian resistance in the occupied territory. Based on its fundamental nature, the law of occupation must acknowledge a certain level of armed resistance.

Additionally, since the modern law of occupation developed and defined belligerent occupation as a *tentative* status during armed conflicts, not as a formal transfer of sovereignty, an Occupying Power cannot exercise its governing power over the territory under its occupation, in the similar way as it does over its own territory. This inevitably affected the extent of authority the Occupying Force exercises in responding to resistance activities. Under the traditional law of war, as indicated in the Lieber Code of 1863, resistance activity by the occupied population – for example, by giving information to the ousted government, the occupied population's home government – was severely punished as war treason. In contrast, under the modern law of occupation, resistance participants could be punished not for violating their inherent duty of obedience or allegiance but because of the material danger to the occupying force.[10]

This interpretation complies with the provisions of the Fourth Geneva Convention of 1949. Article 64 stipulates that the penal laws of the occupied territory shall remain in force. At the same time, the Occupying Power may subject the population of the occupied territory to provisions of its own

partisans temporarily control a part of the occupied territory, see *United States of America v Wilhelm List et al* ('The Hostages Trial'), *Law Reports of Trials of War Criminals*, vol 8, 56.

10 Richard Baxter, 'The Duty of Obedience to the Belligerent Occupant' in Detlev F Vagts, Theodor Meron, Stephen Schwebel, and Charles Keever (eds), *Humanizing the Law of War: Selected Writings of Richard Baxter* (Oxford University Press 2013) 7–36, 33–34.

regulations, including penal or security rules, for very limited purposes: first, when such regulation is essential to enable the Occupying Power to fulfil its obligations under the Geneva Conventions; second, when it is introduced to maintain the orderly government of the territory; and, third, when the regulation is essential to ensure the security of the Occupying Power. The article indicates that the Occupying Power cannot impose obedience on the population of the occupied territory by pursuing criminal charges against the resistance activities just because they are rebellious.

Articles 67 and 68 emphasise that 'when the courts apply regulation imposed by the Occupying Power, or when capital punishment was pronounced, to the population, they shall take into consideration the fact that the accused is not a national of the Occupying Power, and he is not bound to [the Occupying Power] by any duty of allegiance'. In other words, the population of the occupied territory should be dealt with as non-nationals of the Occupying Power; consequently, their allegiance or obedience should not be legally expected vis-à-vis the Occupying Power; thus, revolt against the *de facto* ruler is not prohibited.

2.2 *Responsibility Entrusted to the Occupying Power*

In such uncertain and tentative situations, on the other hand, the law of occupation imposes on the Occupying Power the responsibility to restore, ensure, and maintain security, law, and order in the occupied territory. Article 43 of the Hague Regulations stipulates that 'the authority of the legitimate power having in fact passed into the hands of the occupant, the latter shall take all the measures in his power to restore, and ensure, as far as possible, *l'ordre et la vie publics* [public order and safety], while respecting, unless absolutely prevented, the laws in force in the country.' According to the developed case law, to exercise such authority and power under the Hague Regulations nowadays, the Occupying Power must assume the obligation to ensure the protection of human rights for individuals who fall into its hands as well.[11]

For the Occupying Power, the requirement to effectively control the concerned area is substantiated by exercising such police power, or even by the ability to do so.[12] This assumed authority to exercise police power implies two

---

11 *Armed Activities on the Territory of the Congo (Democratic Republic of the Congo v Uganda)*, (Merits) [2005] ICJ Rep 168, para 178; *Conséquences juridiques de l'édification d'un mur dans le territoire palestinien occupé,* avis consultatif, [2004] ICJ Rep 136, para 109; *Loizidou v Turkey*, App no 15318/89 (ECtHR, 18 December 1996), para 56; *Cyprus v. Turkey* App no 25781/94 (ECtHR, 10 May 2001), para 77. HRC, Concluding Observations (n 5) para 10.

12 Benvenisti (n 7) 43–51.

substantial repercussions. First, the Occupying Power has the power to prevent the obstruction posed by the ousted power or armed resistance to sustain effective control. Second, the assumed responsibility requires, as a matter of fact, a certain degree of 'obedience' by the local population, at least, by complying with the Occupier's regulations. For this reason, while forcing the population to swear allegiance to the Occupier is prohibited by Article 45 of the Hague Regulations, the Occupier still has the authority to promulgate certain rules for the limited purposes indicated above.

This Chapter seeks to clarify whether the premise of the law of occupation that the local population is expected to cohabit orderly with the Occupying Power means that armed resistance by the former is essentially illegal or prohibited under such law.

3 Legitimacy of Armed Resistance?

Armed resistance is undeniably disturbing for the Occupying Power, as it could disrupt the maintenance of security and order in the occupied territory, eventually leading to the termination of the belligerent occupation. For the ousted party or people in the territory, in contrast, it is another naturally expected reaction against the occupation to attempt to terminate the enemy rule by disobedience or active resistance. To harmonise these two contradictory needs, the (il)legitimacy of armed resistance has been at the centre of the debate, leading to codifying the law of occupation.[13]

3.1 *Partial Legitimisation of* franc-tireurs*?*

After the world witnessed widespread use of irregulars in the Franco–Prussian War, some smaller powers started efforts to immunise such irregulars against criminal prosecution by the Occupying Power by granting the status of prisoners of war. The Brussels Declaration of 1874,[14] the Oxford Manual of 1880

13 In this connection, 'legitimacy' has been understood as a situation in which the participants of the resistance movement have equal legal footing with the regular army members, who have the legitimate privilege to participate in hostilities and not be criminally punished for the conduct of hostilities in conformity with the law of war. Thus, it should be noted that admitting legitimacy for certain resistance does not imply any restriction on the use of force against those who qualified as a resistance movement, and members not having such privilege among the movement as well.

14 *Project of an International Declaration concerning the Laws and Customs of War*, Brussels, 27 August 1874.

adopted by the *Institut de droit international*,[15] and the Hague Regulations of 1899 and 1907 were the outcomes of such attempts. However, the well-known fact is that such proposals to grant *franc-tireurs* 'legitimacy' as far as possible were mostly denied. In these documents, the great powers with strong armies conceded that such privilege might be given only to those who fulfilled the four conditions, which were unrealistic for resistance forces that fought secretly in the enemy-controlled territory.[16]

After World War II, in which resistance movements were suppressed severely, mainly by the occupying Axis powers, the Geneva Conventions of 1949 faced the same bitter compromise. It would be somewhat significant this time that the Convention confirmed a previously implicit presumption that resistance movements in occupied territories could be given privileges as prisoners of war if the listed requirements were fulfilled, by explicit reference in Article 4 of the Third Convention to '[m]embers of militias and members of other volunteer corps, including those of *organized resistance movements*, belonging to a Party to the conflict and operating in or outside their own territory, *even if this territory is occupied* [emphasis added].' Only in 1977, when Additional Protocol I (API) was adopted, International Humanitarian Law relaxed the requirements for belligerent status substantially to a level more consistent with the resistance practice in occupied territories. This relaxation of the obligation for belligerents to distinguish themselves from the civilian population was widely criticised by Western powers,[17] while many of these countries accepted that such 'situations in armed conflicts where, owing to the nature of the hostilities, an armed combatant cannot so distinguish himself' could exist 'only in occupied territory or in armed conflicts covered by paragraph 4 of Article 1'.[18]

---

15 *The Laws of War on Land*, Oxford, 9 September 1880.

16 Art 1 of the Hague Regulations of 1907, providing: The laws, rights, and duties of war apply not only to armies, but also to militia and volunteer corps fulfilling the following conditions: "1. To be commanded by a person responsible for his subordinates; 2. To have a fixed distinctive emblem recognizable at a distance; 3. To carry arms openly; and 4. To conduct their operations in accordance with the laws and customs of war".

17 'A Message from the President of the United States regarding Protocol II Additional to the 1949 Geneva Conventions, and Relating to the Protection of Victims of Non-international Armed Conflicts', in Message from the President of the United States, US Government Printing Office, 100th Congress, 1st Session, Treaty doc. 100–2, Washington, 1987.

18 Eg Reservations of Australia, 21 June 1991, Canada, 20 November 1990, and Japan, 31 August 2004, available at https://ihl-databases.icrc.org/, last accessed 31 July 2023.

3.2 *Silence on the Legitimacy*

After all these efforts to legitimise resistance in the occupied area, only limited categories of resistance participants have been designated 'privileged' as understood in International Humanitarian Law. However, this does not mean that armed resistance by 'unprivileged' fighters who do not fulfil the four conditions in the Geneva Conventions or the more 'relaxed' one in Article 44 of the API for prisoners of war are legally prohibited. The fact is seemingly quite contrary: no provision in International Humanitarian Law prohibits armed resistance in the occupied territory *per se.*

This may be rather unsurprising because the law of occupation regulates only occupying powers, not those populations in the occupied territory. As many scholars suggest, international law does not prohibit armed resistance, nor does it give people in the occupied territory the legal *right* to resist.[19] The law of occupation merely acknowledges the reality that in many situations of occupation, people resist the hostile occupier for some understandable but meta-legal motives: patriotism, heroism, or the spirit of sacrifice.[20] The fact that the law of occupation indeed admits, if not sympathises with, such motivated actions, while it recognises the Occupying Power's authority to suppress such uprisings, is confirmed by a curious provision for *levée en masse.*[21] The law here considerably relaxed the requirement for civilian resistance to qualify as privileged status, but only for uprisings 'before' the establishment of belligerent occupation. This does not apply to the time 'after' the establishment of occupation.[22] This imbalance of attitude has no reasonable and consistent explanation but the exceptionality of its occurrence. It may be merely an outcome of a compromise between moral pressure to justify the *just* cause of people's uprising and the military necessity for the occupiers.

4 Use of Lethal Force by Occupying Power in the Occupied Area

While belligerent occupation is characterised as a *stable* situation effectively controlled by the Occupying Power, its establishment does not necessarily terminate all armed resistance. More importantly, neither armed resistance does

19 Marco Longobardo, *The Use of Armed Force in Occupied Territory* (Cambridge University Press 2018) 149.

20 ibid 162.

21 The Hague Regulations of 1907, art 2; The Third Geneva Convention, art 4A (6).

22 Longobardo (n 18) 136–137.

necessarily terminate the belligerent occupation. The belligerent occupation may endure alongside resistance by the ruled population.

In the *Hostage* Case in 1948, the US military court in Nuremberg held as the following:

> While it is true that the partisans were able to control sections of these countries at various times, it is established that the Germans could at any time they desired assume physical control of any part of the country. The control of the resistance force was temporary only and not such as would deprive the German Armed Forces of its status of an occupant.[23]

The high possibility of a certain scale of popular uprising and the necessity of proportional security operations by occupying powers was rightly foreseen as commonplace in the Geneva Conventions.[24] For instance, in paragraph 2 of Article 4, the Third Convention supposes armed resistance in occupied territories. The Fourth Convention also presupposes civilians who engage in activities hostile to the security of the Occupying Power in paragraph 2 of Article 5 and paragraph 2 of Article 68.[25]

The case law and provisions of the Geneva Conventions lead to the conclusion that, as serious resistance may occur in any occupation, even in a firmly established one, it cannot be an easy solution to categorise occupations into either calm or troubled ones, to each of which different paradigms, those of Law Enforcement and Conduct of Hostilities, respectively, apply without confusion.[26] Rather, one has to admit that the fields of application of the two paradigms cannot be neatly delineated. The reality of belligerent occupation is more complex, so the means and methods of warfare under the Conduct of Hostilities paradigm may be employed even for maintaining effective control of the territory, while any police action under the Law Enforcement paradigm taken in the course of the administration in the occupied territory may have certain military value.[27]

---

23 *The Hostage Trial* (n 8) 56.

24 Nils Melzer, *Targeted Killing in International Law* (Oxford University Press 2009) 157.

25 The Fourth Convention, para 2, art 5 reads: 'Where in occupied territory an individual protected person is detained … as a person under definite suspicion of activity hostile to the security of the Occupying Power'. Para 2, art 68 stipulates as follows: 'where the person [a protected person] is guilty of … serious acts of sabotage against the military installations of the Occupying Power or of intentional offences which have caused the death of one or more persons'.

26 Roland Otto, *Targeted Killings and International Law* (Springer 2012) 442–445.

27 Melzer (n 23) 157.

4.1 *Two Paradigms for the Use of Force: Difference*

Thus, a clear exposition of the interplay between those two paradigms of the use of force is critically necessary. Before elaborating on this, however, it is important to confirm what each paradigm denotes and how different they are.

The widely approved definition of the two paradigms is as follows.[28] The Law Enforcement paradigm encompasses all measures to maintain, restore, or otherwise impose public security, law, and order. On the other hand, the Conduct of Hostility paradigm covers all measures aiming to bring about, or defend against, the military weakening or defeat of a party to an armed conflict. In that sense, while military operations are constituted by a mixture of actions guided by either paradigm, the Law Enforcement paradigm would seem to apply to many military missions in armed conflicts, especially for belligerent occupations.

Because of the multifaceted objectives of military operations in enemy territories, belligerent powers must properly switch between the two paradigms based on actual situations. However, as these two paradigms for the use of force have common terminology, such as 'necessity', 'proportionality', or 'precaution', those paradigms are occasionally, and sometimes intentionally, confused, resulting in unfortunate overuse of lethal force, as seen in the *Yesh Din* case. Therefore, fundamental differences between the two paradigms must be firmly emphasised.[29]

First, the two paradigms have different rationales for the lawful use of lethal force. Under the Conduct of Hostilities paradigm, targets recognised as lawful by International Humanitarian Law may be killed at any time unless they surrender or are placed *hors de combat*. These targets are always presumed as militarily necessary to be eliminated, and targetability is decided based on their formal status or membership in certain armed groups. Under the Law Enforcement paradigm, on the other hand, heavily influenced by International Human Rights Law, the use of lethal force is exceptionally permitted only if the target poses an imminent threat to the lives of the attackers or others. Here, no threat is inherently presumed for targeting; thus, neither is militarily necessary to eliminate the target. This is a scenario of the situation- or conduct-based determination for using lethal force.

---

28 Nils Melzer and Gloria Gaggioli Gasteyger, 'Conceptual Distinction and Overlaps between Law Enforcement and the Conduct of Hostilities' in Terry D Gill and Dieter Fleck (eds), *The Handbook of the International Law of Military Operations* (2nd ed, Oxford University Press 2015) 63–92, 76.

29 ibid 77–78.

Second, the concept of proportionality has different meanings in each paradigm. The Conduct of Hostilities paradigm requires the assessment of proportionality between the anticipated military advantage and incidental loss of civilian life or damage to civilian objects. Under the Law Enforcement paradigm, on the other hand, the attacker must assess proportionality between the purpose of the attack and the injury of the targeted persons, which is not legally taken into account for decision-making in the Conduct of Hostilities paradigm.[30]

Third, necessary precautionary measures are implemented differently . The Conduct of Hostilities paradigm requires the attacker to take precautions to minimise the incidental civilian loss, while the Law Enforcement precautionary principle obliges the attacker to minimise the necessity of the use of force as such.[31]

Although, given such fundamental variances in the basic codes of conduct, a clear-cut theory to decide applicable paradigms in changing phases is necessary, the law of occupation is silent on this point. This silence became problematic in assessing the legality of certain practices, such as targeted killings conducted exclusively under the Conduct of Hostilities paradigm, in situations involving occupied territory, where the Law Enforcement paradigm prevails. In this connection, it is helpful to refer to the debate among experts convened by the ICRC in 2011 and 2012.[32] Absent sufficient case law or state practice, the record of this debate might give a good, albeit secondary and theoretical, indication showing how two paradigms function and interplay in occupation situations.

4.2 *Theories for Mutually Exclusive or Simultaneous Applications?*

4.2.1 'Either or' Theory?

At the start of all debates, some experts emphasised that the two paradigms must be mutually exclusive in application to specific situations. This would be the most straightforward answer to the issue, but a large majority of experts did not support this approach. First, the reality of the belligerent occupation reveals that this 'either or' theory could not be sustained, as it presupposes that

---

30 Jan Arno Hessbruegge, *Human Rights and Personal Self-Defense in International Law* (Oxford University Press 2017) 170–174.

31 ibid 146–154.

32 Tristan Ferraro (ed), *Expert Meeting: Occupation and Other Forms of Administration of Foreign Territory* (ICRC 2012); Gloria Gaggioli (ed), *Expert Meeting: The Use of Force in Armed Conflicts, Interplay between the Conduct of Hostilities and Law Enforcement Paradigms* (ICRC 2013).

the classification of situations could be made in a clear-cut manner, which is not the case in most occupation situations as indicated above. Moreover, the Fourth Geneva Convention as such implies to the contrary that 'hot' armed confrontation could exist in the occupied territory when it uses words such as 'evacuation' (Paragraph 2, Article 49) or 'dangers of war' (Paragraph 5, Article 49) in provisions applicable to the belligerent occupation.

Hence, the experts had to start from the basis that two paradigms apply in parallel or simultaneously, and the two paradigms are different; as shown above, a theory distinguishing them or regulating their interplay was thoroughly discussed. The law of occupation was not instructive in this aspect; yet, given that belligerent occupation is comparatively stable in nature, it is an agreed starting point that the Law Enforcement paradigm prevails *in default of* a clear indication of the necessity of the other paradigm.[33] Thus, the matter to be clarified here will be when and how the Conduct of Hostilities paradigm is regarded as pertinent based on objective criteria (Conversion Theory).

4.2.2 Conversion Theories?

Even if it is admitted that Conversion Theory, which supposes that at a particular point, a prevailing paradigm will change from one to another, is more realistic, some experts still reiterate a categorical approach to paradigm conversion. This approach is based on converting a calm part and a troubled or violent part of an occupation grounded in geographical or temporal perspectives. However, as discussed above, it may be unsustainable to distinguish situations through generic or artificial categorisation in many, though not all, cases, as threats to the occupying power exist in a more complex manner. Instead, it should be acknowledged that such conversion of paradigms may occur in proximity in both a geographical and a temporal sense.

4.2.2.1 *Smooth Transition: Sliding Scale Theory?*

Most experts agree that two paradigms are operating in parallel; the applicable or prevailing one for the use of lethal force should be decided on a case-by-case basis depending on the particularity of a given situation. On this assumption, the parameters indicating the paradigm prevalence were examined.

The parameter that was regarded as the most decisive was the *nature of the threat*, which is to be assessed based on the legal status referring to the targetability criteria under the International Humanitarian Law.[34] Accordingly,

33 Melzer and Gaggioli (n 27) 75–76; Longobardo (n 18) 184, 186.

34 Melzer and Gaggioli (n 27) 79–80; Gaggioli (n 31) 59. Darragh Murray, 'The Relationship Between the Law of Armed Conflict and International Human Rights Law' in Elizabeth

the Conduct of Hostilities paradigm prevails when the target of one particular use of force is classified as an enemy combatant, a member of a resistance movement belonging to the enemy party and who fulfils four requirements under Article 4 of the Third Geneva Convention, or an individual civilian participating in hostilities directly, all of whom are targetable persons under the International Humanitarian Law. On the other hand, when the operations are addressed to other, non-targetable persons, it is regulated by the Law Enforcement paradigm.

Although this position was taken by the Israeli Supreme Court in the *Yesh Din* case,[35] it is expected to face difficulty in application, save a case of an open renewed military operation by the enemy armed force to regain occupied territory. As empirically understandable, it is difficult, if not impossible, to identify the overall characteristics of a particular action by a resistance movement or civilians, especially in the initial phase. At least, it is unlikely that such targetability based on individual status can be determined beforehand, and even if it were possible, such a conclusion would change during the event. Additionally, paragraph 1 of Article 50 of the API requires that protection from direct attack be presumed in any case of doubt. This is especially true in the situation of belligerent occupation, in which the Law Enforcement paradigm will apply by default. Indeed, belligerent occupation is part of an armed conflict in which International Humanitarian Law applies. However, this does not automatically mean the prevalence of the Conduct of Hostilities paradigm, with which the other paradigm interplays. Therefore, the theory presuming the threat based on the target's status is unsustainable.

The second parameter was the *correlation of the intensity of violence and the degree of control over the area or circumstances*. On this basis, the Conduct of Hostilities paradigm can be triggered by the fact that the Occupying Power has lost the factual capacity to mount effective law-and-order operations in a particular area.[36] This theory is based on the presumption that the less control the Occupying Power can exercise, the more violent the armed opposition becomes, and vice versa, on which serious doubts can be cast. This may be the case in many cases of belligerent occupation, but not always. In some cases, the Occupying Power does not provide heavy control because of the relatively

Wilmshurst, Françoise Hampson, Charles Garraway, Noam Lubell, Dapo Akande (eds), *Practitioners' Guide to Human Rights Law in Armed Conflict* (Oxford University Press 2016) 79–108, 99–100.

35 *Yesh Din v IDF Chief of Staf* (n 2) para 45.

36 Ferraro (n 31) 114; Longobardo (n 18) 232.

stable status of a particular area. In contrast, much tighter control may sometimes be exercised for a tense area in the occupied territory.[37]

The third parameter discussed by the experts was the *duration of the occupation*. This is based on a similar uncertain premise: the longer the occupation lasts, the less tense the situation becomes. The argument in the preceding paragraph applies here again.

The discussion above shows that it is hardly possible to present a clear-cut point of conversion relying on objective parameters, without which any theory for smooth conversion of the paradigms could not be successful. A more problematic outcome is that such a theory grounded in the unwarranted presumptions can induce an easy and premature conversion of the paradigm from the Law Enforcement to the Conduct of Hostilities based on a cursory assessment of the situation. The devastating result of this shift was demonstrated in many events, including those of the Gaza Strip in 2018.

4.2.2.2 *Jump Theory?*

Failing to find a decisive parameter for smooth conversion, some experts came to argue that the difference between the two paradigms for the use of lethal force was too large for a smooth transition being an expected result; thus, the conversion would be triggered instantaneously like a jump, when the situation crossed a specific threshold.

Regarding the threshold for this jump theory, Longobardo and some of the convened experts suggest that criteria to assess the existence of a non-international armed conflict (NIAC), the intensity of violence and organisation of a party to the conflict, may be satisfactory candidates for the threshold.[38] This theory may have a certain persuasiveness because these requirements are similar to an established condition by which a state could switch the paradigm for using armed force inside or possibly outside its territory in the case of NIACs. The Law Enforcement paradigm exclusively governs the situation below this threshold. Beyond that, the situation is classified as a NIAC, in which the two paradigms apply in parallel or sometimes the Conduct of Hostilities paradigm comes to the forefront.

However, this does not mean an armed confrontation that reaches the threshold is necessarily classified as a NIAC.[39] As discussed in the next section,

---

37 Longobardo (n 18) 232–233.

38 Ferraro (n 31) 115; Longobardo (n 18) 237.

39 Longobardo does not conclude that such a high-intensity confrontation with the organised armed group in the occupied territory constitutes an NIAC; nevertheless, he considers that those two criteria may function as the trigger for the Conduct of Hostilities paradigm. Longobardo (n 18) 237.

it is widely argued that a separate NIAC could exist between the Occupying Power and a local non-state armed organisation. Yet this proposed threshold of the jumping conversion of the paradigm can apply not only to military operations against an independent movement that is not related to the party to the original International Armed Conflict (IAC), but also to that against a resistance group belonging to the ousted party, which is regarded as part of the original IAC, not as a separate NIAC.

Another issue to be considered is whether crossing the threshold and the jumping conversion of the paradigm terminates the belligerent occupation as such. As the answer depends on each case's circumstances, it is impossible to draw a conclusion in the abstract. According to the case law,[40] however, it may be observed that the two constitutive elements of the threshold of NIAC are not low, and they exclude 'situations of internal disturbances and tensions, such as riots, isolated and sporadic acts of violence or other acts of a similar nature.'[41] Therefore, in most cases, the belligerent occupation situation may not be legally sustained in such a high-intensity armed confrontation.

One of the points that should be emphasised for this theory invoking the NIAC threshold is a strong indication of the continuing prevalence of the Law Enforcement paradigm over the armed confrontation between the Occupied Power and armed resistance unless the armed confrontation unquestionably reaches such a high threshold for the paradigm change, and, thus, the belligerent occupation as such would be terminated in most cases. This scenario may anticipate that the less permissive rule for the use of force should prevail far more widely than contended by some occupying forces. In most cases, it should last as long as the belligerent occupation lasts.

5 Consequence of the Conversion: Classification of the Situation

Traditionally, the law of occupation has solely anticipated armed opposition by the population in the occupied territory *in line with* efforts by the ousted

40 For instance, in the *Limaj* case, Trial Chamber II of the International Criminal Tribunal for the Former Yugoslavia (ICTY) deliberately examined the organisation of the Kosovo Liberation Army (KLA) and the intensity of armed confrontation in Kosovo in 1998 and concluded, partially rejecting the Prosecutor's argument, that the NIAC existed only after the KLA possessed a highly sophisticated scheme of command and control, and the armed confrontation represented a certain level of intensity. See *Prosecutor v Limaj et al.*, (Trial Judgment), ICTY-03-66-T (30 November 2005) paras 171–173.

41 Para 2 (d) and (f), art 8 of the Rome Statute of the International Criminal Court. Similar wording may be found in Additional Protocol II, para 2, art 1.

government to recapture the territory.[42] In this scenario, whether the armed confrontation between the Occupying Power and the opposition might be classified as a part of the original IAC was not seriously questioned. Similarly, the privileged status as prisoners of war of some resistance movement members was recognised provided they belonged to the ousted party to the conflict and met the four requirements.

However, in modern-day scenarios, occupying powers may confront armed groups that are not related to, and sometimes opposed to, the ousted party, such as in the case of the Shiite opposition to the occupying powers in Iraq, 2003-2004, or the armed opposition by Hamas, which broke with the Palestine Authority, against Israel. In the case in which the Occupying Power's use of lethal force against such independent armed groups exceeds the threshold for the paradigm change, should this be regarded as a part of the original IAC or as another NIAC in parallel with that IAC?

Assessing whether an armed group in the occupied territory belongs to the ousted party to the conflict is a complex task that can be based on a formalistic or institutional relationship between them. In situations of occupation, the armed forces of the ousted party are usually dismantled; nevertheless (or therefore), they seek to mobilise resistance groups that continue fighting within the occupied area via less formal channels without a *de jure* link. The Geneva Conventions of 1949 seem to have endorsed a liberal interpretation of this point, which reflected the experience of the resistance movements in World War II, by adopting the term 'belong to' in Article 4 of the Third Convention to indicate the minimum connection necessary to relate a resistance group to the ousted party, to classify individuals' status. Pictet's Commentary for the Conventions maintains that the 'belonging' requirement can be satisfied when there is 'a *de facto* relationship between the resistance organization and the party', which may be demonstrated merely by tacit agreements, 'if the operations are such as to indicate clearly for which side the resistance organization is fighting.'[43] Such a *weak* tie might be theoretically incoherent with other principles and rules of international law, such as the law of state responsibility or the rule regulating the internationalisation of NIACs, but the space constraint

42 In exceptional cases, such as Yugoslavia during World War II, partisan forces *not* related to the ousted government may be recognised as entities representing (the people of) the occupied country, where the government controlling the territory before the occupation is completely dismantled. See *Military Conclusions of the Tehran Conference*, 1 December 1943, available at https://avalon.law.yale.edu/wwii/tehran.asp, last accessed 31 July 2023.

43 Jean S Pictet (ed), *The Geneva Conventions of 12 August 1949, Commentary, III* (ICRC 1960) 57.

does not allow us to elaborate on this issue here fully.[44] The point to be clarified for this Chapter concerns the classification of an armed confrontation between the Occupying Power and armed groups that lack such weak ties with the ousted party. Some claim the appropriate classification is as another NIAC parallel to the original IAC. In contrast, others contend that the armed confrontation should be regarded as a part of IAC insofar as it occurs within the occupied territory.

For the former camp, the armed confrontation between the occupying power and independent armed groups acting within the occupied territory should be classified as a separate NIAC, provided two constitutive requirements for establishing NIAC are substantiated. The basis for this argument is straightforward: as an IAC could exist only between two or more entities with an international legal personality under public international law, the law of NIAC should apply to any hostilities in an occupied territory not involving two states. This idea posits that as the classification of an armed conflict depends on the status of the parties,[45] as long as armed groups do not belong to the ousted party, their hostilities against the Occupying Power should fall under the law of NIAC.[46]

The latter camp criticises the former and contends that such armed confrontation must be seen as a part of the original IAC, even when it does not satisfy the requirements of 'belonging', regardless of the interpretations of the word, whether the liberal one by Pictet's Commentary or other stricter ones. Longobardo takes this position and argues that the supporters of the previous view do not consider the existence of a situation of occupation, which may be created only in an IAC. He wonders how the law on NIAC would be required to apply.[47] He does not admit the possibility of the parallel existence of IAC and NIAC within a single occupied area and with a single occupying power fighting against different parties, the ousted one, and a separate non-state actor.

From a practical point of view, applying the law of NIAC to such confrontations is criticised. Longobardo points out that it is highly impracticable to classify hostilities in the occupied territory into two parallel armed conflicts. This is because this theory imposes upon the Occupying Power the burden of making a threefold complicated distinction: not only between law enforcement and conduct of hostilities but also between different types of hostilities

44 See Katherine Del Mar, 'The Requirement of "Belonging" under International Humanitarian Law' (2010) 21 *European Journal of International Law* 105–124.

45 *Hamdan v Rumsfeld*, 548 US 557 (2006) 630–631.

46 Ferraro (n 31) 125, 127.

47 Longobardo (n 18) 217.

based on the personal status of the enemy fighters depending on whether they 'belong' to the ousted party or not, and between hostilities against various armed groups in the occupied territory, which act as co-belligerents against the common enemy, the Occupying Power, on an *ad hoc* basis one day, while fighting each other the other day.[48]

Theoretically and practically, classifying the armed confrontation between the Occupying Power and independent armed groups as a single IAC may seem convincing. However, it contains a critical defect: it lacks consistency with the common understanding of states regarding the concept of *extraterritorial* NIACs. Absent the occupation, a state may be involved in IAC and NIAC simultaneously in the territory of another state.[49] However, it is difficult to find a sound reason why this could not apply to hostilities involving the occupation of that country.[50]

As observed above, the debates among experts on the classification of such situations as either IAC or NIAC are inconclusive. Even if such academic discussion came to a clear conclusion, its actual application to the occupation scene would be tangled. Thus, some countries encountering such problems invoke an evasive situation classification. The Israeli military and judiciary, for instance, have characterised Israel's armed confrontation with Hamas in the Gaza Strip, which cannot be seen as a constituent part of the single entity of the Palestine Authority, as an 'armed conflict' without clarifying whether it was an IAC or a NIAC. For that conflict, the IDF pledged to conduct itself under the rules of the Law of Armed Conflicts, commonly applied in IAC and NIAC.[51] Surely, the 'unification' of the law of IAC and that of NIAC since the 1990s[52] validates Israel's attitude. However, the most significant result of this Israeli approach in the context of this Chapter was separating a new 'armed conflict' with terrorist organisations from the original IAC with the Palestinian Authority, to which the law of occupation applies. In the Gaza Strip, the *non-application* of the law

48 ibid 218.

49 *Military and Paramilitary Activities in and against Nicaragua (Nicaragua v United States of America)*, (Merits) [1986] ICJ Rep 14, para 219; *Prosecutor v Tadic*, (Appeals Chamber Judgment), ICTY-94-1-A (15 July 1999), para 84.

50 Longobardo (n 18) 225–226.

51 *IDF Report, The 2014 Gaza Conflict: Factual and Legal Aspects (7 July – 26 August)*, May 2015, available at: http://mfa.gov.il/ProtectiveEdge/Documents/2014GazaConflictFullReport.pdf, last accessed 31 July 2023; *Jaber al Bassouini Ahmed et al v Prime Minister and Minister of Defense*, HCJ 9132/07, 30 January 2008, opinion of President Beinisch, para 12.

52 The ICRC's study on Customary International Humanitarian Law is said to be evidence of such 'consolidation'. Jean-Marie Henckaerts and Louise Doswald-Beck, *Customary International Humanitarian Law Vol I: Rules* (Cambridge University Press 2005).

of occupation and the resulting legal vacuum was intentionally brought about by the IDF's unilateral withdrawal of ground forces.[53]

It was through this exclusion of the Gaza Strip and Hamas from the belligerent occupation of the whole territory of Palestine that Israel could have an excuse to evade the Law Enforcement paradigm, which is interpreted strictly to limit the use of lethal force in exceptional situations, and to apply instead the more robust paradigm, which gives its soldiers a wider margin of appreciation to use deadly force. After all, the Israeli approach resulted in the situation being *reclassified* as one in which the Conduct of Hostilities paradigm exclusively applies.

A similarly arbitrary switching of the prevailing paradigm by segregating parties in the occupied territory may occur when an armed confrontation between the Occupied Power and an armed resistance group is classified as a separate NIAC. An unwarranted classification of armed revolts not related to the ousted party as an independent armed conflict, which is usually NIAC, and the exclusion of those people from the broader legal protection based on the law applicable to the original IAC, clearly has an adverse effect on people in the occupied territory.

6 Conclusion

In codifying the law of occupation, the most critical but divisive issue for the drafters was how the law should address resistance movements. However, the resulting conventions tended to be almost silent but made exceptional allowances for prisoner-of-war status to a limited extent within such movements. The legal framework applied to the belligerent occupation nowadays, however, does not marginalise the legal protection for those resistance members. Unlike in the past, the Occupying Power now cannot handle them oppressively and mercilessly. Instead, as shown above, along with other humanitarian rules of International Humanitarian Law and applicable rules of International Human Rights Law, the modern law of occupation should be interpreted as respecting, to some extent, the *cause* of disobedience of the people residing in the

53 As to the legal status of Gaza Strip after the disengagement, see Iain Scobbie, 'Gaza' in Elizabeth Wilmshurst (ed), *International Law and the Classification of Conflicts* (Oxford University Press 2012) 280–316; Yuval Shany, 'Faraway, So Close: The Legal Status of Gaza after Israel's Disengagement' (2005) 8 *Yearbook of International Humanitarian Law* 369–383.

occupied territory, as long as the security of the Occupying Power and the endurance of the belligerent occupation are not disturbed.

However, apart from the legal protection of resistance fighters when they are in the hands of the Occupying Power, the diverse perceptions on the paradigm for the use of lethal force against civilians who take up arms against the Occupiers are troubling factors in some cases of occupation. The theory of paradigm change or interplay is so complicated and twisted that lethal force is easily overused. This adversely affects the fate of those civilians, and the legal protection for them may be made meaningless by treating those cases of armed resistance as if civilians directly participate in hostilities under the Conduct of Hostilities paradigm.

In conclusion, it should be noted that this critical observation does not depart far from the traditional views and a faithful interpretation of the law of occupation. Under this interpretation, less permissive rules based on the Law Enforcement paradigm in conformity with Human Rights Law ought to prevail in the occupied territory unless, by a massive armed campaign through civilian uprisings, an armed confrontation with the enemy force resumes. Though frequently misused, the paradigm change should occur only in highly intense scenarios that could eventually terminate the belligerent occupation.

PART 4

Constructive Resistance through International Legal Institutions

CHAPTER 7

International Organisations and Contestation: Reconsidering Democratic Control in Global Constitutionalism

Ryuya Daidouji

1 Introduction

Democracy, the rule of law, and human rights are the trinity of global constitutionalism (GC).[1] In particular, at the heart of the rule of law is the idea of democratic control, according to which power should be constrained by law enacted through democratic procedures, whatever 'democracy' or 'constraining power' precisely means. Insofar as GC is concerned with the rule of law on the international plane, it must incorporate democracy beyond states. However, the arguments on global democracy within GC have lagged in comparison to other tenets such as human rights. Thus, it is compelling to ask:

- How have global constitutionalists (including Professor Mogami) dealt with global democracy?
- What are the global constitutionalist conceptions of democratic control?
- What is missing from GC, and what should be done to supplement it?

To answer these questions, this chapter pays particular attention to international organisations (IOs) for two reasons. First, while there has been an intensive debate over the extent to which IOs are – or should be – democratic,[2] IOs' potential contributions to the democratisation of global governance have not been examined. Second, some IOs that allow individuals' participation may play a role as a nexus between international institutions and those affected by their policies.[3]

1 Anne Peters, 'Global Constitutionalism' *The Encyclopedia of Political Thought* (Wiley 2015) 1.

2 Eg, Andrew Moravcsik, 'Is There a "Democratic Deficit" in World Politics? A Framework for Analysis' (2004) 39 *Government and Opposition* 336–363.

3 This chapter distinguishes 'international organisations' and 'international institutions'. The former refers to the autonomous organs established mainly by governments based on international law, while the latter is a more encompassing notion referring to the set of international rules or norms.

 | DOI:10.1163/9789004681477_009

This chapter critically reviews the existing literature on GC, claiming that it suffers from a 'contestatory deficit': scholars on GC have failed to adequately consider *ex post* political contestation against international power, while some theorists of 'norm contestation' in turn neglect the potential of the concept of contestation in realising democratic control. It then argues that the contestatory deficit can be partly rectified by the idea of contestatory democracy originally proposed by Philip Pettit,[4] a political philosopher. This chapter extends Pettit's conception of republican global democracy and proposes 'global contestatory democracy', wherein some IOs may function as institutional paths that empower individuals vis-à-vis international power (Section 1). This argument is illustrated by two empirical studies: the European Union (EU) asylum policy and the United Nations (UN) targeted sanctions (TS; Section 2). Finally, some implications for the role of IOs in global governance are suggested (see Concluding Remarks).

Methodologically, the topic of democratic control in GC requires combining political science and law, although GC tends to be dominated by lawyers.[5] When GC problematises the *status quo* of international law – as Professor Mogami does, as critical constitutionalism[6] – institutional change inevitably becomes a relevant topic. At this point, political scientists' wisdom on institutional change can help enrich GC. Thus, the empirical part of this chapter specifically analyses IOs' documents and case laws, employing the process-tracing method,[7] with particular attention to ideas and discourse.[8]

---

4 Philip Pettit, *Republicanism: A Theory of Freedom and Government* (Oxford University Press 1997); Philip Pettit, 'Democracy, National and International' (2006) 89 *The Monist* 301–324; Philip Pettit, 'Republican Freedom and Contestatory Democratization' in Ian Shapiro and Casiano Hacker-Cordón (eds), *Democracy's Value* (Cambridge University Press 1999) 163–190.

5 It is an exaggeration that political scientists have not engaged in GC. The editors of a journal, *Global Constitutionalism*, once distinguished 'normatively oriented disciplines', such as moral philosophy, political theory, and legal theory, from 'positively oriented disciplines' like political science, arguing that GC includes both 'method[s]'. Anthony F Lang Jr, Mattias Kumm, Antje Wiener, James Tully and Miguel Poiares Maduro, 'Interdisciplinarity: Challenges and Opportunities' (2013) 2 *Global Constitutionalism* 1–5.

6 Toshiki Mogami, 'Towards Jus Contra Oligarchiam: A Note on Critical Constitutionalism' (2012) 55 *Japanese Yearbook of International Law* 371.

7 Alexander L George and Andrew Bennett, *Case Studies and Theory Development in the Social Sciences* (MIT Press 2005).

8 Vivien A Schmidt, 'Taking Ideas and Discourse Seriously: Explaining Change through Discursive Institutionalism as the Fourth "New Institutionalism"' (2010) 2 *European Political Science Review* 1–25.

2 Global Constitutionalism and Democracy

2.1 *Contestatory Deficit in Global Constitutionalism*

How has GC dealt with global democracy and democratic control? Under the single label of GC, there are divergent ontologies, epistemologies, methodologies, and conclusions. Thus, the conceptions of global democracy and democratic control must be examined differently.[9]

Some authors understand constitutionalisation as the centralisation of power or the supranationalisation of polity. For example, Bardo Fassbender interprets the UN Charter as *the Constitution* of the international community.[10] Such a 'big-C' approach assumes that an international community exists, and is governed by a written Constitution superior to other laws in that legal system. In this case, democratic control refers to certain procedures inherent in the Constitution. When applied to the UN Charter, it implies that the General Assembly (GA) should constrain the Security Council (SC), just as a domestic legislature constrains the government. However, in reality, the drafters of the Charter did not intend to enshrine such control of the SC by the GA. In short, this 'big-C' approach puts greater emphasis on the supremacy of the Constitution over other laws than on constraining power through democratically enacted law.

Instead, a functional approach to GC explores the functional equivalents to constitutional laws from existing laws – including hard law, soft law, doctrines, interpretations, and so on – rather than a single written Constitution.[11] In distinguishing ordinary norms from constitutional ones, it presupposes that some values that are more fundamental to others, including democracy. In this line, Anne Peters intensively argues that GC envisages 'global constitutional order' whose membership includes not only sovereign states but individuals, NGOs, IOs, and firms.[12] In that order, she continues, democracy has two tracks: statist and individual. The statist track refers to the realisation of people's will

9 For different conceptions of democratic conceptions, see for example Philip Pettit, 'Three Conceptions of Democratic Control' (2008) 15 *Constellations* 46–55.

10 Bardo Fassbender, *The United Nations Charter as the Constitution of the International Community* (Brill 2009).

11 Jeffrey L Dunoff and Joel P Trachtman, 'A Functional Approach to International Constitutionalization' in Jeffrey L Dunoff and Joel P Trachtman (eds), *Ruling the World?: Constitutionalism, International Law, and Global Governance* (Cambridge University Press 2009) 3–36.

12 Anne Peters, 'Membership in the Global Constitutional Community' in Jan Klabbers, Anne Peters and Geir Ulfstein (eds), *The Constitutionalization of International Law* (Oxford University Press 2009) 153–262.

through diplomacy between states: sovereign states should be democratised, and these states should deliberate on an equal footing in diplomatic arenas. By 'democratisation' GC has meant this inter-state democracy, but Peters rightly points out that it needs to be complemented by the individual track, allowing the participation of various stakeholder groups and individuals in global law-making and implementation.[13] She successfully enhances the notion of global democracy by combining these tracks, implying that the institutional paths of effective democratic control can vary, allowing different kinds of actors to input their views and opinions. Thus, in contrast to the widespread misunderstanding of GC as promoting a single-value system, Peters in effect assumes that diverse views would provide input into global governance.

The most fascinating point of Peters' argument is simultaneously its Achilles' heel: some values, which Peters acknowledge as 'constitutional', are obviously challenged in contemporary world politics; however, her approach fails to take *ex post* political contestation seriously.[14] Global constitutionalists usually do not pay attention to participation in, and challenge against, global governance *after* the law and/or policy is enacted. Relatedly, the meaning and methods of democratic control in Peters' 'dual democracy' model remain unclear. According to the distinction between statist and individualist tracks, the global constitutional order should be equipped with statist and individualist mechanisms of democratic control. The former seems relatively clear: international institutions are democratically controlled to the extent that sovereign states, which themselves are democratically constituted, exert influence on decision-making on equal footing. In the meantime, it is questionable what the 'individualist' democratic control looks like, and whether and how it would be realised.

If GC is concerned about constraining international power, this lack of consideration of contestation – which may be termed a contestatory deficit – should be fulfilled for two reasons. First, it is almost impossible to foresee and prevent the negative consequences of activities by, for example, powerful IOs or giant multinational corporations. Their malfunctions can be problematised and rectified through contestations only after negative consequences are brought about. Second, in many cases, the wrongdoings of international

13 Anne Peters, 'Dual Democracy' in Jan Klabbers, Anne Peters and Geir Ulfstein (eds), *The Constitutionalization of International Law* (Oxford University Press 2009) 263–341.

14 This critique also applies to what this chapter calls the 'big-C' approach. From a political scientist's perspective, it is worth reminding that Michael Zürn intensively analyses the politicisation of, and challenge against, global governance. See Michael Zürn, *A Theory of Global Governance: Authority, Legitimacy, and Contestation* (Oxford University Press 2018).

powers are not intentional. For example, as demonstrated later, TS led by the UNSC caused a fundamental rights violation, but it was not intended by the drafters of the Charter or the planners of the sanctions; on the contrary, TS were first invented to avoid the collateral negative effects on ordinary citizens' lives in the sanctioned state.[15] Therefore, the rectification of problematic conducts of international powers afterwards needs to be envisaged.

At this point, some of the works by Professor Mogami, published in Japanese, deserve attention. He emphasises the necessity of democratic control of IOs in relation to the philosophical foundation upon which IOs have relied in the aftermath of WWII. According to him, the idea of creating supranational power to resolve international issues – 'philosophy of power creation' – underlies IOs, and this thought prevails over what he calls 'philosophy of power control'.[16] To fill the gap between the two philosophies, he underlines the importance of civil society actors.[17] In the UN's context, he identifies two phenomena. First, he proposes the 'popularisation of the UN', arguing that it is partly and embryonically realised. For example, he points to the cooperation between UN organs and NGOs and the institutionalisation of Arria-formula meetings in the SC.[18] Second is the 'constructive resistance' against the UNSC as 'international oligarchy': the importance of some values like human rights prevails over the formal hierarchical structure enshrined in the UN Charter in the course of law implementation, as in the *Kadi I* case delivered by the Court of Justice of the EU (CJEU).[19]

His arguments obviously constitute an important exception to 'contestatory deficit', because he pursues the rectification of the global structure of governance grounded in the 'philosophy of power creation'. In the meantime, from the viewpoint of political science, he has not offered how resistance results in normative/institutional change; therefore, his arguments can be further advanced by analysing the micro-level political process of resistance. Since

15 Arne Tostensen and Beate Bull, 'Are Smart Sanctions Feasible?' (2002) 54 *World Politics* 373–403.

16 Toshiki Mogami, 'Shiso to shiteno Kokusai Kiko [International Organisations as Philosophy]' in Mogami Toshiki, *Kokusai Rikken Syugi no Jidai* [The Age of International Constitutionalism], (Iwanami Shoten 2007), 96; Toshiki Mogami, *Kokusai-kiko-ron Kogi* [Lecture on International Organisation] (Iwanami Shoten 2016).

17 Mogami, *Kokusai-kiko-ron Kogi*; Mogami Toshiki, 'Kokusai Kiko to Minsyu Syugi [International Organisations and Democracy]' in *Kokusai Rikken Syugi no Jidai* (n 16) 157.

18 Mogami, *Lecture on International Organisation* (n 17) 150–151.

19 Mogami, 'Towards Jus Contra Oligarchiam' (n 6). This judgment will be closely examined later.

this critique applies to other global constitutionalists, doing so paves the way for a more dynamic GC.

2.2 *Two Conceptions of Contestation and Democratic Control*

While the global constitutionalists discussed so far – mainly legalists – have not sufficiently considered *ex post* political contestation, it is worth noting the recent developments in International Relations that focus on contestation. Its core meaning is objection to norms or institutions, but there are two different, but interrelated, ways of understanding the term: contestation as *competition of norms* and as *a challenge to power*.[20]

The former conception is advanced by Antje Wiener, a leading scholar of norm contestation theory, explaining it as follows:

> Contestation is a social activity. While mostly expressed through language not all modes of contestation involve discourse *expressis verbis*. Thus, among the distinct modes of contestation, including justification, deliberation, arbitration or contention, especially the latter does not necessarily involve language. [...] As a social practice contestation entails objection to specific issues that matter to people. In international relations contestation by and large involves the range of social practices, which discursively express disapproval of norms.[21]

Normatively, she underlines 'the principle of contestedness', which warrants regular access to contestation for involved stakeholders.[22] In a subsequent book containing further empirical analyses, she emphasises that different ideas may compete with each other, and highlights the continuous questioning of the legitimacy of international institutions after their establishment.[23]

This idea of norm contestation is helpful in overcoming contestatory deficit in GC because it assumes the existence of multiple alternative norms proposed by various 'affected stakeholders',[24] thereby opening the possibility of

---

20 There are different understandings of the term. For example, for Ian Hurd, it simply means the indeterminacy and disputability of the meanings of law. While it is to some extent correct that the meanings of law are politically determined, he crucially underestimates the potential of law in problematising and rectifying injustices in reality. Ian Hurd, *How to Do Things with International Law* (Princeton University Press 2017).

21 Antje Wiener, *A Theory of Contestation* (Springer 2014) 1 [emphasis in the original text].

22 ibid.

23 Antje Wiener, *Contestation and Constitution of Norms in Global International Relations* (Cambridge University Press 2018).

24 ibid 9.

challenging the norms in place. This possibility constitutes the necessary conditions of *ex post* democratic control, because norm contestation theory 'centr[es] on the "agency of the governed"'.[25] For self-rule by the addressees of the law is, in general, an essential component of democracy, norm contestation by 'affected stakeholders' can ameliorate contestatory deficit in GC. Indeed, Wiener rightly concludes that 'countering injustice depends on access to all three practices of [formal, social, and cultural] norm validation so as to enable affected stakeholders to engage in both "objection" [...] and "creative engagement" [...] with the norms that govern them'.[26]

However, Wiener's framework suffers from theoretical and empirical problems. While she successfully explains how a norm is contested, the policy implications of the contestation remain unclear. Admittedly, she mentions the 'transformative effects of contestation' and 'co-constitution of normative change',[27] but what she actually exhibits is normative *competition* rather than normative change. More precisely, by normative change, she means competition between actors who attempt to justify their own behaviours in different ways. Therefore, although she successfully illustrates how a norm is relativised, she fails to explain how institutional change is caused by norm contestation. Thus, in effect, she downplays the potential of norm contestation to realise the democratic control of international power. This problem makes her empirical assessments less convincing (see Section 2.2.).

Considering the problems of norm contestation theory as such, another conception of contestation that emphasises the challenge to power comes into play. In particular, Philip Pettit's conception of contestatory democracy is useful in exploring what global democratic control looks like.[28] He problematises the relationship of 'domination', which exists to the extent that

1. they [the dominators] have the capacity to interfere
2. on an arbitrary basis
3. in certain choices that the other is in a position to make.[29]

This domination is well illustrated by the famous allegory of master and slave:

25 ibid 10.

26 ibid 225.

27 ibid 222–225.

28 Pettit, 'Republican Freedom and Contestatory Democratization' (n 4); 'Democracy, National and International' (n 4); Pettit, *Republicanism: A Theory of Freedom and Government* (n 4).

29 Pettit, *Republicanism: A Theory of Freedom and Government* (n 4) 20.

> I may be dominated by another – for example, to go to the extreme case, I may be the slave of another – without actually being interfered with in any of my choices. It may just happen that my master is of a kindly and non-interfering disposition. Or it may just happen that I am cunning or fawning enough to be able to get away with doing whatever I like. I suffer domination to the extent that I have a master; I enjoy non-interference to the extent that that master fails to interfere.[30]

In countering such domination, he continues that

> it must always be possible for people in the society, no matter what corner they occupy, to contest the assumption that the guiding interests and ideas really are shared and, if the challenge proves sustainable, to alter the pattern of state activity. Unless such contestability is assured, the state may easily represent a dominating presence for those of a certain marginalized ethnicity or culture or gender.[31]

In another article, he employs another metaphor of 'author' and 'editor': he distinguishes 'authorial' democracy, wherein people collectively form and control their government by election, from 'editorial' democracy, in which people challenge governmental decisions through a broad kind of contestation. He also argues that this distinction can be maintained in the international scene.[32]

This idea of contestatory democracy is useful in exploring how to constrain international power for two reasons. First, the 'domination' of international powers may be formally institutionalised, such that control from *outside* is necessary. In other words, 'editorial' democracy is required for global settings. For example, the UNSC may 'dominate' states, other IOs, and notably, individuals because of the broad discretion and competence enshrined in Article 103, in tandem with Article 25, of the UN Charter. Therefore, to change the SC's behaviour, it is reasonable to expect not only the existence and interpretation of certain legal provisions but also the specific challenges outside the UN. This is what contestatory democracy envisages. Second, in Pettit's conception of democracy, where the contestability of a specific law or policy is critical, democratisation is understood not as an overhaul of an institution, but as an incremental, *ex post* policy change reflecting the voices of the affected. Contestatory democracy allows consideration of the formal establishment/

30 ibid 22–23.

31 ibid 63.

32 Pettit, 'Democracy, National and International' (n 4) 317.

amendment of an institution and the informal influences of various stakeholders. As such, *ex post* contestation may serve to demand an international power to consider its own negative consequences, thereby indirectly constraining it.

The importance of political contestation is not necessarily shared within GC. Peters explicitly denies the usefulness of contestatory democracy, claiming that it 'lack[s] a clear account of how the powerless are able to entrench their claims institutionally'; thus, it is 'no real substitute for formal democracy'.[33] However, in the first place, contestatory democracy does not attempt to be a 'substitute' for existing democratic mechanisms; rather, it supplements other democratic credentials. Therefore, Peters' criticism should rather be read as indicating the agenda to be addressed: how should the surrounding contestations outside formal institutions be institutionalised?

2.3 *IOs' Role in Global Contestatory Democracy: Inter-organizational Contestation*[34]

Considering the institutionalisation of political contestation against international power, this chapter argues that IOs may play a significant role in realising democratic control by what the author elsewhere conceptualised as 'inter-organizational contestation'.[35] It is 'the process where an IO makes an accusatory claim concerning another organization's specific rule or policy'.[36] It is identified by examining the documents issued by an IO for features suggesting that the IO takes another organisation into consideration: *reference* (*to norms*), *criticism*, and *indirect review*, for example.[37] This occurs when there is a 'violation of the contesting organization's core norms or principles'.[38] This notion contributes to addressing the theoretical problems identified thus far. First, it partly overcomes the contestatory deficit by focusing on how IOs organise voices of the affected: 'the contesting IO aggregates and organises

33 Peters, 'Dual Democracy' (n 13) 270. Although it is possible to imagine that someone pretends to be affected by a policy, contestation by such an actor is hardly effective; it seems that, for such a person, a better strategy is to claim to be a legitimate representative of those who are actually affected.

34 The idea of 'global contestatory democracy' is elaborated elsewhere: Ryuya Daidouji, 'The case for "global contestatory democracy": Individuals' contestation against global governance' in Japan Association for United Nations Studies (JAUNS) (ed), *Evolution of the United Nations System: An East Asian Perspective* (Routledge 2023) 206–221.

35 Ryuya Daidouji, 'Inter-Organizational Contestation and the EU: Its Ambivalent Profile in Human Rights Protection' (2019) 57 *Journal of Common Market Studies* 1130–1147.

36 ibid 1133.

37 ibid 1134.

38 ibid 1135.

opinions, voices, or information concerning another, *which are otherwise not easily heard*'.[39] Stated differently, the concept offers a hypothesis on how contestatory democracy can be institutionally realised on the international plane. Second, by explaining policy change, inter-organizational contestation does pay attention to democratic control. Contestation by an IO tends to be politically and legally more relevant to the contested organisation than, for example, individuals or NGOs.[40] This may raise the contested organisation's concerns about the legitimacy and/or effectiveness of the policy in question, urging it to modify that policy. Finally, inter-organizational contestation assumes that it is grounded in objective, formalised norms. For example, when the UN High Commissioner for Refugees (UNHCR) criticises other IOs for their potential maltreatment of asylum seekers, such criticism entails an evaluation of legality in light of the Refugee Convention and other relevant norms. Therefore, this framework is not identical to Wiener's *competitive* model of norm contestation.

While GC has thus far adopted a static approach exploring constitutionalist readings of international law, inter-organizational contestation focuses more on the process of specific policy change. It attempts to explain, rather than interpret, a micro-level dynamism leading to a change in policy, law, or institution. If a certain institutional change can be explained by contestation by other IOs, the international power at stake is controlled, and contestatory democracy in Pettit's sense is to that extent realised. Therefore, the appropriate research method should be a causal inference based on a case study, such as qualitative process tracing.[41] To show that a policy change is not an accidental coincidence but a result of inter-organizational contestation, it must be exhibited that the contested IO takes the specific challenge into consideration. To do so, discourse analysis based on a detailed document analysis is helpful.[42]

The rest of this chapter illustrates the framework of inter-organizational contestation using two examples: EU asylum policy and UNTS. These cases are selected because both illustrate domination (in Pettit's sense) on the international plane and the contestation against it.

---

39 ibid 1133 [emphasis added].

40 The scope of the concept of 'international organisations' is a potential problem in this context. On the one hand, it may include certain civil society actors whose activities are transnational in nature (eg Médecins sans frontières); on the other hand, enhancing the notion as such risks making it all-inclusive, thereby downplaying IOs' potential in 'organising' voices that have difficulty in being heard. Thus, this chapter conventionally equates IOs as intergovernmental organisations (IGOs).

41 George and Bennett (n 7).

42 In this sense, this chapter aligns with what political scientists call 'discursive institutionalism'. Schmidt (n 8).

3 Democratic Control via Inter-organizational Contestation

3.1 *Example 1: the Making of the Dublin System*

Asylum seekers are one of the most prominent examples of global domination in the sense identified above. The interferences in them are arbitrary because, legally speaking, states essentially have the discretion to determine whether to allow them in their territory. Nevertheless, they have no voices over the immigration policies that affect them. As such, the all-affected principle – or what Wiener calls the principle of contestedness – is not fulfilled. This is particularly the case in the EU where the Common European Asylum System (CEAS) is in place because the EU's decision-making process is significantly distant from the affected. Therefore, how the EU can be contested and thereby controlled deserves attention.

On 11 September 1997, the Convention determining the State responsible for examining applications for asylum lodged in one of the Member States of the European Communities entered into force (Dublin I). Soon after, the legislative process to incorporate it into EU law as Dublin II regulation was initiated. During this process, the UNHCR contested the EU (in particular, the European Commission) to affect the content of the new legislation. The responsibility for examining an application lodged by an asylum seeker is frequently allocated to the state of first entry, not taking the asylum seekers' will into account. The UNHCR criticised the EU in 2001 in this regard:

> [The] UNHCR considers it wholly inappropriate to derive any responsibility for considering an asylum application from the fact that the applicant has been merely present in the territory of a Member State. Mere presence in a territory is often the result of fortuitous circumstances, and does not necessarily imply the existence of any *meaningful link or connection*.[43]

By contrast, the European Commission emphasises that 'the general principle is that responsibility for examining an asylum application lies with the Member State which played the greatest part in the applicant's entry into or residence on the territories of the Member States, *regardless of the desire of an asylum-seeker*'.[44] In the final draft issued in July

43 UNHCR, *Revisiting the Dublin Convention: Some Reflections by UNHCR in Response to the Commission Staff Working Paper* (2001) 5 [emphasis added].

44 European Commission, 'Proposal for a Council Regulation Establishing the Criteria and Mechanisms for Determining the Member State Responsible for Examining an Asylum

2001,[45] the Commission made it explicit that it did not reflect the UNHCR's objection by stating that '[i]t would therefore not be realistic to envisage a system […] which diverges fundamentally from the Dublin Convention'.[46] However, this saga vividly illustrates the contrast between the UNHCR emphasising the agencies of the asylum seekers and the Commission that did not do so.

In March 2003, the Dublin II regulation entered into force, which means the initiation of the CEAS. The UNHCR started pointing specifically to the problems in the asylum reception system, especially in Greece, highlighting the insufficient protection of the procedural rights of the asylum seekers and the deteriorating reception condition.[47] In 2008, the UNHCR issued a paper on this issue as follows:

> [The] UNHCR advises Governments to refrain from returning asylum-seekers to Greece under the Dublin Regulation until further notice. [The] UNHCR recommends that Governments make use of Article 3 (2) of the Dublin Regulation, allowing States to examine an asylum application lodged even if such examination is not its responsibility under the criteria laid down in this Regulation.[48]

Following this recommendation, the UNHCR gave an overview of the situation of Greece to point out that 'reception conditions [in Greece] continue to fall short of international and European standards'.[49] Moreover, the UNHCR attributes some responsibilities to other EU member states and EU institutions:

> Strengthening the Greek asylum system so as to ensure consistency with international standards and the EU asylum *acquis* is the primary responsibility of the Greek Government. However, as a matter of solidarity and responsibility sharing, and in order to ensure a fair and effective application of the Dublin Regulation, it is nonetheless an issue concerning all

---

Application Lodged in One of the Member States by a Third-Country National' COM (2001) 447 final, 4 [emphasis added].

45 ibid.

46 ibid 4.

47 UNHCR, *The Dublin II Regulation: A UNHCR Discussion Paper* (2006).

48 UNHCR, *UNHCR Position on the Return of Asylum-seekers to Greece under the 'Dublin Regulation'* (2008) para 4.

49 ibid para 24.

> EU Member States, if a Member State is facing considerable challenges in complying with the relevant standards.[50]

This recommendation reflects the UNHCR's recognition that the problems in Greece are also attributable, to some degree, to other member states and EU institutions.

Remarkably, the UNHCR's approach to the CEAS influenced the Council of Europe (CoE), a latecomer in the debates over EU asylum policy. The Commissioner for Human Rights Thomas Hammarberg visited Greece in December 2008 and issued a report to make a recommendation: '[t]he Commissioner urges the Greek authorities to proceed urgently, in collaboration with competent national and international organizations, to a serious overhaul of the needs and prospects of the national asylum system in order for it to attain a quality level that would effectively safeguard the human rights of all persons in need of international protection'.[51] He explicitly refers to the UNHCR position paper mentioned above:

> The Commissioner has taken note in particular of the Position of UNHCR dated 15 April 2008 which stressed the persistence in Greece of structural shortcomings in the asylum procedure as a result of which 'asylum seekers continue to remain effectively in limbo, unable to exercise their rights, for prolonged periods of time'.[52]

This reference implies the influence of the UNHCR on the CoE. Indeed, a press release in the following year resembles the UNHCR's stance: it requires EU member states 'to halt all transfers of asylum seekers back to countries where they face enormous difficulties in gaining access to the asylum procedure and where they do not enjoy basic safeguards such as interpretation and legal aid'.[53]

Hammarberg also utilised the European Court of Human Rights (ECtHR). In *M.S.S.*, to which Hammerberg intervened as a third-party intervener, the ECtHR declared that the transfer from Belgium to Greece based on the Dublin Regulation was contrary to the European Convention of Human Rights

50 ibid, para 25 [emphasis in the original text].

51 Council of Europe, *Report by Thomas Hammerberg Council of Europe Commissioner for Human Rights following his visit to Greece 8–10 December 2008* (CommDH(2009)6, 2009) para 42.

52 ibid para 11.

53 Council of Europe, '*The "Dublin Regulation" Undermines Refugee Rights*' (Press Release 683(2010), 2010).

(ECHR).[54] The ECtHR 'takes into consideration the applicant's allegations that he was subjected to brutality and insults by the police', on the basis that 'the applicant's allegations are consistent with numerous accounts collected from witnesses by international organisations'.[55] Moreover, it 'attaches critical importance to the letter sent by the UNHCR in April 2009 to the Belgian Minister for Migration and Asylum Policy', containing 'an unequivocal plea for the suspension of transfers to Greece'.[56] This letter informed Belgian authorities about the situation in Greece; it was thus presented as evidence that Belgium recognised the Greek government's inadequate protection of asylum seekers. This reasoning suggests that extra-judicial criticism constitutes a component of inter-organizational contestation.[57]

The *M.S.S.* judgment directly affected the CJEU. In *N.S.*, the CJEU considered the legality of the transfers from the United Kingdom and Ireland, respectively, to Greece, in light of the Charter of the Fundamental Rights of the EU.[58] The CJEU explicitly referred to *M.S.S.* of the ECtHR in finding 'a systemic deficiency in the asylum procedure and in the reception conditions'.[59] Importantly, the CJEU considered not only the conclusion but also the evidence of *M.S.S.*:

> In finding that the risks to which the applicant was exposed were proved, the European Court of Human Rights took into account the regular and unanimous reports of international non-governmental organisations bearing witness to the practical difficulties in the implementation of the Common European Asylum System in Greece, the correspondence sent by the United Nations High Commissioner for Refugees (UNHCR) to the Belgian minister responsible, and also the Commission reports on the evaluation of the Dublin system and the proposals for recasting Regulation No 343/2003 in order to improve the efficiency of the system and the effective protection of fundamental rights.[60]

---

54 *M.S.S. v Belgium and Greece*, ECtHR (Grand Chamber), App no 30696/09, Judgment of 21 January 2011.

55 ibid para 227.

56 ibid para 349.

57 Daidouji (n 35) 1138.

58 Joined Cases C-411/10 & C-493/10, *N.S. v Secretary of State for the Home Department and M E and Others v Refugee Applications Commissioner and Minister for Justice, Equality and Law Reform* [2011] EU:C:2011:865.

59 ibid para 89.

60 ibid. para 90 [reference omitted].

Based on this consideration, the CJEU admitted that EU member states must use their discretion to avoid transfer to a state where there is a deficiency.[61]

The *N.S.* judgment affected the recast process of the Dublin II regulation. The proposal of the Dublin III regulation was issued by the Commission in 2008.[62] Originally, Article 3 (2) of the proposal simply stated that 'the first Member State with which the application for international protection was lodged shall be responsible for examining it'.[63] However, after *M.S.S.* and *N.S.* in 2011, the Council added the following paragraph to Article 3(2):

> Where it is impossible to transfer an applicant to the Member State primarily designated as responsible because there are substantial grounds for believing that there are systemic flaws in the asylum procedure and in the reception conditions for applicants in that Member State, resulting in a risk of inhuman or degrading treatment within the meaning of Article 4 of the Charter of Fundamental Rights of the European Union, the determining Member State shall continue to examine the criteria set out in Chapter III in order to establish whether another Member State can be designated as responsible.[64]

Considering that the CJEU case law was affected by the ECtHR judgment, which relied on various reports issued by several international organs, the recast of the Dublin system can be understood as a result of a chain of inter-organizational contestation. This means that the domination of international power (the EU) over the affected individuals (asylum seekers) may be eased with the help of various IOs and NGOs.

3.2 *Example 2: Targeted Sanctions Saga Revisited*

TS, initiated by the UN, are illustrative of global domination because the SC has the power that may be – indeed, *is* – arbitrarily exercised. It enjoys the

61 ibid para 98.

62 Commission, 'Proposal for a Regulation of the European Parliament and of the Council Establishing the Criteria and Mechanisms for Determining the Member State Responsible for Examining an Application for International Protection Lodged in One of the Member States by a Third-Country National or a Stateless Person (Recast)' COM (2008) 820 final.

63 European Commission (n 62) 27.

64 Council Position (EU) no 5/2013 of the Council at first reading with a view to the adoption of a Regulation of the European Parliament and of the Council establishing the criteria and mechanisms for determining the Member State responsible for examining an application for international protection lodged in one of the Member States by a third-country national or a stateless person (recast) [2013] OJ C177/1, 7.

discretion to determine who to enlist in the so-called terrorist list so as to impose sanctions. It can enlist as terrorist those who are alleged to be 'associated with' terrorist organisation, but the interpretation of that condition is left to the state that requires designating someone (called designating state). Moreover, the delisting procedure also suffers from structural problems in terms of arbitrariness: the decision to delist someone is made by the very actor that enlisted him/her.

A prominent example to challenge this domination is the CJEU's *Kadi I* judgment, which is incredibly famous for international lawyers (but not for political scientists). The plaintiff, Mr. Kadi, requested the annulment of EU Council Regulations 467/2001 and 2062/2001, which implement the SC resolutions that impose TS on him and his company. Rejecting the previous judgments of the Court of First Instance,[65] the CJEU declared that the EU legislations in question were violating fundamental rights, thus suggesting the possibility of suspending the implementation of sanctions. The impact of this judgment was huge enough to urge the SC to introduce some due process, such as the Office of Ombudsperson.

Abundant literature exists on this case.[66] The *Kadi I* judgment was associated with the argument problematising potential human rights violations by the SC[67] and played a significant role in forming and advancing GC.[68] These – mainly legal – studies tend to interpret the relevant judgments and norms, evaluate them, and explore the 'interordinal' relations between UN and EU

65 Case T-315/01, *Yassin Abdullah Kadi v Council and Commission* [2005] EU:T:2005:332.

66 Eg Matej Avbelj, Filippo Fontanelli and Giuseppe Martinico (eds), *Kadi on Trial: A Multifaceted Analysis of the Kadi Trial* (Routledge 2014); Jean d'Aspremont and Frédéric Dopagne, 'Kadi: The ECJ's Reminder of the Elementary Divide Between Legal Orders' (2008) 5 *International Organizations Law Review* 371–379; Gráinne de Búrca, 'The European Court of Justice and the International Legal Order After Kadi' (2010) 51 *Harvard International Law Journal* 1–50; Pasquale De Sena and Maria Chiara Vitucci, 'The European Courts and the Security Council: Between Dédoublement Fonctionnel and Balancing of Values' (2009) 20 *European Journal of International Law* 193–228; Erika de Wet, 'From Kadi to Nada: Judicial Techniques Favoring Human Rights Over United Nations Security Council Sanctions' (2013) 12 *Chinese Journal of International Law* 787–807; Christina Eckes, *EU Counter-Terrorist Policies and Fundamental Rights: The Case of Individual Sanctions* (Oxford University Press 2009).

67 Eg Erika de Wet, Andre Nollkaemper and Dijkstra Petra (eds), *Review of the Security Council by Member States* (Intersentia 2003).

68 De Búrca (n 66); Christina Eckes, 'Individuals in a Pluralist World: The Implications of Counterterrorist Sanctions' (2013) 2 *Global Constitutionalism* 218–236; Ramses A Wessel, 'The Kadi Case: Towards a More Substantive Hierarchy in International Law?' (2008) 5 *International Organizations Law Review* 323–327; Mogami (n 5).

laws.[69] However, they do not pay attention to microscopic political processes and policy changes. Morse and Keohane exceptionally propose a dynamic analysis of the saga using the notion of regime shifting, but their understanding is not well founded, because the CJEU did not offer an alternative venue of judicial review competing with the SC.[70] In relation to norm contestation, Wiener understands the conflict as follows:

> While stakeholder groups 1 (i.e., centring on the EU context) proactively contested the UN Security Council's lack of fundamental rights protection and generated the emergent norm of 'so long as', stakeholder group 2 (i.e. centring on the UN context) defended the moral authority of international law.[71]

This analysis is flawed for four reasons. First, the notion of 'moral authority' of international law is unfounded, and the *Kadi* case was not an issue of morality; moreover, the implicit claim that stakeholders 'centring on the EU context' disregarded international law is not plausible. Second, it is inaccurate from the perspective of EU law that the *Kadi* saga 'generated' the 'norm of "so long as"', not only because that doctrine originates in the German jurisprudence in 1980s, but also because the CJEU finally did not adopt that theory by emphasising autonomy of EU legal order. Third, although she states that 'access' to formal validation (of norms) is fundamentally important (as discussed in 2.2), it is incorrect that legal scholars themselves had it in the process of the *Kadi* saga. If 'access' is a concept broad enough to include 'engagement in debate' (or whatever) then unavoidably, the scope of the notion of 'access' or 'stakeholders' becomes vague. Finally, and most importantly, she does not mention the policy implications of contestations on the UNSC: the policy change on the side of the UNSC is neither explained nor mentioned. As long as democratic control is conceived of as influencing policymakers by the addressees of law, this change must be crucial. Meanwhile, this chapter understands the TS saga as a dialogic process between the regional organisations and the SC, considering how the regional organisations expressed the issue, and how the SC reframed it.

---

69 eg de Búrca (n 66); Luis I Gordillo, *Interlocking Constitutions: Towards an Interordinal Theory of National, European and UN Law* (Hart 2012).

70 Julia C Morse and Robert O Keohane, 'Contested Multilateralism' (2014) 9 *Review of International Organizations* 385–412.

71 Wiener (n 23) 223.

The CJEU emphasised the need for judicial review by the CJEU, stating that 'the Community judicature must [...] ensure the review, in principle the full review, of the lawfulness of all Community acts *in the light of the fundamental rights forming an integral part of the general principles of Community law*'.[72] As far as the EU is 'a community based on the rule of law, of a constitutional guarantee stemming from the EC Treaty as an autonomous legal system',[73] fundamental rights, including the rights to be heard and to effective judicial review, are seen as foundational values necessitating an indirect and substantive review of the SC resolution.

In addition, the non-judicial actors' opinions are also illustrative of the regional organisations' understandings. The European Parliament (EP) criticised the Council of the EU and MS, stressing that 'the present blacklisting procedures at both the EU and the UN levels are deficient from the perspective of legal security and legal remedies'.[74] In the following resolution, whose central issue was the procedural rights in the TS regime, the EP '[r]ecalls that listing and de-listing procedures for the UN and EU sanctions regimes have been strongly criticised as failing to provide satisfactory protection for fundamental rights (both procedural and substantive) and legal certainty'.[75] Moreover, the Parliamentary Assembly of the CoE (PACE) expressed concerns about the potential infringement of procedural rights in TS from the early period. In 2008, the PACE adopted Resolution 1597 and Recommendation 1824, finding 'that the procedural and substantive standards currently applied by the UN [SC] and by the Council of the European Union, despite some recent improvements, *in no way fulfil the minimum standards laid down above and violate the fundamental principles of human rights and the rule of law*'.[76]

As such, the EU and the CoE framed the problem of TS as infringements of certain values, which are often enshrined in law. In other words, the European organisations exhibited value-based contestations.

Inter-organizational contestation as such became a salient issue for the SC; thus, it interpreted and reframed them. In May 2008, the Analytical Support and Sanctions Monitoring Team (MT), a subsidiary organ of the SC, considered

72 Joined Cases C-402/05 P and C-415/05 P, *Yassin Abdullah Kadi and Al Barakaat International Foundation v Council and Commission* [2008] EU:C:2008:461, para 326 [emphasis added].

73 ibid para 316.

74 European Parliament, *The evaluation of EU sanctions as part of the EU's actions and policies in the area of human rights* (P6_TA(2008)0405, 2008) para 54.

75 European Parliament, *Restrictive measures affecting the rights of individuals following the entry into force of the Lisbon Treaty* (P7_TA(2009)0111, 2009) para 10.

76 Council of Europe, *United Nations Security Council and European Union blacklists* (Res 1597, 2008) para 6 [emphasis added].

AG Maduro's opinion in *Kadi I*, expressed concern that a judgment invalidating its sanctions 'would trigger similar challenges that could quickly erode enforcement' and stated that 'it is easy to imagine that the precedent of a decision that invalidated the sanctions, especially one affecting so many States, might lead to similar problems in other States outside the European Union'.[77] As such, the MT was concerned about the spillover effect of the *Kadi* judgment. Notably, the MT report makes no reference to value, such as human rights, transparency, or fairness. The MT was consistently concerned about the impact of the CJEU judgment on the effectiveness of the TS regime. This attitude remained in another report issued after the delivery of the *Kadi I* judgment, in which 'legal challenges' were the main agenda.[78]

> Despite universal recognition of the importance of the sanctions regime, *several factors have undermined its effective implementation*: some States lack the capacity to introduce and enforce the measures; some regard its targets as of marginal national relevance; some grant it a low priority because they believe it ineffective, and *some have questioned its legitimacy*.[79]

The SC's primary concern is the effective implementation of sanctions, and the issue of value or 'legitimacy' is salient only when it is conceived as a threat to the effectiveness of sanctions.

This difference in framing is the background to the introduction of the Office of Ombudsperson. In October 2009, the specific plans of the newly introduced due process were discussed and included the following: a review panel, an ombudsman, time limits on listings, and a regular review of listings and by an existing body.[80] The MT argued that the review panel was not desirable, partly because 'the decision of the Court of Justice of the European Communities in the case of Qadi [=Kadi] and Barakaat suggests that the Court is obligated to conduct its review as a matter of European law, not by the absence of another

77 Security Council, *Report of the Analytical Support and Sanctions Monitoring Team pursuant to resolution 1735 (2006) concerning Al-Qaida and the Taliban and associated individuals and entities* (S/2008/324, 2008) para 40.

78 Security Council, *Ninth report of the Analytical Support and Sanctions Monitoring Team, submitted pursuant to resolution 1822 (2008) concerning Al-Qaida and the Taliban and associated individuals and entities* (S/2009/245, 2009).

79 ibid para 16 [emphasis added].

80 ibid para 39 and following.

appropriate and adequate forum'.[81] In this sense, the CJEU failed to urge the SC to introduce an independent judicial organ by adopting an 'inward-looking' approach.[82] The MT claims that the Ombudsperson would be better, 'as he or she might more easily have access to sensitive or classified information and could evaluate the entire case'.[83]

Against this background, the SC introduced the Office of Ombudsperson in Resolution 1904. It is notable that the SC

> [e]ncourages Member States and relevant international organizations to inform the Committee of any relevant court decisions and proceedings so that the Committee can consider them when it reviews a corresponding listing or updates a narrative summary of reasons for listing.[84]

Having so stated, the SC elaborates on the rules regarding the Office of Ombudsperson. It enables the dialogue between the delisting applicants and the SC, and even makes recommendations for delisting. In the 6247th meeting, where Resolution 1904 was adopted, the SC members acknowledged the correlations between the introduction of the Ombudsperson and what this chapter calls inter-organizational contestation. The previous chairman of the Sanctions Committee Mr. Mayr-Harting states:

> I am also aware of the growing number of cases filed by listed individuals and entities before national and regional courts in various parts of the world. I can therefore also appreciate how very substantially Security Council resolution 1904 (2009) improves the procedures under the sanctions regime under resolution 1267 (1999) in terms of due process.[85]

As such, the SC has understood the developments in Europe and modified the sanctions regime in reaction to contestation. While the European organisations framed the TS saga as a breach of certain values, the SC reframed it as a threat to the effectiveness of a regime. Thus, it is not correct that some universal

81 Security Council, *Tenth report of the Analytical Support and Sanctions Implementation Monitoring Team submitted pursuant to resolution 1822 (2008) concerning Al-Qaida and the Taliban and associated individuals and entities* (S/2009/502, 2009) para 43.

82 de Búrca (n 66) 41.

83 Security Council (n 80) para 46, but the MT did not explain why 'he or she might more easily have access to sensitive or classified information'.

84 Resolution 1904, S/RES/1904 (2009) para 15.

85 Security Council, *Provisional Verbatim Report* (S/PV.6247, 2009).

values, such as human rights, themselves drove the SC. This conclusion might sound pessimistic, but it should be emphasised that procedural rights protection was improved by the establishment of the Office of Ombudsperson. This was because the challenge was done collectively that reframing occurred. In this way, an IO can ameliorate an international institution that embodies global domination by contesting it, meaning that IOs may serve as an institutional path for democratic control.

4 Concluding Remarks

This chapter has identified the problem of the contestatory deficit in GC, proposed the concept of inter-organizational contestation to overcome the problem, and illustrated it with two examples. It has been proposed that an IO may serve as a path for democratic control of another IO, arguing that the challenging IOs aggregate voices, opinions, and information of individuals not heard otherwise, then organise them, and contest an international power on their behalf, thereby improving the situations of individuals affected by international policies. In this sense, international *organisations* may *organise* contestations.

This role of IOs needs further exploration: How do IOs 'organise' contestations? What are the underlying mechanisms? Under what conditions does it succeed or fail? There are many remaining agendas, but the concept of inter-organizational contestation may enrich GC. It is also safe to say that *Legal Rectification of International Injustice* is not a task only for lawyers, but political scientists can and should also contribute to it – this is what the author learned from Professor Mogami.

Acknowledgements

This chapter is part of the outcome of research performed under a Waseda University Grant for Special Research Projects (Project number: 2019E-001) and Grant nos. 20K13437, 20H01467, and 18H03617 of the Japan Society for the Promotion of Science Kakenhi. Its empirical part (Section 3) is partly based on the author's monograph, *Kokusai-kiko-kan Kankei Ron: Ousyu Jinken Hosho no Seido Rikigaku* [Inter-organizational Relations: Institutional Dynamism of Human Rights Protection in Europe] (Shinzansha, 2020). I thank Tetsuya Yamada, Kyo Arai, Masami Maruyama, Makoto Seta, and Yota Negishi for their constructive comments.

CHAPTER 8

Legal Control for the UN Security Council: toward *jus contra oligarchiam* as Critical Global Constitutionalism

Masami Maruyama

1 Introduction

The 'constitutionalization' of international law and international (or global) constitutionalism[1] have been widely discussed in recent years.[2] This chapter examines what the debates and changing perceptions around these phenomena indicate for the powers, functions and activities of the UN Security Council (UNSC) under Chapter VII of the UN Charter.[3] In this sense, this chapter focuses on an empirical study of the UNSC during recent years rather than on the theoretical aspects of constitutionalization and constitutionalism. Nevertheless, it is necessary, to some degree, to provide an overview of the theoretical aspects, which will be outlined in the following section.

While there is no doubt that one of the triggers of the debate on constutitionalization and global constitutionalism lies in the revitalization of the UNSC,[4] the debate reaches far beyond the UNSC itself; it can also be abstract and ambiguous in nature. This chapter, however, limits the discussion to the

1 Although some authors distinguish between *international* and *global* constitutionalism in a meaningful way, this article use 'global constitutionalism' except for citing other materials.

2 As the general overview of prof. Mogami's ideas on global constitutionalism, Toshiki Mogami, '*Perpetuum Mobile* before and after Global Constitutionalism' in Takao Suami, Anne Peters, Mattias Kumm and Dimitri Vanoverbeke (eds), *Global Constitutionalism from European and East Asian Perspectives* (Cambridge University Press 2018) 29–57. More specifically, Toshiki Mogami, 'Towards *Jus Contra Oligarchiam*: A Note on Critical Constitutionalism' (2012) 55 *Japanese Yearbook of International Law* 371–402, 371–379.

3 This article is based on Masami Maruyama, 'The UN Security Council and "Constitutionalization" of International Law: Emerging 'Legal Control' Mechanism?' (2014) 33 *Yearbook of World Law* 65–93 [in Japanese]. This chapter has attempted to observe the subsequent international practices and secondary materials after the original publication, but has not been thoroughly implemented.

4 Eg Tetsuo Sato, 'The Legitimacy of Security Council Activities under Chapter VII of the UN Charter since the End of the Cold War' in Jean-Marc Coicaud and Veijo Heiskanen (eds), *The Legitimacy of International Organizations* (UN University Press 2001) 309–354.

 | DOI:10.1163/9789004681477_010

possibility of constitutionalism within the UNSC. This means that global constitutionalism, for example, being discussed in the context of the European Union (EU)[5] and the World Trade Organization (WTO)[6] is set aside for the time being. While it is true that each debate puts the entire international community or international legal order(s) within reach, it is a matter for other opportunities to discuss their differences, consistencies, and potential connections. With those debates in mind, this chapter examines the possibility of constitutionalism in the context of the UNSC from the perspective of the broader concept of legal controls, which is not confined to judicial review. The objects of analysis are limited to a few practices related to targeted sanctions, international criminal justice, and the responsibility to protect. The limited issues to be considered and the ongoing nature of the debate itself is likely to give this chapter a patchwork-like impression. With this in mind, rather than presenting a firm conclusion as to what constitutionalization and constitutionalism might influence on the functions of the UNSC, I would like to find some budding elements of those influence worthy of further discussion in the future.

2 Critical Global Constitutionalism and the Concept of Legal Control

2.1 *The Constitutionalization of International Law and Global Constitutionalism*

When constitutionalization or constitutionalism is talked about in terms of the functional aspects of the UN, two major positions emerge. In the first, the UN Charter is regarded as the constitution of the 'International Community' (not just of the UN as an international organization), and its legal nature as a constitution is discussed.[7] This is referred to as a comprehensive constitutionalist position, and it pursues the unity of the international community with the UN Charter at the apex of its legal hierarchy. This position is oriented toward institutional integration and centralization with the UN at the top. Suspicion and criticism of this position abounds, as mainly do concerns about such a constitutionalism losing its abilities to restrain power.[8]

5 There are wide variety on global constitutionalism even in Europe which is the centre of the debates. Takao Suami, 'Global Constitutionalism and European Legal Experiences. Can European Constitutionalism Be Applied to the Rest of The World' in Suami *et al* (n 2) 123–167.

6 Eg Joel P Trachtman, 'The Constitution of the WTO' (2006) 17 *European Journal of International Economic Law* 623–646.

7 Bardo Fassbender, *The United Nations as the Constitution of the International Community* (Martinus Nijhoff 2009).

8 Mogami *Jus Contra Oligarchiam* (n 2) 373–375.

Rather than arguing whether the UN Charter is a constitution, the second position considers the implications of constitutionalism for the UN as a space of global governance, and proposes basic elements to be applied there. For example, the leading constitutionalist Peters, highlights the elements of global constitutionalism that complement national constitutionalism, such as the rule of law, restraint and balance of powers, human rights protection, and democracy.[9] Although certainly a proposal as *lex ferenda*, this position advocates global constitutionalism and constitutionalization as a *process* that seeks precedent in established law and distinguished between *lex lata* and *lex ferenda*. It attempts to develop a constitutional paradigm in which the requirements for consent of states to international legislation are mitigated, the concept of the international community is centered on individuals, and political power is regulated through the legal system.[10]

Dunoff and Trachtman criticize this second position on methodological grounds, arguing that it is a 'top-down' (or definitive) approach that prescribes the elements of constitutionalism a priori and is not based on real state practices.[11] In defending the position, Peters counters that such elements are extracted from the existing precedent, that she takes a prescriptive (normative) approach, and real state practices are open to a wide range of interpretation.[12] It is clear that, such epistemological conflicts will remain unresolved for some time, and may reflect the weakness of global constitutionalism.

2.2 Jus contra oligarchiam *as Critical Global Constitutionalism*

Amid the debates around what constitutes constitutionalism, the concept of 'critical constitutionalism' presented by Mogami is useful for the purpose of this chapter. According to Mogami, critical constitutionalism enables us to capture 'some of the current norms and institutions which may no longer correspond to reality and thus may no longer legitimized' and to conceive the

---

9 Anne Peters, 'Compensatory Constitutionalism: The Function and Potential of Fundamental International Norms and Structures' (2006) 19 *Leiden Journal of International Law* 579–610, 583. See also Mogami, Towards *Jus Contra Oligarchiam* (n 2) 400–401.

10 Anne Peters, 'Conclusions' in Jan Klabbers, Anne Peters, and Geir Ulfstein, *The Constitutionalization of International Law* (paperback edn, Oxford University Press 2011) 342–352. This was first published in 2009 and paperback edition in 2011 incorporated the attractive dialogue done in *Debate on EJIL Talk! Blog*.

11 ibid 372–373. See also Jeffrey L Dunoff and Joel P Trachtman, 'A Functional Approach to International Constitutionalization' in Jeffrey L Dunoff and Joel P Trachtman (eds), *Ruling the World?: Constitutionalism, International Law, and Global Governance* (Cambridge University Press 2009) 3–36, 9.

12 ibid 388–389.

reconstruction of those norms and/or institutions based on 'the constitutional principles of democracy, human rights, rule of law, and constraint of power'.[13] Therefore we can assume that it still lies within the sphere of positive law.[14]

The norms and institutions in modern international law which deviate from the facts mentioned above can be summarized by the following two points in light of the functional aspects of the UNSC. The first is the normative (rather than institutional) unity of the fragmented international legal order, and the second is the mechanisms for restraining the power of international organizations involved in the governance of the international community, which means the development of *jus contra oligarchiam*. As will be evident from the examination in sections II and III below, these two points may seemingly conflict with each other, and the key to global constitutionalism is whether or not it can provide means to realize both. Moreover, global constitutionalism is often invoked for external relations purposes, such as responding to fragmentation and building mutually complementary relations between the UN and domestic and regional legal orders based on human rights norms. This consideration is equally important. Based on the above, I employ the concept of legal control as a critical perspective from, which we can narrow the concept of global constitutionalism down to an operational level.[15]

2.3 *The Concept of Legal Control*

As the previous sections indicate, the link between the functions of the UNSC and constitutionalism becomes most conspicuous when examining aspects of legal control. It is appropriate to define legal control, a concrete mechanism of global constitutionalism, as a multi-layered process in which various actors verify that the given decisions of an organ of an organization are in accordance with certain norms and exert an influence on the organ in order to protect those norms. By this definition, legal control is a broader concept than judicial review and assumes a process that is feasible in the current UN system.[16] It does

13 Mogami, *Jus Contra Oligarchiam* (n 2) 400–401.

14 However, we should be careful that prof. Mogami derives the origin of critical constitutionalism from the conceptual framework of 'the World Order Models Project (WOMP)'. Furthermore, he points out that 'if global constitutionalism, aiming either to be equipped with an overall explanatory power for international law or to consolidate the value basis for it, was not in itself truly innovative and not further advanced than its predecessors such as WOMP, then we should say that global constitutionalism as an academic movement has had limits which it has no overcome'. Mogami, *Pepetuum Mobile* (n 2) 51–54.

15 This is inspired from Mogami, ibid 41.

16 ibid 37. The definition was largely inspired from M.a Eugenia López-Jacoiste Díaz, *Actualidad del Consejo de Seguridad de las Naciones Unidas: La legalidad de sus decisiones*

not assumed that a process has already been realized, but rather does assume that it can be realized earlier than the establishment of a judicial review system. In this sense, this definition places legal control within the realm of an applicable method while maintaining the distinction between *lex lata* and *lex ferenda* mentioned above.

The above definition may require some additional clarification. First, it assumes the existence of a hierarchy of norms (in a loose sense). Within this hierarchy, it is assumed that there is a conflict between obligations to uphold specific norms (in the strictest sense), and that certain norms are superior to others. However, in recent years, the hierarchy of norms has been discussed in a very broad sense, including conflicts of the obligations and rights, and conflicts of the interests and values reflected in the norms.[17] In the narrow sense, when a specific (genuine) conflict arises, one may need to resolve it by establishing the superiority of one norm over another, while in the broad sense, a harmonious interpretation of norms is required in order to prevent and avoid both apparent and genuine conflicts. In the case of the latter, the 'normative hierarchy' can be avoided in principle.[18] However, even in the case of an apparent conflict, values and interests are bound to conflict as long as the norms reflect certain values and interests. Both must be interpreted in a preferential manner. Therefore, this definition also presupposes hierarchy in a broad sense.

Second, the various ways and means to preserve and protect the normative hierarchy should be noted. Foremost, it is difficult for a judicial body to exert legal controls on an assumption of invalidity or illegality. While normative claims (made through statements, reports, court decisions, and so on) reflect the interests and values of the International Community, they are not uniform. Rather, they depend on the position of the parties involved, who are extremely diverse.[19]

It is important to note here that both judicial *and* non-judicial bodies may use their respective roles to exert legal control by making prescriptive claims. Such a diversity of actors is in line with the UNSC expansion of the concept of 'threats to peace' as well as the expansion of its sphere of activity under Chapter

y el problema de su control (Editorial Civitas 2003). See also the book review by Aristotle Constantinides (2005) 16 *European Journal of International Law* 787–791.

17 Erika de Wet and Jure Vidmar, 'Introduction' Erika de Wet and Jure Vidmar (eds), *Hierarchy in International Law The Place of Human Rights* (Oxford University Press 2012) 1–12.

18 Antonios Tzanakopoulos, '*Human Rights and United Nations Security Council Measures*' in ibid 42–70, 44–48.

19 Here, 'involvement' assumes a very broad and open-ended meaning of having relations to UNSC activities in some way.

VII powers. It is an unending task to fully clarify the relationships between the involved parties and the UNSC and their respective legal positions.[20]

Thus, this chapter poses the following questions: can the process of legal control be an indicator of the 'constitutionalization' of international law, and can it be enriched as *jus contra oligarchiam*? Before examining these questions, possibility of normative integrity, which is the precondition of legal control will be explored by observing three areas of UNSC practices in the next section.

3 Toward Normative Integrity?

3.1 *Practices I: Targeted Sanctions*

As is well known, international and domestic jurisprudences are increasingly finding the violations of human rights of persons and entities listed for targeted sanctions or invalidating or squashing the implementation measures. These cases encounter a strict normative conflict between the obligations under the UNSC resolutions on the one hand and obligations to secure the human rights of the listed individuals on the other. Questions about the normative hierarchy of maintaining international peace and security and to suppress international terrorism on the one hand and encouraging respect for human rights on the other are also frequently debated.[21]

Regarding targeted sanctions, the European Court of Human Rights (ECtHR) ruling in the case of Nada v. Switzerland is informative. The court

20 Although the term of control has various meanings and risk for confusion, I use this for some positive reasons. One is strength of the term as critical perspective. Control means the ability or power to make someone or something do what the subject of control want to. Another is the expectation for an effect of the logic. For example, 'contrôle international' often expressed as 'international supervision' in English are mainly led by international organizations and they are one of symbols for aggrandizement of international organizations. The logic functions: the more international organizations expand their powers and influence, the more they need to respect the rule of law and human rights etc. Or, the more international organizations take control against other actors such as States and individuals, the more they should be controlled.

21 See Mogami Towards, *Jus Contra Oligarchiam* (n 2) 393–394. In the same context, he states as follows: "It is not simply a matter of a conflict between EU Law and UN Law, between regional constitutionalism and 'universal' (conterminous with the UN) constitutionalism, but rather ostensibly on between human rights norms and international security norms. The Kernel agendum is what kind of norms the international legal order is called to possess in order to be a truly universal legal order, and through what process those norms would be discovered. This is what international constitutionalism, at least from the author's standpoint, intends to seek".

found that the rights of Nada, a resident of Italian enclave in Switzerland who was placed on a list for sanction, were abused.[22] The ruling represents a continuation of a series of national and international courts decisions issued in opposition to the UNSC's targeted sanctions. However, a slightly more detailed comparison with the European Court of Justice (ECJ) decisions in the cases of Kadi[23] and the Human Rights Committee (CCPR) views on Sayadi v. Belgium[24] reveals some of the differences in approach to normative conflicts. Article 103 of the UN Charter is critical in responses to allegations of human rights abuses, which can be broadly divided into dualistic and monistic types.

A dualistic approach prioritizes human rights and avoids the application of Article 103 in domestic law or in an autonomous legal order such as the EU. The ECJ's decisions in the Kadi cases and the Canadian Federal Court's decision in the case of Abdelrazik[25] took this approach. The CCPR's views in the case of Sayadi is also a dualistic one, albeit with some reservation.

A monistic approach directly takes into account the issues of Art. 103 and prioritizing the obligations to implement the UNSC resolutions. The decision of the Swiss Federal Court's decision in Nada, for example, confirms Switzerland's obligations under Articles 25 and 103 of the Charter, stating that Member States cannot circumvent obligations under UNSC resolutions because to do so would put them in a position of non-compliance with the Charter.[26] The Federal Court's judgment does not stop there, also confirming that obligations to implement UNSC resolutions can be defined by peremptory norms of general international law.[27]

On the other hand, the monistic response of the ECtHR decision, while also taking into account the requiring compliance with the obligations under

22 *Nada v Switzerland*, ECtHR (Grand Chamber), App no 10593/08, Judgment of 12 September 2012 (Nada, ECtHR).

23 Joined Cases C-402/05 P and C-415/05 P, *Case of Yassin Abdullah Kadi and Al Barakaat International Foundation v Council and Commission*, Judgment of the Court (Grand Chamber), 3 September 2008 (Kadi, ECJ).

24 *Sayadi and Vinck v Belgium*, Human Rights Committee, Comm no 1472/2006, Views of 29 December 2008 (*Sayadi*, CCPR).

25 *Abousfian Abdelrazik v the Minister of Foreign Affairs and the Attorney General of Canada*, the Supreme Court of Canada, Judgment of 4 June 2009.

26 *Nada*, ECtHR (n 22), para 46.

27 The Swiss Federal Court noted as the examples of *jus cogens* norms: the right to life, protection from torture and inhuman or degrading treatment, prohibition of slavery, prohibition of collective punishment, the principle of individual criminal responsibility and the *non-refoulement* principle. On the other hand, it stated that the enjoyment of possessions, economic freedom, the guarantees of a fair trial or the right to an effective remedy were not included in the category of *jus cogens*. Cited in ibid para 47.

Articles 25 and 103 of the Charter, nevertheless provides the Swiss government discretion in implementing UNSC resolutions. Or in other words, the logical structure of the decision determines that there is a violation of human rights obligations that can be remedied within the purview of the Swiss government. Important to this decision is what is called a human rights-compatible interpretation. This is explained as follows according to the judgment: the objectives of the UN include not only maintaining peace and security but also encouraging the promotion of respect for human rights and Article 24 (2) requires the UNSC to act in accordance with UN objectives and principles. Thus, in interpreting UNSC resolutions, it should be presumed that unless explicitly stated, the UNSC has no intent to impose obligations that undermine basic human rights principles. If ambiguity remains in the resolution, then one must choose the interpretation that is most consistent with international human rights law and that avoids conflicts of obligation.[28]

In the case of Al-Dulimi (a member of the Iraqi secret services under the regime of Saddam Hussein) and Montana Management Inc. v. Switzerland, the Second Chamber of the ECtHR applied the 'equivalent protection' test. It concluded that Switzerland could not ignore its responsibilities under the European Convention on Human Rights (the Convention), insofar as the UNSC system of blacklists and targeted sanctions failed to offer to individuals a rights protection equivalent to that provided by the Convention and determined a violation of Article 6 (1) of the Convention.[29]

The Subsequent Grand Chamber Judgment also determined a violation of Art.6 (1) on the basis that the Swiss Courts did not effectively review the listing of the applicants by the UN Sanctions Committee. However, the legal reasoning of this judgment is slightly different from that of the Second Chamber. In a nutshell, UNSC Resolution 1483 does not contain any clear or explicit wording excluding the possibility of judicial supervision of measures taken for its implementation, thereby requiring an understanding that the courts of the respondent State are authorized to exercise sufficient scrutiny in order to avoid arbitrary application. By limiting scrutiny to arbitrariness, the ECtHR was able to strike a fair balance between the obligation to ensure respect for human rights and the imperatives of the protection of international peace and

---

28 ibid para 171. See also *Al-Jedda v the United Kingdom*, ECtHR (Grand Chamber), App no 27021/08, Judgment of 7 July 2011, paras 101–102. This could be seen on the extension of 'systemic integration' which consider on 'any relevant rules of international law applicable in the relations between the parties' provided in the art 31–3 (c) of VCLT.

29 *Al-Dulimi and Montana Management Inc v Switzerland*, ECtHR (Chamber), App no 5809/08, Judgment of 26 November 2013.

security. And any inability of the listed persons to access information on the listing is capable of constituting a strong indication that the impugned measure is arbitrary, especially if the lack of access is prolonged, thus continuing to hinder any judicial scrutiny. Accordingly, any State Party whose authority gives legal effect to the addition of a person to a sanctions list, without first ensuring that the listing is not arbitrary will engage its responsibility under Article 6 of the Convention.[30] The decision effectively affirms the powers of domestic courts and the ECtHR to judicially review through the arbitrariness test. This test can be considered as the more elaborated criteria to evaluate the acts of the UNSC, enabling a harmonious interpretation.

However, in the case of targeted sanctions, such a harmonious approach seems to be unreasonable. For example, Judge Malinverni, in his concurring opinion of *Nada* case, criticized the court's decision to maintain discretion in Switzerland and while he adopts the approach taken by the Swiss Federal Court, he reaches the opposite conclusion. In other words, addressing Article 103 head on, he suggests that the UNSC resolutions are a secondary legislation, and that the obligation to respect human rights take precedence because it is directly derived from the UN Charter, the primary law.[31] In light of the prevailing view that the UN Charter does not directly oblige Member States to respect human rights, and in contrast to the fact that the fundamental rights of the EU are incorporated into the EU's primary law as a general principle of law, such an interpretation might be somewhat impossible. However, considering that the Universal Declaration of Human Rights is an important complement to the UN Charter, and that it is regarded as a legally binding document at least for the UN organs and agencies *ipso facto*, it may be worth considering.

Regardless of whether courts take a dualistic response or a monistic response, we can recognize that the UNSC and Member States are required to respect the rights of individuals based on international human rights norms.[32] On

30 *Al-Dulimi and Montana Management Inc v Switzerland*, ECtHR (Grand Chamber), App no 5809/08, Judgment of 21 June 2016, paras 145–147.

31 *Nada* ECtHR, *Concurring Opinion of Judge Malinverni*, paras 21–22. See also Bruno Simma *et al* (eds), *The Charter of the United Nations: A Commentary*, vol 2, (3rd ed, Oxford University Press 2012) 2120–2121.

32 Following the ECJ ruling on Kadi, the hearing for Kadi and Al-Balakaat was conducted, and the basis for listing by the Sanctions Committee was notified, but they were once again listed. Kadi filed a complaint again, but the General Court and the Court of Justice considered the content of the basis for listing of Kadi and determined that the grounds were insufficient and invalidated the regulation again. It can be said that the series of this case are very aggressive judgments based on the substantive and full review in the light of standards of human rights norms. Joined Cases C-584/10 P, C-593/10 P and C-595/10 P, *Case of the European Commission, the Council of the European Union and the United*

the whole, it seems that human rights protection is seen more important than terrorism prevention measures. It can also be said that obligations to protect human rights promote improvements by the UNSC itself, such as the establishment of ombudspersons. It should be noted, however, that many legal decisions and documents, including that of Nada case, have criticized the current mechanism as insufficient in the light of human rights protection and remedies for its abuse.[33] On the other hand, it remains as a matter for consideration as to whether the human rights norms on which each court relies are recognized as 'universal'. For example, the ECJ has only determined the internal legality of its rules according to the 'fundamental rights' under the EU law, while the ECtHR has found violations of the obligations of State Parties in accordance with the European Convention on Human Rights and its own case law. As is well known, any universality of national court decisions is not automatically recognized, as national courts decide cases according to a legal framework that strongly reflects their own constitutional traditions and cultures.[34]

3.2 *Practices II: International Criminal Justice*

We run now to cases related to international criminal justice. Needless to say, the UNSC has established International Criminal Tribunals for the former Yugoslavia (the ICTY) and for Rwanda (the ICTR), and has been involved in various international criminal trials from the perspective of maintaining and restoring international peace and security. As is well known, the UNSC has also referred the situation of Darfur in Sudan and of Libya to the International Criminal Court (ICC).[35] In particular, when the ICC issues arrest warrants to incumbent state leaders, such as it did for President Al-Bashir in 2009, the

---

Kingdom v Yassin Abdullah Kadi, Judgment of the Court (Grand Chamber), 18 July 2013 (*Kadi II*), paras 97–134.

33 ibid para 133. See also *United Nations Security Council and European Union blacklists*, Parliamentary Assembly of the Council of Europe, Resolution 1597 (2008) para 6, *The Sixth (final) Report of the Special Rapporteur on the promotion and protection of human rights and fundamental freedoms while countering terrorism*, UNGA, UN Doc A/65/258, 6 August 2010, paras 51–58.

34 On the other hand, the ECJ could have examined the SC sanctions in the light of human rights norms *under the UN Law* in conjunction with Art 103 of the UN Charter. In that sense, *Sayadi* Case should be more important from the perspective of international law. See Individual opinion of Committee member Mr. Yuji Iwasawa (concurring) of *Sayadi*, CCPR (n 24) 34–35.

35 As to the comprehensive review of the relationship between the UNSC and ICC and provocation for improvement within UNSC, David Kaye *et al*, *The Council and the Court: Improving UNSC Support of the international Criminal Court* (2013) 1–30, available at https://www.international.ucla.edu/media/files/The-Council-and-the-Court-ms-sz2.pdf, last visited on 28 August 2023.

UNSC must balance goals of justice, in the sense of judging serious international crimes, and peace, in the sense of ending any armed conflict. Indeed, the relationship between justice and peace is often actively debated within the UN and academia. Generally speaking, in the 1990s, the contradiction between justice and peace was emphasized, and an overall tone of prioritizing peace dominated international politics as internal conflicts erupted in many countries, particularly on the African continent. However, in recent years, effective ways of achieving peace (or reconciliation) through the realization of justice have been actively sought. Here, the relationship between the ICC, which strives to achieve justice, and the UNSC, whose mandate is to uphold peace, is hotly debated.[36] Such debates can be re-evaluated from the perspective of the normative unity. In this regard, the ICC Pre-Trial Chamber decisions on non-cooperation, not only for Sudan, but also in African Union (AU) countries such as Malawi and Chad, are informative.[37]

Regarding the relationship between justice and peace, the UNSC itself has, on various occasions, confirmed that so-called impunity or exemption from jurisdiction for state leaders is not to be granted and has urged Member States to cooperate with the ICC.[38] African Union countries, however, have relied on

---

36 Generally, Lutz Oette, 'Peace and Justice, or Neither?: The Repercussions of the al-Bashir Case for International Criminal Justice in Africa and Beyond' (2010) 8 *Journal of International Criminal Justice* 345–364, Janine Natalya Clark, 'Peace, Justice and the International Criminal Court: Limitations and Possibilities' (2011) 9 *Journal of International Criminal Justice* 521–545, James D Meernik, 'Justice, Power and Peace: Conflicting Interests and the Apprehension of ICC Suspects' Dawn L Rothe, James D Meernik and Thordis Ingadóttir (eds), *The Realities of International Criminal Justice* (Martinus Nijhoff 2013) 169–190.

37 *The Prosecutor v Omar Hassan Ahmad Al Bashir*, Corrigendum to the Decision Pursuant to art 87(7) of the Rome Statute on the Failure by the Republic of Malawi to Comply with the Cooperation Requests Issued by the Court with Respect to the Arrest and Surrender of Omar Hassan Ahmad Al Bashir, ICC-02/05-01/09, 13 December 2011.

38 For example, the presidential statement as the result of thematic debate on 'Strengthening international law: rule of law and maintenance of international peace and security' held in June 2006 emphasizes the responsibility of States to comply with their obligations to end impunity and to prosecute those responsible for the core crimes and draws attention to the full range of justice and reconciliation mechanisms to be considered, including national, international and 'mixed' criminal courts and tribunals and truth and reconciliation commissions. S/PRST/2006/28, 22 June 2006, para 4. And later, in 'Cooperation between the United Nations and regional and subregional organizations in maintaining international peace and security' held in August 2013, the presidential statement also clearly expresses its general policy as follows: 'The Security Council recalls that justice and rule of law are of key importance for promoting and maintaining peace, stability and development in the world. In this regard, the Security Council emphasizes that ending

the decisions of the AU Assembly not only to refuse cooperation with the ICC, but also to demand that the UNSC defer prosecution under Article 16 of the ICC Statute.[39] They also argue that it is not possible to waive the exemptions granted by international law for officials of countries that are non-Parties, relying on Art. 98 of the Statute.[40] Here, one can see examples of normative conflicts, such as that between the purview of an international court to criminally prosecute an individual and the immunity from jurisdiction granted to incumbent heads of state. Complicating such conflicts is the ambiguity that can be found in UN resolutions due to political considerations. For example, paragraph 2 of UNSC Resolution 1593, which referred the situation in Darfur to the ICC, on the one hand clearly states the obligations of the Sudanese government and other Parties to the conflict to cooperate, while on the other, affirms that non-Parties to the ICC have no obligations under the Statute, but rather are merely requested by regional organizations to cooperate.[41] In response, the ICC has confirmed the irrelevance of official qualifications as provided for in Article 27 of the Statute, and has given its obligation to cooperate with the ICC in light of the inapplicability of Article 98 and the referral of UNSCs under Article 13 (b).[42] Although the UNSC has to date failed to produce an effective

impunity is essential in a conflict and post-conflict society's efforts to come to terms with past serious crimes under international law, and in preventing future serious crimes under international law. In this regard, the Security Council highlights that regional and subregional organizations and arrangements can contribute to accountability through support for enhancing the capacity of national justice systems, as appropriate, and through cooperation with international mechanisms, courts and tribunals, including the International Criminal Court'. S/PRST/2013/12, 6 August 2013, para 27. Cf David P Forsythe, 'The UN Security Council and Response to Atrocities: International Criminal Law and the P-5' (2012) 34 *Human Rights Quarterly* 840–863. He properly points out that the double standard of the permanent members, especially the United States, China and Russia, for their national interests in the narrow sense and for the desire of other States to do what they do not want, have hindered the credible and consistent policy decisions of the UNSC.

39 See for example, *Decision on the Progress Report of the Commission on the Implementation of the Assembly Decisions on the International Criminal Court* (ICC), Assembly/AU/Dec.397(XVIII), 29–30 January 2012, paras 3, 7–8.

40 ibid para 6.

41 S/RES/1593, 31 March 2005, para 2: 'Decides that the Government of Sudan and all other parties to the conflict in Darfur, shall cooperate fully with and provide any necessary assistance to the Court and the Prosecutor pursuant to this resolution and, while recognizing that States not party to the Rome Statute have no obligation under the Statute, urges all States and concerned regional and other international organizations to cooperate fully'.

42 For example, the Pre-Trial Chamber of the ICC in the non-cooperation decision for Malawi (n 33) emphasised that the 'Arrest Warrant Case' in the ICJ was concerned solely with immunity across national jurisdictions, and that the ICJ's majority discussion of customary international law immunity was therefore distinct from the present circumstances,

response to such non-cooperation decisions, a normative claim by the ICC is now regarded as something that cannot be neglected, thus prompting a response of the UNSC.

From a different perspective, the decision of the Special Tribunal for Lebanon (the Tribunal) on the legality of its own establishment issued in October 2010 is also instructive. The Tribunal was established in 2005 by UNSC Resolution 1757 to prosecute the suspects of Lebanon's former prime minister's assassination. Defendants requested that the Tribunal's legality be reviewed, arguing that the manner in which the establishing Statute was made entry into force violated Lebanon's sovereignty.[43] The Tribunal was initially supposed to be established by concluding the statute between the UN and Lebanon. However, as the ratification was not possible because the Lebanese Parliament did not approve, the UNSC had adopted Resolution 1757 with the Statute as an annex.

In the decision, the First Trial Chamber rejected the claim that the Tribunal is not authorized to review actions taken by the UNSC; it affirmed that the Tribunal was purely a creation of UNSC resolution, and; found that the Statute had no provisions to authorize the Tribunal to review UNSC resolution.

as here an *international court* was seeking arrest for international crimes (para 45). And then, it referred to the finding of the Appeals Chamber of the Special Court for Sierra Leone: 'A reason for the distinction, in this regard, between national courts and international courts, though not immediately evident, would appear due to the fact that the principle that one sovereign state does not adjudicate on the conduct of another state; the principle of state immunity derives from the equality of sovereign states and therefore has no relevance to international criminal tribunals which are not organs of a state but derive their mandate from the international community' (para 46). As a result, 'the immunity of either former or sitting Heads of State can not be invoked to oppose a prosecution by an international court. This is equally applicable to former or sitting Heads of States not Parties to the Statute whenever the Court may exercise jurisdiction. In this particular case, the Chamber notes that it is exercising jurisdiction following a referral by the United Nations Security Council made under Chapter VII of the United Nations Charter, in accordance with art 13(b) of the Statute' (para 36).

Thus, the chamber concluded, based on the understanding that 'the international community's commitment to rejecting immunity in circumstances where international courts seek arrest for international crimes has reached a critical mass', that 'customary international law creates an exception to Head of State immunity when international courts seek a Head of State's arrest for the commission of international crimes and that there is no conflict between Malawi's obligations towards the Court and its obligations under customary international law; therefore, article 98(1) of the Statute does not apply' (paras 42–43). On the contrary, there are persistent opposition to this positive attitude, eg Dire Tladi, 'The ICC Decisions on Chad and Malawi: On Cooperation, Immunities, and Article 98' (2013) 11 *Journal of International Criminal Justice* 199–221.

43 José E Alvarez, '*Tadić* Revisited: The Ayyash Decisions of the Special Tribunal for Lebanon' (2013) 11 *Journal of International Criminal Justice* 291–302.

The Appeals Chamber essentially affirmed the decision of the First Trial Chamber.[44] The difference between this decision and that of the ICTY in the Tadic case and similar decisions of the ICTR is that the latter decisions actively examined the UNSC resolutions on which they established. In this regard, Judge Baragwanath in his partially dissenting opinion argued that, even without explicit provisions, the review for defendants was the tribunal's inherent power and it should have reviewed and found to be lawful.[45] This conclusion is based on the premise that if the legality of establishment by UNSC resolution is weighed against the rights of the accused, that is, the right to a fair trial, the latter should be given priority. Furthermore, it is emphasized that the right to a fair trial is the peremptory norm in the jurisprudence of the Tribunal.[46] Although whether the right to a fair trial is a peremptory norm remains controversial, the decision asserts that the Tribunal established under Chapter VII of the UN Charter also requires consideration of human rights norms. Critical to this assertion is that the legitimacy of the establishment partly depends on whether or not it violates the human rights of the defendants and if it breaches the sovereignty of s state. While Judge Baragwanath's argument is an individual opinion, it may be an important indication of an emerging mechanism for legal control based on human rights norms.

In any case, it can be pointed out that while the UNSC is actively stepping into the area of international criminal justice, its implementation has been half-hearted due to political liquidity. While no clear normative direction can be found in this area as with targeted sanctions, normative claims presented by the criminal courts do appear to send a certain signal (priority of achieving justice, human dignity and human rights norms) to the UNSC.

3.3 *Practices III: Responsibility to Protect*

The doctrine of responsibility to protect is also said to be a symbol of global constitutionalism, and it represents a shift in precedence from the right of

44 *Decision on the Defence Appeals Against the Trial Chamber's 'Decision on the Defence Challenges to the Jurisdiction and Legality of the Tribunal'*, STL-ll-OIIPT/AC/AR90.1, 24 October 2012, paras 32–54.

45 ibid, *Separated and Partially Dissenting Opinion of Judge Baragwanath*, paras 45–81.

46 ibid, para 68: 'the *jus cogens* character of fair trial, accepted by the Security Council in Article 16(2) of our Statute, must expose the Resolution, on which the existence of the Tribunal depends, to assessment of its compliance with the fundamental norms of the Purposes, Principles and Article 24(2) of the Charter. Not to do so could be seen as abdicating the judicial responsibility to ensure the 'highest standards of international criminal procedure' stipulated in Article 28(2) of the Statute'.

state sovereignty to the duty of the state.[47] Under the doctrine, states no longer have a duty to avoid third-party actions and interference, but, conversely, may in fact have a duty to act internationally. The essence of this doctrine emphasizes the dignity of individuals and protection of civilian populations. Here, the role of international organizations, including the UNSC as a representative body of the international community, comes to the fore. In other words, if the primary responsible state is unable to provide protection, the responsibility is transferred to the international community, which in today's terms has no other choice but to assume an international organization, typically the UN.

There is general agreement that the doctrine has not yet become positive international law, not least because of discrepancies about the scope of the responsibility to protect, including who perceives when and how to implement responsibilities, and prescriptive content, such as the parameter of intervention by an individual state without the authorization of the UNSC. The UNSC's contradictory responses to the situations in Libya and in Syria are often pointed to as illustrative examples of the doctrine's immaturity.[48] Even in the case of Libya, which is considered an example of the application of the concept of responsibility to protect, scepticism and criticism persist as to the ability to successfully apply the doctrine.[49]

Despite this, several interesting points emerging in the debate around the enactment of new obligations of the UNSC to intervene. For example, Peters confirms that the responsibility to protect has been established as a strong legal norm for the countries where damages actually occurs and as an 'emerging' norm for other countries and the UN. She argues that 'responsibility' in the doctrine refers to a primary, not secondary norm, and that the duty to protect as a primary norm can therefore be violated by inaction, omission, or inadequate response. She further argues that if responsibility to protect is owed to an individual, and damages occur due to insufficient action, then it follows that there is also a secondary obligation to compensate the individual.[50] In

---

47 Peters also expresses this as shift from 'non-intervention' to 'non-indifference'. Anne Peters, 'The Security Council's Responsibility to Protect' (2011) 8 *International Organizations Law Review* (2011) 15–54, 18–21.

48 This contradictory response is due to the veto system or collective security system itself. The culmination of these contradiction has led to a lively debate on the possibility of constraining veto power (the so-called illegal veto) and an attempt to relatively increase the role of the UNGA based on the 'Uniting for Peace' resolution. This is a secondary effect which the debates on the responsibility to protect have brought.

49 As the concise overviews of those practices and debates, eg Ramesh Thakur, 'R2P after Libya and Syria: Engaging Emerging Powers' (2013) 36 *The Washington Quarterly* 61–76.

50 Peters (n 47) 26–27.

this way, the UNSC and its members (especially permanent members) are held accountable to their duties. In other words, without this secondary obligation, the doctrine has little teeth.

The logic of such doctrine may be understood as follows: even though the international community is composed of states, its legal interests are no longer necessarily those of sovereign states. The international community is a 'cognitive community'[51] that has shared values and common interests, which in turn come with obligations and duties for inaction. Currently, the international community is in the process of determining whether values other than sovereign identity, such as individual dignity, are recognized by international law and if so, how they are then to be enforced. In other words, a process is underway to consider these values beyond the existing interstate framework and integrate them into international law.

If the enactment of new obligations, such as the responsibility to protect, is synonymous with a process of constitutionalization, it would seem to require a move toward normative unity. Attempts to build such a unity are ongoing. Can human rights and democratic legitimacy as universal values and interests surpass traditional national sovereignty and the principle of non-interference in internal affairs? If so, can this form a normative basis for mandating the UNSC? These are complicated questions. The doctrine of responsibility to protect is seen as part of a US-led liberal constitutionalism and carries with it the dangers of posed by interventionist and hegemonic international law.[52] There is no doubt that concerns about such dangers have hindered the doctrine from becoming established law. Both the UNSC's response to future situations and General Assembly (UNGA)'s deliberations will be strong indicators of the doctrine's prospects.[53]

51 Jure Vidmar, 'Norm Conflicts and Hierarchy in International Law: Towards a Vertical International Legal System' in de Wet and Vidmar (n 17) 13–41, 15–16.

52 Mogami, Towards *Jus Contra Oligarchiam* (n 2). This is also pointed out in relation to the practices of 'international legislation' typical of res 1373 and res 1540. Eg Daniel H Joyner, 'The Security Council as a Legal Hegemon' (2012) 43 *Georgetown Journal of International Law* 225–257.

53 On the other hand, it seems that the viewpoint of normative unity can be utilized in response to the implementation level. 'Responsibility while protecting', which is currently being discussed at the UNGA, is likely to encourage the formation of norms that must be considered in implementation, primarily in terms of protecting civilians. The main issues are the restrictions on duties and periods when permitting the use of force, the minimum and equilibrium of the use of force, and the establishment of a monitoring system by the UNSC. As can be seen from the fact that the UNSC, which dislikes restrictions, has refused to set standards for humanitarian intervention, it is undeniable that it is difficult to enact

3.4 *Towards Normative Integrity Based on International Human Rights Norms and the Principle of Subsidiarity*

3.4.1 International Human Rights Norms

Three major areas of UNSC activity have been discussed from the viewpoint of normative integration. Despite some differences, in each area, normative conflicts can be found, and in each case a search for a certain level of hierarchy seems to be directed. Indeed, there is evidence that that discussions around such a hierarchy are underway. The notion that human rights, humanitarian considerations, and individual dignity should take precedence over other norms emerges in each area. Moreover, various normative claims coalesce around human rights norms, even though the activities of the UNSC cannot be viewed with a lens of institutional unity. At a minimum, human rights are increasingly regarded as a norm that should be prioritized while maintaining international peace and security.[54]

However, the issue of whether human rights norms bind the UN in the first place, and which 'legal order' such human rights norms derived from, remains. Without delving deeply into the theoretical problems here, I offer the following observations. Based on Article 103 of the UN Charter and its public nature of collective security system, the UNSC can take certain human rights-restricting measures. However, since the objectives of the UN Charter includes respect for human rights, human rights consideration is required. On the other hand, considering that implementation of UNSC resolutions by Member States has required conformity with human rights norms, it is necessary to gradually specify what human rights norms should be considered within the framework of the UN law.

Despite the significant volume of studies accumulated, confusion regarding binding and restrictions by human rights norms also remains. At this juncture, it is useful to distinguish between 1) the 'specific contents of human rights

---

a law, but it seems likely to be established earlier as an *internal* customary law within the UN rather than the 'duty' of intervention.

54 See also Mogami Towards *Jus Contra Oligarchiam* (n 2) 389–392. It is important to consider this in the broader context of 'humanization or human rights-ization of international law', and there are many studies in Japan from this perspective. See Koji Teraya, 'Individuals-Based Constitutionalism as a Response to Fragmentation: with a Special Focus on the Relationship between International Human Rights Law and International Humanitarian Law' (2009) 28 *Yearbook of World Law* 42–76 [in Japanese]. Kimio Yakushizi, 'The Potential of International Human Rights to Develop into World Constitutinal Rights' (2010) 29 *Yearbook of World Law* 1–49 [in Japanese]. Koki Abe, 'Human Rights-ization of International Law: A Critical Analysis of the "Ethical Turn"' (2013) 111 *Journal of International Law and Diplomacy* 1–28 [in Japanese].

norms and the legal sources from which they derive' and 2) 'constraints to UN activities by human rights norms in practice'. It may be possible to aim for the convergence through the dialogue between legal orders as a process.

3.4.2 Potential of the Principle of Subsidiarity

It may be useful to explore the potential of the subsidiarity principle as another approach to realize the human rights and democratic legitimacy required by global constitutionalism in the context of the UNSC.[55] The subsidiarity principle, in its simplest sense, prioritizes decision-making at the most immediate (local) level. Therefore, if this principle functions in the UNSC, it may be possible for the body to achieve a certain degree democratic legitimacy. At a minimum, the principle may provide a practical means to establish and clarify the relationship between the UN and its Member States. Upon examining the role of the subsidiarity principle in the UNSC legislation, Tsagourias views it as 'a structural principle that sits at the intersection of United Nations' and member states' powers and informs the manner in which their respective powers should be exercised'[56] and find that Article 2 (7) of the UN Charter endorses the subsidiarity principle. Certainly, it appears that in practice domestic jurisdiction of Member States is undergoing a continuous process of reduction and that Article 2 (7) has become devoid of juridical meaning or purpose in the UN system. Tsagourias continues that while Article 2 (7) 'has place in the UN system and a role to play, what is needed is to revisit its underlying principle and its "spirit"'.[57] Originally, Article 2 (7) was introduced in order to protect the jurisdictional autonomy of Member States; its role is to regulate the exercise of jurisdictional authority by the UN and States, not to define the realm of jurisdictional authority enjoyed by both. According to the 'spirit' of the Article, the jurisdictional interaction between the UN and States is open to interpretation, relational and not fixed or organically separated, and its nature is political rather than juridical (marking a stark contrast with Article 15 (8) of the Covenant of the League of Nations). Thus, Article 2 (7) functions as a sort of filter at the intersection of UN and Member State powers in the pursuit of the common goals of peace and security.[58]

---

55 Masami Maruyama, 'The Principle of Subsidiarity in the UN Security Council: A Tentative Observation' (2018) 6 *Tokyo Review of International Law* 47–73 [in Japanese].

56 Nicholas Tsagourias, 'Security Council Legislation, Article 2(7) of the UN Charter, and the Principle of Subsidiarity' (2011) 24 *Leiden Journal of International Law* 539–559, 541.

57 ibid 549.

58 ibid 550.

Certainly, if Article 2 (7) is understood as such, it can be recognized as endorsing the subsidiarity principle. However, the degree to which the purpose is achieved is critical to the 'filter' function of the principle, particularly as 'international peace and security' is very broad and ambiguous concept and can therefore be biased in favor of the UNSC. With this in mind, it becomes even more important to envision and implement the subsidiarity principle from the perspective of human rights and democratic legitimacy.[59]

Thus, through a series of trials and errors, the following five criteria have emerged as conditions for allowing the UNSC to exercise Chapter VII powers as a result of applying the subsidiarity principle:[60] (1) the triggering situation has a transnational aspect, (2) a UNSC intervention meets the common objectives pursued by the UN and the Member States, (3) exercising Chapter VII powers can achieve the objectives more efficiently than the normal law-making process of the Member States, (4) the powers are not be used excessively in an intervening manner against the States to achieve their purpose, and (5) considerations are given to human rights and democratic legitimacy. Strictly speaking, criteria (1) to (3) are narrowly defined in terms of whether or not the powers can be exercised. On the contrary, (4) and (5) relate to *how* to exercise the powers, and therefore involve the principle of proportionality. According to the practices of the EU and ECtHR, subsidiarity and proportionality tend to be applied as a unit, and therefore criteria (4) and (5) affect not only how the powers are exercised (or, the type of measures) but also the possibility of exercise.[61] In this sense, it may be possible to consider these criteria as the subsidiarity principle in a broad sense and to position the principle as a 'filter', and as a basis for pursuing normative unity.[62]

---

59 This is inspired from Follesdal's idea on the principle of subsidiarity based on cosmopolitan normative individualism. Andreas Follesdal, 'The Principle of Subsidiarity as a Constitutional Principle in International Law' (2013) 2 *Global Constitutionalism* 37–62.

60 These five criteria are tentatively set based on the current practices of the UNSC, with reference to examples of the EU and ECtHR. Therefore, it may become a kind of tautology, but it is unavoidable to some extent in the present situation where the principle of subsidiarity in the UNSC is unclear. On the contrary, it seems that the substance and criteria of the principle will be clarified by further accumulation of studies.

61 For example, in the sense that if democratic legitimacy and protection of human rights are not properly considered, it leads to the argument that they should not be exercised as a whole.

62 In the context of the ICC, the principle of complementarity may have potential. The principle of complementarity provided in the Statute is said to be 'the solutions […], reflecting the concerns of States over national sovereignty and the potentially intrusive powers of an international institution'. John T Holmes, 'Complementarity: National Courts *versus* the ICC' in Antonio Cassese, Paola Gaeta, John R W D Jones (eds) *The Rome Statute of the International Criminal Court A Commentary*, vol I (Oxford University Press 2002) 668.

4 Towards Legal Control Mechanism?

4.1 *Judicial Control*

When discussing judicial control at the international level, it is necessary to examine the judicial review powers of the International Court of Justice (ICJ), first of all. Although the ICJ itself has clearly stated that it has no authority of judicial review, it has been recognized in previous cases that incidentally reviewing the acts of political organs is an inherent judicial function of the ICJ.[63] As a result of the Lockerbie case, the ICJ's power to review was seemingly lost, but the possibility to reassert this function remains. The ICJ's position has basically been maintained since 2003 when the Lockerbie case was removed from the Court's General List.

For example, in the case of the ICJ's advisory opinion on construction of walls in occupied Palestinian territory, it was claimed that the UNGA's request for an advisory opinion was beyond its power, based on the fact that the UNSC had long been involved in the situation in Palestine.[64] The ICJ, after confirming the precedent that 'primary responsibility' under Article 24 of the UN Charter was not an exclusive power, denied the claim based on its interpretation of Article 12 (1) and 'Uniting for Peace' Resolution 5/377 and practices of the UNGA. The ICJ also rejected the Israel's claim on the right of self-defence against terrorist attack (the UNSC Resolutions 1368 and 1373 were further grounds that the claim was justified). The ICJ, in avoiding interpretation of the resolutions, rejected Israel's claim since the construction of the wall was for neither an attack from outside the territory nor by States, it had no relevance to Article 51 of the Charter.[65] Perhaps more important than findings on the legality of the alleged acts consulted was its strong message to the UNSC that, 'especially the General Assembly and the Security Council, should consider what further

---

I wonder whether it is not possible to extend it a bit further and to guide it in considering the role of the UNSC in conducting activities related to the international criminal justice. The principle might be applied in utilization of mandatory powers for non-cooperation of each State, responsibilities of UN (or multinational forces authorized by the UNSC) and other personnel in investigating and collecting evidence, and so on. Would it be difficult to assume the principle of complementarity as the coordinating principle for balancing peace and justice in the context of the ICC and the UNSC, regional organizations, and states, including how to evaluate the decisions of regional international organizations?

63 Erika de Wet, *The Chapter VII Powers of the United Nations Security Council* (Hart 2004) 79–116.

64 *Legal Consequences of the Construction of a Wall in the Occupied Palestinian Territory*, Advisory Opinion, ICJ Report 2004, paras 26–28.

65 ibid paras 138–139.

action is required to bring to an end the illegal situation resulting from the construction of the wall and the associated regime'.[66]

The ICJ's advisory opinion on the Declaration of Independence of Kosovo, which was requested by the UNGA, not by the UNSC. The UNSC had addressed for more than a decade and had adopted resolutions under Chapter VII. A claim was raised that this UNSC's involvement was a 'compelling reason' for denying the request for an opinion, but this claim was rejected following the Wall opinion.[67] In examining whether Kosovo's Declaration of Independence conformed to international law, the ICJ confirmed that UNSC Resolution 1244 was an applicable law, considered interpretations of the resolution, and concluded that 1) the Declaration did not contradict the resolution and 2) Resolution 1244 had no bearing on Kosovo's final status.[68] While recognizing that addressees of UNSC resolutions may generally include various actors other than Member States, the ICJ found that Resolution 1244 does not include a prohibition on a declaration of independence that binds the issuer as an addressee. It therefore concluded that Kosovo's Declaration of Independence did not violate Resolution 1244.[69]

The above decisions are not exhaustive of ICJ precedents and do not overturn UNSC's resolutions. However, from these cases we can infer the ICJ stance toward the UNSC in a broad sense.[70] For example, Wellens notes that since the Lockerbie decision, the ICJ has developed its role in *harmony*, not in *concert*

---

66 ibid para 160.

67 *Accordance with international law of the unilateral declaration of independence in respect of Kosovo*, Advisory Opinion, ICJ Report 2010, paras 36–48.

68 ibid paras 94–100. In this context, the court analyses the acts of the UNSC as follows: 'contemporaneous practice of the Security Council shows that in situations where the Security Council has decided to establish restrictive conditions for the permanent status of a territory, those conditions are specified in the relevant resolution. For example, although the factual circumstances differed from the situation in Kosovo, only 19 days after the adoption of resolution 1244 (1999), the Security Council, in its resolution 1251 of 29 June 1999, reaffirmed its position that a 'Cyprus settlement must be based on a State of Cyprus with a single sovereignty and international personality and a single citizenship, with its independence and territorial integrity safeguarded' (para 11). The UNSC thus set out the specific conditions relating to the permanent status of Cyprus. By contrast, under the terms of resolution 1244 (1999) the UNSC did not reserve for itself the final determination of the situation in Kosovo and remained silent on the conditions for the final status of Kosovo'. ibid para 114. This way of presumption seems to be closely related to the human rights-compatible interpretation stated above.

69 ibid paras 115–119.

70 However, as can be seen from the debate over whether the ICJ have power of judicial review over the Lockerbie case, it should be noted that there are aspects that take the same point but reach to opposite conclusion. Eg. de Wet (n 63) 74–79.

with the UNSC, but in many cases in line with UNSC decisions. He views this as a reflection of the distinct but complementary roles of the two institutions, an illustration of the ICJ according to the will of the UNSC while clearly maintaining its own conclusions.[71] In other words, the ICJ is not purely subservient to the UNSC, and, if necessary, is able to assert its own jurisdiction against claims of invalidity or illegality, as it did, for example in the Lockerbie case. From such cases, we can see that the ICJ is in a position that reserves the right to make such assertions.[72]

Regardless of whether the decisions come from the ICJ, the ECJ, the ECtHR, or other judicial bodies such as the ICC, the effects of each decision are not legally binding for the UNSC, but rather a series of precedent that support, delegitimate, or further elucidate UNSC resolutions. These accumulated precedents are the only mechanism for invalidating or revoking a UNSC resolution, as current international law provides no other. Such decisions can be seen as an exercise of influence. While in theory the ICJ may have the power to invalidate UNSC resolutions, it rarely does so in practice. At the same time, the other regional or international judiciaries can exert substantial influence (in whether they provide a sound function or paralysis to the UNSC), providing a stark, even ironic contrast.[73] The ECJ judgments in the Kadi cases are clear illustration of this. On the whole, however, such decisions are extremely exceptional, otherwise seem to be evaluated as maintaining a humble position similar to the ICJ.

Nevertheless, it appears that a legal control mechanism through a judicial body and the underlying logic to justify it is being formed. A typical manifestation of this is the equivalent protection doctrine, which was created to guide the relationship between the ECJ and the ECtHR, but whose basic ideas apply at various levels.[74] In short, unless the UN introduces similar or equivalent

71 Karel Wellens, 'The Legal Significance Given to the Security Council in the Court's Jurisprudence since Lockerbie' (2012) 55 *Japanese Yearbook of International Law* 134–175, 175.

72 There is the analysis that in addition to the Lockerbie case, the Kosovo case was also alluring opportunity for judicial review. See James Sloan and Gleider I Hernandez, 'The Role of the International Court of Justice in the Development of the Institutional Law of the United Nations', Christian J Tams and James Sloan (eds), *The Development of International Law by the International Court of Justice* (Oxford University Press 2013) 193–235, 226.

73 On the other hands, from a different point of view, the ICJ has also begun to deal with cases directly related to human rights of individuals in the context of inter-state trials, and as a result, necessarily the domestic implementation of judgments and orders has become a specific issue as well as like in the case of the UNSC resolutions. Considering such emergence, we could see the ICJ's aggressiveness in that sense.

74 For example, Judge Malinverni in *Nada* case assert, citing one commentator, that 'for as long as the United Nations has not introduced a human rights protection mechanism

human rights protection mechanisms at the UN level, national and regional courts have powers to verify whether the implementing acts of UNSC decisions are in accordance with fundamental rights. The idea is that if the protection of those rights is inadequate or flawed in the context of the UN system, those courts should fill in any gaps in protection should there be a violation of rights.

4.2 *Non Judicial Control*

Judgments of various judicial bodies play a central role in debates around global constitutionalism. However, various legal subjects and actors other than judicial bodies can also claim a certain level of influence in restraining power by asserting their own norms or values as reflected in the grounds or rationale of their case. Indeed, some may argue that non-judicial bodies, by their acts, can have a greater influence given the realities of international politics. These include actors such as the UNGA, the Human Rights Council (HRC) and its special rapporteurs, the Secretary-General, the High Commissioner for Human Rights, the Ombudsperson, and international commissions of inquiry as overviewed in section II.[75]

Here the general role of the UNGA should be reconfirmed. At the High Level Meeting on the Rule of Law held in September 2012, the UNGA reconfirmed itself as 'the chief deliberative and representative organ of the United Nations', and expressed its will to positively contribute to 'the rule of law in all its aspects through policymaking and standard setting, and through the progressive development of international law and its codification'.[76] Active contributions to the rule of law could include the formation of legal norms that the UNSC should respect, and the Assembly could express its views in light of the conducts of the UNSC in each case. These functions seem to be more similar to the legal controls referred to in this chapter than to political controls.

With regard to targeted sanctions, the Parties in the various trials have relied on reports from the Special Rapporteur appointed by the HRC, which assert

---

… comparable or equivalent to that introduced in the Member States and at European level, the domestic and European courts remain competent to verify that acts implementing Security Council decisions respect fundamental rights'. *Nada,* ECtHR, Concurring Opinion of Judge Malinverni, para 24.

75 Although the viewpoint is slightly different from the legal control in this article, various subjects are considered from the viewpoint of realizing accountability through political and administrative control as well as judicial control in: Guglielmo Verdirame, *The UN and Human Rights: Who Guards the Guardians?* (Cambridge University Press 2011) 320–393.

76 *Declaration of the High-level Meeting of the General Assembly on the Rule of Law at the National and International Levels,* A/RES/67/1, 19 September 2012, para 27. See also paras 28 and 29.

that the measures of the UNSC are in excess of power, as well as resolutions of the Parliamentary Assembly of the Council of Europe, to present their claims.[77]

Regarding the 'international legislation' represented by Resolutions 1373 and 1540, committees and groups of experts established by the UNSC respond cautiously to the implementation aspects of these resolutions from the perspective of the rule of law and human rights, thereby contributing to increasing their legitimacy and gaining support of Member States. It can also be confirmed, though briefly, that the efforts of other UN organs such as the UNGA and the HRC (including appointed special rapporteurs), have had considerable influence in promoting improvement of implementation process.

In situations such as those in Sudan and Libya, in which activities of the International Independent Inquiry Commission, led by the HRC and the High Commissioner for Human Rights, led to the referral of events to the ICC, also imply a strengthening of legal control.[78] For example, Alston points out that the actions of the Darfur Commission, organized by the High Commissioner for Human Rights, have led to an increase in the transparency, legitimacy, and accountability of the UNSC response, although the Commission itself was established by the UNSC.[79]

Furthermore, it cannot be overlooked that the HRC activities have the effect of encouraging the UNSC to act under Chapter VII, as they implicitly and sometimes explicitly blame the UNSC for acts of omission, thus undermining its legitimacy.[80] From these and other examples we can see a pattern in which organs and actors have been able to exert some influence by expressing their views on human rights *norms* rather than by acting based on their *powers*.

On the other hand, caution should be noted when considering decisions made by political and/or regional organizations. For example, the AU has demonstrated the significance of its role in various international incidents.[81]

---

77 See (n 33).

78 Eg Micaela Frulli, 'Fact-Finding or Paving the Road to Criminal Justice?: Some Reflections on United Nations Commissions of Inquiry' (2012) 10 *Journal of International Criminal Justice* 1323–1338.

79 Philip Alston, 'The Darfur Commission as a Model for Future responses to Crisis Situations' (2005) *Journal of International Criminal Justice* 600–607, 607.

80 A series of actions by the HRC and the UNGA in Libya and Syria, more recently North Korea and Myanmar etc., where there are grave breaches of human rights obligations could pave a way to enforcement functions by the UNSC. The point is to positively mobilize these actions in a meaningful way.

81 Eg Eki Y Omorogbe, 'The African Union, Responsibility to Protect and the Libyan Crisis' (2012) 59 *Netherlands International Law Review* 141–163. Theresa Reinold, 'Constitutionalization? Whose Constitutionalization?: Africa's Ambivalent Engagement

However, although States dealing with non-cooperation decisions by the ICC rely primarily on the decisions of the AU, the legality and legitimacy of each decision needs to be considered separately.[82]

On the whole, various claims, reports, and resolutions may have *de facto* effect, or at a minimum send a signal to the UNSC. From the perspective of normative integrity, however, the specific content of legal claims is most important. In other words, whether such claims can pressure the UNSC depends on the persuasiveness of the content in terms of the human rights and interests of individuals rather than those of States. In addition, as is evident in the context of the responsibility to protect (in the case of Libya and Syria), there is a role for non-judicial control actors to evaluate UNSC actions from the perspective of human rights norms. It should be reiterated that not only do such evaluations encourage the UNSC to intervene, but they also promote, and to some degree help advance, normative unity.

In any case, the importance of judicial institutions to global constitutionalism is not always aligned with the current state of the international community, and is often omitted from consideration. International relations are too complicated to enable simple resolutions of the seemingly confrontational relationship between political bodies, the UNSC, and judicial organs, which are supposed to promote constitutionalism. Moreover, even judicial bodies have no clear judicial review powers in relation to the UNSC. In such a situation, it would be more constructive to seek more flexibility in legal control mechanisms, including in the role of non-judicial actors (focusing on the functions they perform, not the nature of the institution). Nevertheless, global constitutionalism remains challenged by how to theorize influential decisions and normative claims. The most obvious example of this challenge is 'the right of last resort' of Member States.

---

with the International Criminal Court' (2012) 10–4 *International Journal of Constitutional Law* 1076–1105.

82 The AU's insistences might be summarized as follows: the Rome Statute, which allows jurisdictions to the citizens of non-parties, is inconsistent with the VCLT; the exemption is applicable under art 98 of the Statute (as argued above); only African nations are subject to prosecution; the Security Council has the discretion to prevent prosecution pursuant to art 16 of the Statute, but has not exercised it; the Prosecutor has the discretion not to conduct an investigation that does not contribute to the 'interest of justice', but has not exercised it. I cannot afford to go into detail here, but they all seem to be legally lacking the foundation. See Simon M. Weldehaimanot, 'Arresting Al-Bashir: The African Union's Opposition and Legalities' (2011) 19 *African Journal of International and Comparative Law* 208–235, 225–233. In successive years, the AU has often requested that the Member States of AU to submit the proposal for the UNSC to defer the prosecution based on art 16.

4.3 *'The Right of Last Resort'*

It goes without saying that effective function of the UNSC ultimately depends on the implementation by the Member States, and the most effective control on the UNSC is a refusal to comply (with UNSC decisions) by Member States. Global constitutionalism can be thought of as a position that seeks legally persuasive grounds in permitting such refusals.

Tzanakopoulos a leading scholar in this field, asserts that because there is no final review mechanism by a third party, there is no system to invalidate UNSC resolutions. He adds, however, that disobedience based on the system of international responsibility in the decentralized international community (such as through countermeasures, as illegality by non-compliance of resolutions is precluded), can occur.[83] In such cases, the resolution itself is not invalid under the UN law. Although this needs more careful examination, it is worth considering whether disobedience as a countermeasure under general international law is legally possible. On the one hand, the right of Member States will not be recognized because each Member State cannot invalidate UNSC Resolutions, and on the other hand, countermeasures based on a decision of each Member State will be permitted. What must not to be forgotten is that Tzanakopoulos argument does not to encourage Member States to disobey UNSC resolutions, but rather it attempts to establish legal consequences for such a disobedience.

From a slightly different perspective, Hamamoto in observing Member State actions to date, confirms that while many actions support the recognition that each country has the right (pouvoir) to refuse implementation, it is incorrect to refer to it as a 'right'.[84] He argues that refusal of implementation by a Member State is instead a 'unilateral claim (prétention unilatérale)' that the resolution presumed to be valid is invalid. The rationale for admitting the rights of the Member States are that (1) the powers of an international organization are based on an *acte constitutif*, which is an international treaty, (2) the treaty is an agreement of the Parties' will, therefore the powers of the international organization shall also be based on the agreement, and (3) the wills of Member States can only be interpreted by the Member States themselves, so that the scope of powers of the international organization may also be determined by each Member State. Regarding (3), he raises logical deficiencies from the viewpoint that the 'self-interpretation' of the constituent document of an

83 Antonios Tzanakopoulos, *Disobeying the Security Council Countermeasures against Wrongful Sanctions* (Oxford University Press 2011) 154–200.

84 Shotaro Hamamoto, 'Le «pouvoir» de dernier mot Des limites de la présomption de validité des actes des organisations internationales' (2004) 38 *Kobe University Law Review* 21–44.

international organization cannot have objective value.[85] More fundamentally, it seems that the subjective nature of the current international legal order, in which there is no final review body, is the basis for denying the 'right' of last resort.[86] Significantly, Hamamoto notes that although considering the refusal of a Member State to implement a UNSC decision as a one-sided claim and not as a right, is political rather than legal, it nonetheless fulfils a role in that it can lead to the initiation of a 'dialogue' in the legal sphere.[87]

Scholars are divided among those claiming the existence of an objective international law (right) and those insisting on the subjectivity of international law (unilateral claim). It is necessary to consciously consider which position an author takes. For example, de Wet and others, who represent global constitutionalists, presuppose the objectivity of international law.[88] However, as we have already discussed, in order to build a power restraining mechanism while aiming for normative unity, it is necessary to pursue objectivity while taking a pluralist position. From such a standpoint, should we admit the rights of Member States provided that there are legal findings of national or regional courts or decisions of the political organs of regional international organizations, and that they are fully persuasive from the perspective of normative integrity? There may be situations in which the 'rights' of Member States are gradually recognized as rights through 'dialogues' or 'resistance' between the UNSC and various control entities, or between control entities.[89] Can we expect a steady normative convergence based on the requirements of global constitutionalism? Is it too early to determine whether such a multi-layered legal control mechanism is progressively but definitely being formalized?

5 Conclusion

This chapter presented legal control as a concept that operationalize the (critical) global constitutionalism by examining three areas of UNSC activity. The formation of normative unity relies predominantly on normative claims made

85 ibid 39–40.

86 ibid 41.

87 ibid 41–43.

88 Erika de Wet, 'International Constitutional Order' (2006) 55 *International and Comparative Law Quarterly* 51–76.

89 This is one of the important points expressed by prof. Mogami as the perception of *heterarchy*. See the articles by Mogami (n 2).

by various actors based on human rights norms in a broad sense. These claims are often presented as an antithesis or challenge to existing UNSC resolutions.

Thus, the implications and significance for the constitutionalization of international law derived in this way can ultimately be summarized in terms of the importance of human rights norms and the legal position of individuals within the functions of the UNSC.[90] This raises a range of theoretical as well as practical issues, including legal consequences of the addressee of the UNSC resolution being an individual, the direct applicability of such resolutions in domestic jurisdiction, the possibility of remedy, and the democratic legitimacy of the UNSC, not to mention the participation in and transparency of the UN system. Constitutionalization and constitutionalism is positioned as a mindset[91] and cognitive framework to address such issues.

Unfortunately, in terms of legal control as an operationalized concept, a mechanism of power constraint that simultaneously pursues normative unity has yet to be established. In that sense, we cannot conclude that the constitutionalization described in this chapter has been realized. Nevertheless, in evaluating various phenomena, the direction toward normative integration and legal control mechanism seems to be gradually emerged. The seeming inconsistency of normative unity and the constraint of power may be a feature of the process of developing global constitutionalism (or, the constitutionalization of international law) in the context of the UNSC. In this regard, this chapter suggests that normative assertions that encompass the entire international community could have the potential to constrain the power of the UNSC.

In addition, the UNSC itself has repeatedly stated (specifically at the general meetings on the rule of law) that it will respect the rule of law.[92] The UNGA has also declared the importance of carrying out activities based on international law and is trying to exert some control over the UNSC. The declaration confirms that human rights, the rule of law, and democracy are interconnected and mutually reinforcing, and that they can be considered universal

90 Peters examines individuals as a member of 'the Global Constitutional Community' and the recent expansion of international human rights as a manifestation of the constitutionalization of international law. Peters, (n 10) 157–179.

91 Martti Koskenniemi, 'Constitutionalism as Mindset: Reflections on Kantian Themes about International Law and Globalization' (2007) 8 *Theoretical Inquiries in Law* 9–36.

92 See for example, thematic debate on 'the strengthening of international law' held in June 2006 already introduced (n 38), and *The Promotion and Strengthening of the Rule of Law in the Maintenance of International Peace and Security*, S/PRST/2012/1, 19 January 2012, see in particular paras 2 and 15.

and inseparable core values (that may form the basis of a normative unity).[93] Although the term of constitutionalism is not directly used, including in the Secretary-General's report on the rule of law prepared for the high-level meeting,[94] those can be seen as a move towards constitutionalization in practice. International law scholars have an important role to play in organically linking such movements in practice with the formation of a cognitive framework such as global constitutionalism.

The formation of a *normative* multilateralism, a concept that Mogami enthusiastically worked on,[95] has become increasingly important in the face of recent crises of multilateralism. It is hard to imagine that the necessity of international organizations, particularly normative ones that Mogami emphasized, will disappear. Certainly, in the face of Russia's aggression of Ukraine, we can't help but envision a setback in multilateralism, even if not demise of it. Each practice examined above has carried various changing (not necessarily new) aspects to be debated. Targeted sanctions are increasingly imposed by a single group of states, not by the UNSC, raising questions on the legality and legitimacy of such measures. The possibility of the ICC collaborating with the UNSC to achieve justice, especially in accordance with Article 13(c) of the ICC Statute, is becoming increasingly remote. Similarly, implementation of R2P by the UNSC will also be hampered by disagreements among P5. In these situations, will main focus of critical constitutionalism be shifted again into *jus contra anarchiam*?[96] The answer may be partly yes, but there seems to be no option to abandon multilateralism, even if it is imperfect, for humankind in the 21st century. In order to recover and advance multilateralism, it is essential to promote the discussion on the legal control as *jus contra oligarchiam*. We must inherit and further his great works.

---

93 *Declaration of the High-level Meeting of the General Assembly on the Rule of Law at the National and International Levels*, A/RES/67/1, 19 September 2012, paras 1–2 and 5.

94 *Delivering justice: programme of action to strengthen the rule of law at the national and international levels*, A/66/749, 16 March 2012. This resolution defines the rule of law as 'a principle of governance in which all persons, institutions and entities, public and private, including the State itself, are accountable to laws that are publicly promulgated, equally enforced and independently adjudicated, and which are consistent with international human rights norms and standards. It requires, as well, measures to ensure adherence to the principles of supremacy of law, equality before the law, accountability to the law, fairness in the application of the law, separation of powers, participation in decision making, legal certainty, avoidance of arbitrariness and procedural and legal transparency' (para 2). This statement should not be overlooked since expressed as the consensus in the international community and starting point for every activities within and outside the UN.

95 Mogami, *Perpetuum Mobile* (n 2) 51–54.

96 Mogami, *Jus Contra Oligarchiam* (n 2) 380–384.

PART 5

Constructive Resistance in International Law by Sovereign States?

CHAPTER 9

The United Nations and the Big Powers at a Time of 'Patriotic Unilateralism' and 'Global Governance'

Tetsuya Yamada

1 Introduction

The Russian invasion of Ukraine on 24 February 2022 was an outrage that negated the régime under the UN Charter. At the time of writing, the armed conflict is still ongoing and the future is uncertain. On the other hand, the relationship between international organisations and major powers, and in particular between the UN and major powers, has been the subject of much debate. In many cases, international organisations are established at the initiative of major powers. On the other hand, major powers can complete their foreign policy without international organisations. For this reason, major powers have often ignored international organisations. In many cases, the policy of disregard for the UN by the US has been criticised, but this time it was Russia, the successor to the former Soviet Union, which was a major power when the UN was established, that trampled on the basic principles of the UN Charter. With this in mind, I would like to reflect once again on the relationship between the UN and the major powers.

Of special interest is the current tendency for politicians as well as academics to talk about 'Patriotic Unilateralism' on the one hand and about 'Global Governance' on the other. Clearly, these two phrases suggest totally different directions and policy preferences. The latter implies building a world based on multilateral cooperation where actors include international organizations, non-governmental organizations (NGOs), multi-national companies, sovereign states, and individual persons. Global Governance is a way of thinking which has great affinity with international organizations like the UN. However, 'Patriotic Unilateralism', especially unilateral behavior of the Big Powers, undermines the raison d'être of international organizations. In fact, under the Trump administration, the United States made public that it would withdraw from the Universal Postal Union (UPU) and the World Health Organization (WHO). Also, it stopped participating in meetings of the UN Human Rights Council. These actions could be understood as a challenge to the UN system as a whole. The withdrawal of the United Kingdom (UK) from the European

 | DOI:10.1163/9789004681477_011

Union (EU) in the so-called Brexit, could be also motivated by the its unilateral preference. Even among the EU members, xenophobic policies were deployed against asylum seekers from the Middle East, mostly from Syria and Libya. Japan also withdrew from the International Whaling Treaty in order to protect its whaling industry, bucking the international trend of conservation of whales from environmental points of view.

This chapter focuses on the current situation where several Big Powers are showing attitudes of what could be called 'Anti-' or 'Non-multilateralism'. The possible resulting influence of this on the UN will be made clear. This explanation would make it possible to predict the future of other international organizations as well as the world order. In addition, such an explanation leads to a reconsideration of the significance of Global Governance, both as a theory and as a practice. However, we must keep in mind that this is not the first time the UN has had its *raison d'être* questioned. Clearly, except for some peacekeeping operation (PKOs), the Cold War made the UN virtually unworkable until 1989. Also, at the time of the US and UK attack against Iraq in 2003, the suggested measures needed to be taken by the Security Council (SC) were ignored. And there is no doubt that Russia's aggression in Ukraine also tramples on the UN Charter in various aspects. By looking at these examples, we can find that the history of the UN is that of a tense relationship with the Big Powers. This chapter could also be regarded as a search for a possible answer to the problem that the historian Mark Mazower has raised in his book on the topic. In the very final paragraph of the Introduction, he stated:

> Anticolonialism and antiracism quickly lost their radical edge once states won independence – at that point they often turned into defenders of the status quo and the Indian government was to resist UN intervention in its internal affairs as strongly as the South Africans had done earlier. The UN expanded further and more rapidly than its founders had thought possible. But it remained suspended between its twin function as great power talking shop and supporter of national self-determination across the world. What had started out as a mechanism for defending and adapting empire in an increasingly nationalist age has turned into a global club of national states, devoid of any substantial strategic purpose beyond the almost forgotten one of preventing another world war. Freezing intact the power configuration at the end of the last one, it looks – so far in vain – for a political raison d'être more suited to the needs of the present.[1]

1 Mark Mazower, *No Enchanted Palace: The End of Empire and the Ideological Origins of the United Nations* (Princeton University Press 2009) 27.

What Mazower wrote gains great importance and meaningful significance in light of the current rivalries between the Big Powers.

2 Big Powers Politics and the International Order

2.1 *The UN in History*

The UN does not exist independently from history. As Toshiki Mogami pointed out in his book, *International Organization,*[2] the view that the Concert of Europe was the precursor of the international organization and could be considered as the first international organization has been well recognized. However, the Concert of Europe has also been criticized because it was based on a balance of power among the Big Powers and it did not hesitate to suppress the middle and small powers. Also, this agreement among the Big Powers has come to be understood as a system of suppression of the liberal and/or national movement. However, this common view of history studies can be paradoxically understood that there is a mutual relationship between the establishment of any international organization and the very existence of the Big Powers. The Big Powers would, undoubtedly, try to keep their advantageous positions against the middle and small powers. In theory, according to Hiroshi Nakanishi, the image of international politics which urged international society to be organized is the System of Sovereign States.[3] What is important here is the fact that, in addition to the 18th century balance of power system, states learned to settle their disputes through congresses or conferences during a time of peace.

Additionally, in the 19th century, international society invented the so-called international administrative unions in various technical, social, and administrative fields which further influenced international organizations. Moreover, two peace conferences in the Hague are also regarded as roots of the emergence of the League of Nations (LN). The Hague Conferences, held in 1899 and in 1907, have contributed to the expansion of international society because the conferences invited various countries outside of Europe like China, Japan, and Latin American countries.

---

2 Toshiki Mogami, *Kokusai-kiko-ron Kogi* [*Lecture on International Organisation*] (Iwanami Shoten 2016) 26–30 [in Japanese].

3 Hiroshi Nakanishi, *What Is International Politics?: Human Beings and Order in Global Civil Society* (Chuokoron Shinsya 2003) 21–22 [in Japanese].

It is clear from the detailed studies of Yuichi Hosoya, an expert on diplomatic history, the Concert of Europe played the role of predecessor to the foundation of the LN.[4]

According to Hosoya, Charles Webster, historian and diplomat, was commissioned by the UK government to provide a plan for post-world war international order and Webster tried to find answers from the Concert system. Therefore, it would be fair to say that both in academic history and in practice there were clear and strong ties with both Big Power relations and politics and the establishment of the LN.

Then, what is the relation between the LN and the UN? As far as academic history in Japan is concerned, there has seemed to exist a tacit understanding that emphasizing the rupture between the two organizations would guarantee the legitimacy of the UN.[5] However, such an understanding has been reconsidered in Japan in various studies of international organizations. In those studies, the authors tend to focus on and emphasize the historical, material, and human continuity between the two organizations. In addition, the parents of the UN, as an international organization, are apparently the group of several nations, namely, the UK, US, and Soviet Union. These countries planned to establish the UN in order to overcome the 'failure' of the LN. To be sure, the two organizations were totally different, both in their functions and in their organizational structures. But these differences were based on the experience of the LN; the UN was not born from nothing. Therefore, it should be noted that at the core of the idea of the establishment of the UN, this very intention of the three Big Powers did play an important role. If this interpretation is correct, the question inherent in 'The UN and the Politics of the Big Powers' would become significant as a part of the bigger question involved in 'International Organizations and the Politics of the Big Powers'.

2.2 *The Question 'the UN and Big Powers Politics' Matters*

According to Thomas Weiss and others, the UN has three 'faces'.[6] According to them, '[t]he first UN is an institutional framework of member states that bring their different aspirations, values, ideologies, and capability to the table'. This

---

4 Yuichi Hosoya, 'The Design of the Establishment of the United Nations: Charles Webster and his Idea on the World Order' (2011) 84 *The Study of Law (Keio University)* 91–128, 94 [in Japanese].

5 Shunsuke Obiya, *The League of Nations: Its Universality and Regionality* (University of Tokyo Press 2019) 1 [in Japanese].

6 Thomas G Weiss, David P Forsythe, Roger A,Coate and Kelly-Kate Pease, *The United Nations and Changing World Politics* (8th ed, Westview Press) 2–6.

means that the UN is a forum to discuss among the member states the various matters of concern. In this 'first' UN, how each Big Power tries to maximize its state's interests as far as possible would matter and its goal is to 'utilize' the UN for this purpose.

On the other hand, even under the System of Sovereign States, there are various common interests among states. In order to pursue such interests, all the states, including the Big Powers, try to cooperate with the UN apart from their own interests. This situation may be understood as the 'International Community' rather than the 'International Society' in the sense that the common values are shared among states. Under this circumstance, the roles of the 'second' and the 'third' UN may become more important. Again according to Weiss and others, the 'second' UN, which means the body of the international civil service headed by the Secretary-General, 'is an important actor in its own right because the UN bureaucracy provides expertise, knowledge, and independent diplomatic skills'.[7] Moreover, the 'third' UN, composed of the network of NGOs, independent experts, corporate executives, media representatives, and academics, may 'work closely with the first and second UN'.[8] The 'second' UN does not only support the 'first' UN administratively, but also works independently under the theory of 'principal-agent relationship'[9] with its own knowledge and experience. Protecting refugees, development assistance, and various peace operations are listed as examples. Through the activities on the ground by the agents (the UN and its subsidiary organs), their organizational memories and experiences may provide feedback to their principal (in this case, all the member states in a collective sense). This may cause a change in the principal's understanding of the existing norms and may lead to the change of, or even the establishment of norms. Therefore, at the analytical level, the System of Sovereign States and the International Community are neither completely separated nor exist independently. Rather, both are mutual influences at the norm level thanks to the existence of the 'second' and the 'third' UN. This means that each Big Power, as well as each state, always chooses its policies and actions in the balance by weighing its own interests and the common interests of the whole world. In general, it could be said that a state will cooperate with or utilize the UN when the state's interest matches with the common interests.

7 ibid 4.

8 ibid 5.

9 For the deeper understanding of this theory, see, for example, Darren G Hawkins, David L Nielson and Michael J Tierney (eds), *Delegation and Agency in International Organizations* (Cambridge University Press 2006).

However, on the other side, 'Patriotic Unilateralism' can be understood as the situation in which a particular state wants to maximize its own domestic interest while turning its back on the common interest of the international community. UN studies have tended unconsciously to fix their eyes on the roles of the 'second' and the 'third' UN which work for the realization of the 'ideal' international community which is emphasized in the charter of the UN, mainly in Article 2. In this tradition, the policies and actions of any member state which are contrary to the realization of common interests were the targets of criticism. At the same time, the view focusing on the balance or relationship between state interest and the cooperation to the UN was treated very lightly. Therefore, it can be said that the spread of 'Patriotic Unilateralism' poses questions on 'what the UN really is' and 'why a state cooperates with the UN or not'. In this light, Russia's actions defy the pledge agreed in 1945 not to change the territorial *status quo* by military force, and Putin's decision is the ultimate of Patriotic Unilateralism in the worst and most inhumane manner.

3 About the Universality of the UN

3.1 *Geographical Universality*

Without doubt the world regards the UN as a 'universal' international organization. As the author has already stated, the 'first' UN is a forum of the member states, each having different aspirations, values, ideologies, and capabilities. Under these circumstances, we cannot expect a sort of harmony of interests in a cooperative manner and atmosphere among the member states in discussions. It also means that whether the sharing of values or norms through negotiation can be achieved or not is uncertain and unforeseeable. It is certain that geographical universality does not guarantee harmony of interests among the member states at all.

3.2 *Realization of Universal Value*

On the other hand, each international organization has its own objectives to achieve (functionality). In the case of the UN, Article 1 of its charter provides four purposes. Article 2 provides principles to be observed both by the UN and by the member states in pursuit of the purposes stated in Article 1.

The first purpose of the UN is 'to maintain international peace and security'. Though the LN clearly failed in this field, international society again wanted to establish a new international peace organization whose main effort is to build so-called collective security. Attention should be paid to the main reason of the failure of the LN in collective security which was that it was a system led by the then Big Powers. On this point, the UN Security Council (SC) was given greater prominence than that of the LN Council. Furthermore, under Article 43, a so-called 'UN Force' was planned, which could be regarded as ambitious and innovative. Also, the UN charter stated that member states must accept decisions made by the SC as an international legal obligation under Article 25. Also, Article 2, Paragraph 6 even requires that '[t]he Organization shall ensure that states which are *not Members* of the United Nations act in accordance with these Principles so far as may be necessary for the maintenance of international peace and security' (italics added). Compared with the LN, the UN, or its collective security system, was given far stronger power.

In addition, the respect of basic human rights and self-determination of people and socio-economic cooperation among the member states were added to the purpose of the UN. Toshiya Hoshino once pointed out that the UN tried to achieve not only a 'passive' peace but also a 'positive' peace from the beginning.[10] Though the Covenant of the LN did not set similar objectives, the LN later came to recognize the importance of socio-economic cooperation and for that purpose the so-called Bruce Report recommended the establishment of a special Committee in 1939. But it failed simply because of the German aggression against Poland some months after the publication of the report. This fact clearly shows that the UN was established in an innovative and creative manner.

On the other hand, the UN Charter is at the same time conservative and seeking status quo in the sense that the sovereign equality principle remained (Article 2, Paragraph 1) and the UN has no power to intervene in matters essentially within domestic jurisdiction (Article 2, Paragraph 7). In sum, the UN was founded with two different characters; innovative and creative on one hand and based on the traditional view of international order on the other.

4 'Patriotic Unilateralism' and Order

4.1 *Structural Background of 'Patriotic Unilateralism'*

According to Sakai and others, structural background which brought about 'patriotic unilateralism' is the very character of the modern international order in the sense both of the sovereign state system and of the international community. In other words, we should understand that international order and

10 Toshiya Hoshino, 'International Organization' in Akio Watanabe and Jitsuo Tsuchiyama (eds), *Global Governance* (University of Tokyo Press 2001) pp 182 (fig 7–2) [in Japanese].

the rule of international law are the normative reflection of such order as an expression of a real power relationship at the time of its establishment. At the same time, states could protest the existing order or the existing rules for the purpose of adjusting to reflect the interest of states in accordance with the change of political, economic, and military relations.[11] This is not an odd situation because in international society, there is no single legislature and it is quite difficult to change treaty provisions in accordance with the change of time and circumstances. This causes a withdrawal from a particular treaty or the creation of a new treaty or régime in order to maintain the state's own interest.

The Russian amendment of its Constitutional Law in July 2020 was the most excessive example and this was also a legal foreshadowing of the current invasion. The old Constitutional Law provided that, under Article 17, Russia 'observes the norms of international law'. However, the amended version provides that no international law, treaty, or decision of international organizations will restrict the rights and freedoms of Russian nationals, and that such things are valid only when they are in conformity with the Russian Constitutional Law. As Russia is a party of the Vienna Convention of the Law of Treaties, it must observe its provisions, *inter alia*, Article 27 providing '[a] party may not invoke the provisions of its internal law as justification for its failure to perform a treaty'. This amendment would cause a dramatic increase of international legal disputes with Russia over the interpretation and application of various treaties. In addition, Russia has not accepted the compulsory jurisdiction of the International Court of Justice (ICJ). Therefore, the parties of treaties with Russia would face extreme difficulties when attempting to solve legal disputes. The Russian case may be an exception; however, it could be concluded that the international order, which is also provided by international organizations, namely the UN, is challenged and may need to be changed or amended by 'Patriotic Unilateralism' of Big Powers.

As was mentioned in the introduction, the US and UK attack against Iraq was also a 'violation of international law' and 'the negligence of the UN's role of the maintenance of international peace and security', which provoked many international legal debates and a discussion about the relationship between the UN and the Big Powers. Also, in the General Debate of the UN General Assembly, then-President Trump made a speech and pointed out that the UN had become already 'out of date'. It is uncertain on which points Trump

11 Hironobu Sakai, Tadashi Mori and Yumi Nishimura, 'Patriotic Unilateralism and International Order: Introduction' (2019) 30 *Ronkyu Jurist* 4–6, 4 [in Japanese].

regarded the UN as 'out of date'. Still, it is quite easy to understand that Trump felt hostility toward multilateralism. However, the situation in 2003 was totally different. In 2003, the US attended the SC debate to assert its 'legality' of the attack by explaining that Iraq was developing and hiding weapons of mass destruction. This might be 'rough legalization', as Mogami has put it;[12] still, at least the US tried to explain that its attack was 'not illegal'. Putin also called the invasion a 'special military operation' and claimed that it was an exercise of the right to self-defense under Article 51 of the UN Charter. This was another rough legal justification. However, in a series of speeches, Putin has tried to dodge accusations by the US and the UK with the legal arguments surrounding the NATO bombing of Kosovo in 1999 in mind. While that argument is still rough and erroneous, it must be borne in mind that the bombing of Kosovo, which was assessed as 'illegal but legitimate' and with many legal grey areas, is a 'bad precedent' that led to the current aggression.

On the contrary, what should be mentioned as remarkable is that the current 'patriotic unilateralism' is a clear violation of rules of international law or the withdrawals from existing international organizations and régimes.

4.2 *China as a New Big Power: Its Possible Impact on Multilateralism*

It is well known that China (the People's Republic of China or PRC) is adopting its own unique diplomatic policy represented by the Belt and Road Initiative (BRI). Also, China established the Asian Infrastructure Investment Bank (AIIB) in 2013, which is regarded as a rival to the existing Asian Development Bank (ADB). In addition, at the very beginning of the spread of COVID-19, the World Health Organization (WHO), especially its Director-General Dr. Tedros Adhanom Ghebreyesus, was criticized alleging that WHO and Ghebreyesus had been influenced too much by China. That begs the question: What is the Chinese view on the UN and the UN system as a whole?

Contrary to our general expectation, Xi Jinping and his administration have attached great importance to the UN system in their diplomatic policies.[13] Although the details and possible impacts will be touched upon later, it could be pointed out here that it has not been well known that historically China has put emphasis on multilateral diplomacy.[14] Even in the era of the Qing

12 Toshiki Mogami, *The United Nations and the United States* (Iwanami Syoten 2005) 13 [in Japanese].

13 Shin Kawashima, 'The Xi Jinping Administration's View of the International Order' (2019) 1 *Security Studies* 13–26, 13 [in Japanese].

14 Due to the author's linguistical limitation, this part relies on Shin Kawashima, 'The Long-term Target on Chinese Diplomatic History to Enhance Its International Status on Hague

Dynasty, China sent a delegation to the Hague Peace Conferences. Also, after the Xinhai Revolution, China, then known as the Republic of China, became a member state of the LN. However, partly because its government in Beijing had not being founded strong and effective enough, there had been questions and doubts of who or which governments represented China. Nevertheless, at the time of the Manchurian Incident in 1931, China referred the case to the LN Council, under Article 11 of the LN Covenant, in order to settle it through its multilateral mechanism.

At the time of the establishment of the UN, under Article 23, Paragraph 1, China became an original member state as the Republic of China. However, after the establishment of the PRC, the question of the right of representation had arisen again. At last, in 1971, the General Assembly (GA) decided to invite PRC as a legitimate representative of China. Since then, China, represented as PRC, has kept its permanent seat at the SC. However, when the right of representation took place, PRC was not considered a Big Power. In reality, the PRC itself was economically poor and underdeveloped. Therefore, the PRC behaved as 'the biggest developing country' and as the representative and 'leader of the developing world'.

However, thanks to its dramatic economic growth, China has become the second largest economy in the world and as a result it is also the second largest financial contributor to the UN. According to Shin Kawashima, the Xi Administration, from the beginning, has recognized the importance of the UN since Xi became the leader in 2012.[15] Especially after 2016, China came to distinguish between the existing 'world order' and the 'international order' which China aimed to realize. In Chinese understanding, world order is a synonym for Pax Americana which is backed by the US and Western values and military power. However, the international order, which China seeks, is the order led by the UN 'with the various principles of international law' and these two orders are distinguishable.[16] Then, what are the contents or reality of the UN 'with the various principles of international law'? As has been stated above, the UN Charter contains both innovative and progressive aspects, like the strengthened mechanism of collective security, the respect of basic human rights and self-determination, and socio-economic development, and also contains conservative aspects like sovereign equality and non-intervention in domestic jurisdictions. The Xi administration made public its desire to replace

Peace Conference, the League of Nations and the United Nations' (2006) 145 *International Relations* 17–35 [in Japanese].

15 Shin Kawashima, 'The Xi Jinping Administration's View' (n 13), especially 18.

16 ibid 20–21.

the 1954 Five Principles of Peaceful Coexistence between China and India and the principle of non-intervention with a policy of domestic jurisdiction as the Chinese traditional principles of its diplomacy since the days of Zhou En-lai's administration.[17] Therefore, it should be clear that the UN 'with the various principles of international law' means that the UN should be based more upon those conservative norms. If so, no one can expect that China, within the UN system, will take the lead in innovative and progressive fields of activities. Rather, China will keep its position friendly to the developing states in order to maintain its influence on them.[18] The Chinese attitude is different from the 'Patriotic Unilateralism' with xenophobia, which can be observed in the position of the US and in some European states in their refugee policies. However, the Chinese diplomacy towards the UN would also undermine the UN's innovative and progressive aspects. In this sense, China is also poisoned by 'Patriotic Unilateralism' and 'Anti-/Non- multilateralism'.

5 Conclusion

There are multiple answers to the question of why we need to study international organizations, including the UN. Here, provisionally, let us understand that the purpose of this study 'is to seek what kind of norm structure would be preferable in order to manage this world in a way that observes norm and peaceful manner, instead of being managed unilaterally or violently'.[19] If this definition is appropriate, it becomes clear that the prevailing 'Patriotic Unilateralism' does not stand together with international organizations.

On the contrary, as was stated at the beginning of this chapter, the expression 'Global Governance' is frequently used when we talk about current international relations. Global Governance was defined as follows in the final report of the Commission on Global Governance.

> Governance is the sum of the many ways individuals and institutions, public and private, manage their common affairs. It is a continuing process through which conflicting or diverse interests may be accommodated

17 ibid 17.

18 For example, Xi visited Myanmar and proposed to extend economic cooperation based upon its BRI. At the same time, he expressed his support for the Myanmar Government's policy to settle the Rohingya issue through its internal procedure and process. (The Yomiuri Shinbun, 19 January 2020 [in Japanese]).

19 Mogami (n 2) 9.

> and co-operative action may be taken. It includes formal institutions and regimes empowered to enforce compliance, as well as informal arrangements that people and institutions either have agreed to or perceive to be in their interest.[20]

Based on this definition, the theory and the study of Global Governance were born and developed as the academic field dealing with the creation and realization of norms dynamically. The theory of Global Governance, while considering the sovereign state system as a premise, regards various subjects as stakeholders and new norms will be created and implemented through mutual influence among stakeholders. By connecting this understanding with the UN studies by Weiss and others, we could understand that the 'second' and 'third' UN would also contribute to the creation and implementation of new norms.

However, when we think about the origin of this concept, we can understand that it did not come from positive beginnings. The Report of the Commission on Global Governance was published in 1995, longer than a quarter century ago. This was a year after the world ignored the genocide in Rwanda in 1994. At the same time, in December 1995, the Dayton Agreement was concluded that ended the civil conflict in Bosnia-Herzegovina. Therefore, we need to understand the word 'Global Governance' not as a result of positive analysis of the real world but as an expectation of how the world 'ought to be'. In any case, in 2020, the study of Global Governance became more popular than the study of international organizations and UN study. Does this mean that the traditional theory of multilateralism is not as popular as the concept of multilateralism with various stakeholders which the theory of Global Governance considers as its premise?

Within the context of the UN Charter, this means that the UN has failed to become 'a center for harmonizing the actions of nations in the attainment of these common ends' as stated in Article 1, Paragraph 4. 'Patriotic Unilateralism' positions of various Big Powers may accelerate the disintegration of the very multilateralism which the UN has tried to initiate. No one can foresee when the behaviors of the Big Powers based on their 'Patriotic Unilateralism' will come to an end and it is beyond the scope of this chapter. What could be expected here is only that the Sovereign State system would restore multilateralism based on the concerted effort of sovereign states. In this context, the UN's 'Sustainable Development Goals' (SDGs) might provide momentum for

20 The Commission on Global Governance, *Our Global Neighborhood* (Oxford University Press 1995) 2.

the restoration of multilateralism. The SDGs clearly are based on the ideas both of multilateralism and of multilateral cooperation. As is well known, the Millennium Development Goals (MDGs), the predecessor of the SDGs, aimed at improving the situation of developing countries, especially the Least Developing Countries (LDCs). In contrast, the SDGs have set up 17 goals with 169 targets and some of these goals and targets require the efforts not only by the developing countries but also by the developed countries (for example, 'Goal 11: Sustainable Cities and Communities'). Also, 'Goal 13: Climate action' and the remaining goals are essentially 'global' subjects.

From a Mazower-like point of view, the SDGs might be regarded as proof of the 'failure' of the past UN positions since it failed to realize them after 1945 despite the existence of the above-mentioned provisions like Article 1, Paragraph 4. Therefore, leading toward the 'success' of the SDGs may prove a political *raison d'être* of the UN, which Mazower pointed out that the UN has yet to establish. While the UN is geographically universal, the purposes, provided in Article 1 of the UN, have never been achieved fully and satisfactorily. What the international community requires today is to restore the liberal international order. In this multi-layered international order, the UN Charter still survives as the symbol of the realization of a fundamentally normative international order.[21]

21 The original and longer version of this chapter appears in 'Great Powers and the UN (The United Nations Studies, No 21)' (June 2020) in Japanese. In this Chapter, Russian aggression and its impacts on the topic of this Chapter was inserted to the original manuscript submitted to the Editor before the aggression on minimal basis.

CHAPTER 10

The Role of Universal Jurisdiction in Achieving International Legal Justice: a Global Constitutionalism Perspective

Makoto Seta

1 Introduction

Since the end of the 20th century, international criminal law has dramatically developed insofar as it can be regarded as one of the most developed fields of public international law. Corollary to this, the principle of universal jurisdiction has likewise developed. In the *Arrest Warrant* case decided by the International Court of Justice (the ICJ) in 2001, the Democratic Republic of Congo (the DRC) contested the legality of the exercise of universal jurisdiction by Belgium. In particular, the DRC argued that the arrest warrant against its incumbent Minister of Foreign Affairs, which alleged crimes against humanity, was issued without any valid grounds. However, since the DRC changed its legal strategy and did not raise the aforesaid argument in its final submission, the ICJ did not address the legality of the Belgian exercise of universal jurisdiction.[1] Nonetheless, some judges, in their separate opinions, criticized the decision of the majority for failing to examine whether Belgium could validly exercise universal jurisdiction over crimes against humanity.[2] At that time, the judges were remarkably divided on the controversial issue, which could explain why the ICJ did not rule on it in the decision.[3]

As of 2024, the exercise of universal jurisdiction over core crimes such as genocide, crimes against humanity, and war crimes, seems to be respected both

1 *Mandat d'arrêt du 11 Avril 2000* (*République démocraique du Congo c. Belgique*), arrêt, CIJ Recueil 2002, paras 45–46.

2 *Mandat d'arrêt du 11 Avril 2000* (*République démocraique du Congo c. Belgique*), arrêt, CIJ Recueil 2002, Opinion Individuelle de Mme Higgins, M Kooijmans, et M Buergenthal, para. 16.

3 Wouters indicates 'The real reason may be that the judges were very much divided on this controversial issue'; Jan Wouters, 'The Judgment of the International Court of Justice in the Arrest Warrant Case, Some Critical Remarks' (2003) 16 *Leiden Journal of International Law* 253–267, 263.

 | DOI:10.1163/9789004681477_012

by most States and academic scholars.[4] Professor Toshiki Mogami's scholastic work on universal jurisdiction published in 2009 is premised on the belief that universal jurisdiction over such core crimes is established under customary international law. According to Mogami, universal jurisdiction is necessary in the period of transition from domestic criminal jurisdictions to international courts and tribunals.[5] He emphasized the fact that universal jurisdiction is anchored on the concept of *jus cogens* in the sense that both concepts regard some criminal acts as international crimes.[6] Actually, these two concepts originate from Europe. It is well known that the term 'genocide' was invented and criminalized as a result of the Holocaust, an infamous European experience.[7] In the same vein, the grave breach of international humanitarian law was internationally criminalized by the 1949 Geneva Convention, the result of a great effort exerted by the International Committee of the Red Cross (ICRC),[8] which is mainly based in Switzerland.

Nevertheless, nowadays, such criminalization seems to be supported by non-European States. The idea to universally prosecute and punish international crimes is widely accepted, as evinced by the establishment of the International Criminal Court (ICC), the permanent international criminal court. The idea to establish such court dates back to the drafting of the Genocide Convention.[9] However, due to the Cold War, it was after 50 years of the Nuremberg and Tokyo trials that new international criminal tribunals were created, namely, the International Criminal Tribunal for the former Yugoslavia (ICTY) and the International Criminal Tribunal for Rwanda (ICTR). In 1998, the ICC was finally established, which fulfilled the dream of the international community to have a permanent international criminal court.[10]

---

4 As for State Practices, see, for example, Trial International, *Universal Jurisdiction Annual Review 2023* (2023) <https://www.ecchr.eu/fileadmin/user_upload/01_TRIAL_UJAR_2023_DIGITAL_27_03.pdf> (accessed 30 July 2023); Also, see for example, Cedric Ryngaert, *Unilateral Jurisdiction and Global Values* (Eleven International 2015) 111.

5 Toshiki Mogami, 'Introduction of Universal Jurisdiction: Tangled and Revolutionary Structure' in Shigeki Sakamoto (ed), *Forefront of the International Law-Making* (Yushindo 2009) 3–28, 26–27 [in Japanese].

6 ibid 21–25.

7 William A Schabas, *Genocide in International Law: The Crime of Crimes* (2nd ed, Cambridge University Press 2009) 14–50.

8 Roger O'Keefe, 'The Grave Breaches Regime and Universal Jurisdiction' (2009) 7 *Journal of International Criminal Justice* 811–831, 819–823.

9 Schabas (n 7) 400–490.

10 Robert Cryer, Håkan Friman, Darryl Robinson and Elizabeth Wilmshurst, *An Introduction to International Criminal Law and Procedure* (4th ed, Cambridge University Press 2019) 144–146.

Following its establishment 20 years ago, the criticism against the ICC grew due to the different perceptions among non-European regions. One of the striking examples is the withdrawal from the ICC by Burundi and the Philippines.[11] In addition, some African and Asian states criticize the unilateral exercise of universal jurisdiction by third states that do not have any connection with the committed crimes. These circumstances can be interpreted in the following two ways: First, some African and Asian states do not share the same stance on legal justice with European states, and second, the withdrawal and criticism are merely a coincidental and transitory reaction. The latter position suggests that Burundi and the Philippines, in harmony with European legal justice, would eventually join the ICC again. Stated differently, the difference in the suggested meanings stems from the uncertainty on whether legal justice can be shared in the international community.

This paper resolved this issue in the context of universal jurisdiction. For this purpose, Section 2 tackled the concept of universal jurisdiction and the possibility of regional universal jurisdiction. Then, Section 3 discussed the adverse movements by African and Asian regions against international criminal law led by Europe. Next, Section 4 evaluated the consequences of these movements and how universal jurisdiction could be exercised from a perspective of global constitutionalism. Lastly, the conclusion emphasized the democratization of international law, which has been the focus of Professor Mogami's academic career.

2 Jurisdiction Exercised by States and International Courts

2.1 *Universal Jurisdiction and Its Theoretical Foundation*

Under contemporary international law, the concept of universal jurisdiction has been recognized and used extensively in the manner as defined by the Princeton Principles.[12] According to principle 1.1,

11 In 2023, for the purpose of allowing Russian President Vladimir Putin, against whom the ICC issued an arrest warrant, to visit their territory without any fear of being arrested, both South Africa and Brazil took the position that they would review the ICC membership, but they have not decided to withdraw from it.

12 The definition of Princeton Principle is used in the following documents; Amnesty International, *Universal Jurisdiction: The Duty of States to Enact and Implement Legislation*, (IOR:53/003/2001) (2001) 2; Zdzislaw Galicki, 'Preliminary Report on the Obligation to Extradite or Prosecute ('*aut ded-ere aut judicare*')', UN Doc A/CN.4/571, 7 June 2006, para 19.

> universal jurisdiction is criminal jurisdiction based solely on the nature of the crime, without regard to where the crime was committed, the nationality of the alleged or convicted perpetrator, the nationality of the victim, or any other connection to the state exercising such jurisdiction.[13]

While there has been no dispute over the origin of universal jurisdiction (i.e. piracy),[14] its current scope, specifically the crimes now cognizable, remains controversial. Under customary international law, it has become widely accepted that gross human rights offenses (GHROs) such as genocide, crimes against humanity, and war crimes are subject to universal jurisdiction.[15] Although all three crimes are subject to the jurisdiction of the ICC, it does not mean that the ICC Statute itself obliges contracting parties to exercise universal jurisdiction.[16] Universal jurisdiction over such crimes has been established under customary international law crime by crime basis.

Aside from under customary international law, some treaties have provided for universal jurisdiction. To some extent, the term 'universal jurisdiction' is misleading because even treaties by which only the contracting parties are bound can establish universal jurisdiction.[17] However, given its definition, universal jurisdiction may be established irrespective of the forms of sources of law. In fact, many treaties provide for universal jurisdiction in the form of the obligation to extradite or prosecute. Although this is still a debatable idea, the ICJ said that this obligation is premised on the universal jurisdiction,[18] because it obliges a custody state whose territory suspects physically exist, to prosecute, in other words, exercise jurisdiction, even when there is no connection between that State and the crime committed by these suspects.

13 Princeton Project on Universal Jurisdiction, *The Princeton Principles on Universal Jurisdiction*, 28, <https://icj2.wpenginepowered.com/wp-content/uploads/2001/01/Princeton-Principles-Universal-Jurisdiction-report-2001-eng.pdf> (accessed 30 July 2023).

14 Mark Chadwick, *Piracy and the Origins of Universal Jurisdiction* (Brill 2018) 2–3.

15 Robert Cryer *et al* (n 10) 56–57.

16 Although there is no obligation for States to the ICC Statute, the contracting Parties exercise jurisdiction based on complementarity principle, as Philippe indicates; Xavier Philippe, 'The Principles of Universal Jurisdiction and Complementarity: How Do the Two Principles Intermesh?' (2006) 862 *International Review of the Red Cross* 375–398, 384.

17 Michael P Scharf, 'Application of Treaty-Based Universal Jurisdiction to Nationals of Non-Party States' (2001) 35 *New England Law Review* 363–382.

18 *Questions relating to the Obligation to Prosecute or Extradite (Belgium v Senegal)*, Judgment, ICJ Reports 2012, 451, para 74.

2.2 *Bases of ICC's Jurisdiction*

Notwithstanding the exercise of universal jurisdiction by individual states, international crimes like GHROs[19] still fall within ICC's jurisdiction. Universal jurisdiction sometimes incorporates the jurisdiction exercised by ICC and other international criminal tribunals. This is due to the similarity between those two jurisdictions, and the fact that the ICC itself does not have nexus with the crime.[20] On the other hand, legal scholars posit that ICC's jurisdiction arises from the state's jurisdiction, which is anchored on the principles of territoriality and personality.[21]

This basis of the ICC's jurisdiction was discussed during the drafting of the ICC Statute. The deliberations indicate that there is a dichotomy on this point. Some argue that ICC's jurisdiction is based on the consent of states. This argument is supported by the fact that a state may confer its jurisdiction to other states in order for the latter to exercise such jurisdiction on behalf of the former. This practice can be seen when prosecuting and punishing fugitives. This transfer of jurisdiction is employed pursuant to the principle of representation,[22] and should also be done with ICC, especially for member states. However, this transfer of jurisdiction may be difficult for nationals of non-member states, especially the leaders who enjoy immunity under international law.[23] If ICC were to deprive the leaders of non-state parties of such immunity, it would be contradictory with the principle of the law of treaties, namely *pacta tertiis nec nocent nec procunt*, which is provided for in Article 34 of the VCLT as the existing positive law.

---

19 Even crime of aggression might be categorized into GHTOs; See Makoto Seta, 'Expanding the Scope of Universal Jurisdiction through Municipal Law: From Piracy to the Crime of Aggression via Eichmann Trial' (2015) IV *Historical Origins of International Criminal Law* 339–366, 354.

20 For example, Sadat divides universal jurisdiction into two categories: One is 'universal inter–state jurisdiction', the competence of States and the other is 'universal international jurisdiction' which is exercised by international community; Leila Nadya Sadat, 'Redefining Universal Jurisdiction' (2001) 35 *New England Law Review* 241–264, 246; In addition, Michael P Scharf examines the Nuremberg Tribunals under the name of universal jurisdiction; Michael P Scharf, 'Universal Jurisdiction and the Crime of Aggression' (2012) 53 *Harvard International Law Journal* 357–389, 374–379.

21 Ahmed Isau, 'The International Criminal Court (ICC): Jurisdictional Basis and Status' (2015) 6 *Nnamdi Azikiwe University Journal of International Law and Jurisprudence* 34–49, 40.

22 Geoff Gilbert, *Transnational Fugitive Offenders in International Law: Extradition and Other Mechanisms* (Martinus Nijhoff 1998) 102.

23 Lee A Casey and David B Rivkin Jr, 'The Limits of Legitimacy: The Rome Statute's Unlawful Application to Non-State Parties' (2003) 44 *Virginia Journal of International Law* 63–89, 82.

Given all of this, other legal scholars posit that ICC's jurisdiction is based, not on the consent of states, but on its nature as an international organization. Truthfully, ICJ, in the *Arrest Warrant* case, acknowledged that the future ICC (which had not started its mission at that time) would have jurisdiction over state leaders who enjoyed immunity under international law.[24] However, from the perspective of positive law, the reasoning of ICJ's argument is unclear. In fact, there may even be two possible reasonings. First, ICC's jurisdiction over state leaders can be justified by customary international law. Although this theoretical possibility has been noted by Morris from the perspective of *lex lata*, she denies the existence of such customary rules.[25] The more radical approach may indicate the paradigm shift of the international society. So far, most legal scholars have justified ICC's jurisdiction with the jurisdiction of states.[26] However, the second reasoning does not need such an intermediator of states as states have jurisdiction based on territory and nationality, ICC does so as well. To illustrate, all individuals have the nationality of the international community, and all crimes committed by them are considered committed in the territory of the international community. Therefore, ICC which is granted jurisdiction by the international community can justify its jurisdiction.

In this way, several approaches may justify the basis of ICC's jurisdiction. At this stage, it is difficult to conclude which approach is more appropriate and persuasive. However, given that this question is merely theoretical, the answer is not strictly necessary. What is more important here is that ICC's jurisdiction is based on the nature of the crimes over which it has jurisdiction. Since the crimes violate the interest of the international community as a whole, ICC's jurisdiction is directly or indirectly justified through the jurisdiction of states.

2.3 *Regional Universal Jurisdiction?*

Universal jurisdiction is justified on the basis of the nature of the targeted crimes that violate the interest of the international community. This rationale would be important when considering universal jurisdiction in a particular region, among certain regional states. From a practical perspective, any crime

24 *Mandat d'arrêt du 11 Avril 2000 (République démocraique du Congo c. Belgique)*, arrêt, CIJ Recueil 2002, paras 58–61.

25 Madeline Morris, 'High Crimes and Misconceptions: the ICC and Non-Party State' (2001) 64 *Law and Contemporary Problems* 13–66, 35.

26 M Cherif Bassiouni, 'Note Explicative sur le Statut de la Cour penale international (CPI)' (2000) 71 *Revue internationale de droit pénal* 1–41, 8; Michael P Scharf, 'The ICC's Jurisdiction over the Nationals of Non-party States: A Critique of the U.S. Position' (2001) 64 *Law and Contemporary Problems* 67–117, 116.

may be subject to universal jurisdiction for as long as the treaty provides for such. Besides, regional customary law is also recognized.[27] Accordingly, the rules that govern universal jurisdiction within a particular region can be based both on treaties and customary international law.

Its theoretical perspective, however, must still be examined. The basis of jurisdiction may be drawn from the territoriality, personality, and protective principle. These principles share the common idea that states may acquire jurisdiction from the nexus between states and the crime committed.[28] Nevertheless, such nexus is not necessary for universal jurisdiction to be exercised, because a violation of the interest of the international community can already indirectly infringe the interests of all states who are members of the international community.[29] Furthermore, this interest of the international community can be classified into two categories: pragmatic and moral. To illustrate, piracy is subject to universal jurisdiction, because it violates the pragmatic interest. On the other hand, GHROs are also subject to universal jurisdiction, because there is a violation of moral interest due to its heinous character.[30]

Applying *mutatis mutandis*, the rationale to regional universal jurisdiction must be ascertained. Regional universal jurisdiction can be established only for the crimes which violate the common interest for the region, irrespective of whether they are a moral or pragmatic interest. For example, in Africa, the crimes that violate the common interest of the region would be subject to universal jurisdiction among the various African states. However, in order to justify this, it must be confirmed that such common interest indeed exists in the region by determining how it was established in the first place. It can be said that some states establish a common interest by establishing treaties. However, it is unknown whether such treaties truly reflect a regional interest that embodies regional values and justice. Moreover, even if it did, the geographical ambiguity of a region would make the justification of regional universal jurisdiction difficult. The difficulty stems from the fact that criminal law restricts an individual's rights, and as such, must have clear basis.[31] In this sense,

---

27 Anthony A D'Amato, 'The Concept of Special Custom in International Law' (1969) 63 *American Journal of International Law* 211–223.

28 M Cherif Bassiouni, 'Universal Jurisdiction for International Crimes: Historical Perspectives and Contemporary Practice' (2001) 42 *Virginia Journal of International Law* 81–162, 94.

29 Robert Cryer *et al* (n 10) 57.

30 Seta (n 19) 354.

31 Antonio Cassese and Paola Gaeta, Laurel Baig, Mary Fan, Christopher Gosnell and A Whiting, *Cassese's International Criminal Law* (3rd ed, Oxford University Press 2013) 27–28.

if criminal law were applied within a territory or universally, the geographical scope of application would be clearer to some extent.[32] However, if regional justice were to become the basis for criminal law, the boundary setting for that region would become problematic, especially in the Asian region, where the geographical scope of the region is not universally agreed.[33] For example, if Japan recognizes Asian justice and criminalizes certain acts committed within the Asian region, the geographical indeterminacy of the Asian region could entail the challenge of such criminalization, since crimes must have clarity. Given all of this, to establish regional universal jurisdiction, it is essential to create a treaty that can provide the cognizable crimes and the scope of jurisdiction, irrespective of whether it is exercised by states or regional tribunals.

3 Movements against Universal Jurisdiction in the Non-Europe

As discussed in the introduction, non-European States have recently expressed their resistance to the universal jurisdiction exercised by the European States and ICC. This behaviour has been seen in Africa and Asia.

3.1 *African Practices*

As demonstrated in the *Arrest Warrant* case, the unilateral exercise of universal jurisdiction by European States against African leaders frustrated the African States.[34] Other than the Belgian exercise against DRC leaders, Spanish practices also made the African States nervous. In 2008, Andreu Merelles, Investigative Judge of the Spanish Audiencia Nacional, issued arrest warrants against 40 current or former Rwandan officials for charges of genocide, crimes against humanity, and terrorism allegedly committed in Rwanda between 1990 and 2002.[35, 36]

32 Although there are many territorial disputes and territorial borders are vague, this fact does not mean that the application of criminal law becomes vague. This is confirmed by the fact that one of the requirements for Statehood, territory, is fulfilled even if there is a territorial dispute.

33 Asian Development Bank (ADB) notes 'Asia's geographical boundaries are not generally agreed'; ADB, *Emerging Asian Regionalism: A Partnership for Shared Prosperity* (2008) 24.

34 See, for example, Kaitlin R O'Donnell, 'Certain Criminal Proceedings in France (Republic of Congo v. France) and Head of State Immunity: How Impenetrable Should the Immunity Veil Remain?' (2008) 26 *Boston University International Law Journal* 375–416, 404.

35 Commentator, 'The Spanish Indictment of High-Ranking Rwandan Officials' (2008) 6 *Journal of International Criminal Justice* 1003–1011.

36 Julia Geneuss, 'Fostering a Better Understanding of Universal Jurisdiction: A Comment on the AU-EU Expert Report on the Principle of Universal Jurisdiction' (2009) 7 *Journal of International Criminal Justice* 945–962.

AU criticized those unilateral exercises of jurisdiction. Furthermore, the AU's Assembly requested a meeting with the EU to discuss universal jurisdiction and its exercise by European states. At the 10th and 11th AU-EU meetings, Ministerial Troika addressed the issue and concluded to establish a technical *ad hoc* expert group for analysing universal jurisdiction.[37] The conclusive report highlighted both positions of the EU and AU. It also said that immunities needed to be considered, and states exercising universal jurisdiction must 'accord priority to territoriality as a basis of jurisdiction'.[38]

After the report was issued, the AU's Executive Council adopted the African Union Model National Law on Universal Jurisdiction over International Crimes.[39] In Article 4(2) of such, the priority of the territoriality principle was emphasized. Moreover, although the AU-EU expert reports mainly focused on GHROs, the model national law also made piracy, drug trafficking, and terrorism subject to universal jurisdiction.[40] Even though universal jurisdiction over drug trafficking and terrorism was controversial, such crimes could have been subject to African (regional) universal jurisdiction due to African value and justice.

Moreover, the African region has been the harshest critic of ICC's recent activities. This is because most situations wherein ICC is involved happen in the African states. Notably, the evaluation of Africa's criticism is dichotomized among legal scholars. Some post that ICC, which is composed predominantly of Europeans, engages in the new colonialism.[41] Others posit that the tendency to focus on Africa is mostly derived from the African states' self-referral, and not from the initiatives taken by ICC.[42]

---

37 Council of the European Union, *The AU-EU Expert Report on the Principle of Universal Jurisdiction*, 8672/1/09 REV.1, 16 April 2009, Recommendation 9.

38 ibid, Recommendations 8 and 9.

39 The Executive Council of the African Union, 'Decision on the African Union Model National Law on Universal Jurisdiction over International Crimes', adopted 21st Ordinary Session at Addis Abba (Ethiopia), EX.CL/731 (XXI)c, July 2012.

40 African Union Model National Law on Universal Jurisdiction over International Crimes (Model National Law), Arts 8–14 <https://www.un.org/en/ga/sixth/71/universal_jurisdiction/african_union_e.pdf> (accessed 30 July 2023).

41 Joseph M Isanga, 'The International Criminal Court Ten Years Later: Appraisal and Prospects' (2013) 21 *Cardozo Journal of International and Comparative Law* 235–323, 303–304; John Dugard, 'Palestine and the International Criminal Court: Institutional Failure or Bias?' (2013) 11 *Journal of International Criminal Justice* 563–570; Charles Chernor Jalloh, 'Africa and the International Criminal Court: Collision Course or Cooperation Lecture' (2012) 34 *North Carolina Central Law Review* 203–229, 209–210; Patryk I Labuda, 'International Criminal Court and Perceptions of Sovereignty, Colonialism and Pan-African Solidarity' (2014) 20 *African Yearbook of International Law* 289–321.

42 Priya Pillai, 'The African Union, the International Criminal Court, and the International Court of Justice: At the Fault Lines of International Accountability', *ASIL Insight*, vol 22,

Furthermore, the issuance of an arrest warrant against Al Bashir, the Sudanese President and one of the strong African leaders, worsened further the relationship between ICC and African states. The case against Kenyan incumbent leaders such as Kenyatta and Ruto, did the same.[43] When the Security Council referred the Darfur situation to ICC, its Office of the Prosecutor (OTP) initiated investigations against Al Bashir during the internal armed conflict.[44] However, for ICC to be able to prosecute him, he must be within ICC's custody. Similarly to how Cassese describes the ITCY as a giant without arms and legs, the court also has no police power to take him into its custody.[45] For this reason, the Rome Statute contains Article 98, which obliges state parties to assist in obtaining custody of suspects and in bringing them before ICC proceedings.[46]

Because sovereign states are reluctant towards the exercise of police power by outsiders within their respective territories, the aforementioned system is reasonable. However, it would not work if immunity were given to the suspects within each member State. This is because member states cannot then exercise police power due to immunity limitations. On this point, though ICC seems to have different reasonings,[47] it has consistently stated that state parties shall arrest and surrender the suspect to ICC even if the suspect's official capacity normally grants them immunity under customary international law.[48] Since

no 10; It must be noted that there is a view which thinks the opinion is diverse, and the African Region as a whole do not necessarily take the position against the ICC; Elise Keppler, 'Managing Setbacks for the International Criminal Court in Africa' (2012) 56 *African Journal of Law* 1–14, 13–14.

43 Geoffrey Luganol, 'Assessing the Acceptance of International Criminal Justice in Kenya', <https://www.nurembergacademy.org/fileadmin/user_upload/Kenya.pdf>; Laurence R Helfer and Anne E Showalter, 'Opposing International Justice: Kenya's Integrated Backlash Strategy Against the ICC', *iCourts Working Paper Series*, no 83 (2017).

44 See Manisuli Ssenyonjo, 'The International Criminal Court Arrest Warrant Decision for President Al Bashir of Sudan' (2010) 59 *International and Comparative Law Quarterly* 205–225.

45 Antonio Cassese, 'On Current Trends Towards Criminal Prosecution and Punishment of Breaches of International Humanitarian Law' (1998) 9 *European Journal of International Law* 2–17,13.

46 Göran Sluiter, 'State 'Cooperation Issues' in Arresting Al Bashir' in Richard H Steinberg (ed), *Contemporary Issues Facing the International Criminal Court* (Brill 2016) 124–137.

47 See Leila Nadya Sadat, 'Heads of state and other government officials before the International Criminal Court: the uneasy revolution continues' in Margaret M. deGuzman and Valerie Oosterveld (eds), The Elgar Companion to the International Criminal Court, 96–127, 104–126.

48 See, for example, Alexandre Skander Galand, 'Looking for Middle Ground on the Immunity of Al-Bashir? Take the Third 'Security Council Route'', *EJIL Talk!*, Published

the African states are dissatisfied with these decisions,[49] they tried to seek ICJ's advisory opinion.[50] This indicates that African states understand international law differently from ICC.[51]

Aside from the legal conflict, African states are also against ICC politically. In 2008, after the arrest warrant was issued against Al Bashir,[52] the AU Assembly adopted a resolution which objected to ICC's decision and requested the postponement of ICC's investigation of Al Bashir.[53] This, however, was not accepted by the Security Council. As a result, the AU's Assembly adopted a new resolution, which disallowed AU members from cooperating with ICC in attempts to prosecute the president.[54]

Frustrated, the African states established their own regional criminal system. In 2010, based on AU Assembly's 2009 resolution, the AU Commission

---

on 23 October 2018; Asad G Kiyani, 'Al-Bashir & the ICC: The Problem of Head of State Immunity' (2013) 12 *Chinese Journal of International Law* 467–508.

49 See, for example, African Union, Pres Release No. 002/2012 on the Decisions of Pre-Trial Chamber I of the International Criminal Court (ICC) Pursuant to Article 87(7) of the Rome Statute on the Alleged Failure by the Republic of Chad and the Republic of Malawi to Comply with the Cooperation Requests Issued by the Court with Respect to the Arrest and Surrender of President Omar Hassan Al Bashir of the Republic of the Sudan, 9 January 2012.

50 African Union has tried to request such advisory opinion twice so far, in 2012 and 2018 respectively; Assembly of the Affrican Union, 'Decision on the progress Report of the Commission on the Implementation of the Asebly Decisions on the International Criminal Court', adopted 18th Ordinary Session at Addis Abba (Ethiopia), Assembly/AU/Dec.397(XVIII), January 2012; and 'Decision on the International Criminal Court', adopted 30th Ordinary Session at Addis Abba (Ethiopia), Assembly/AU/Dec.672(XXX), January 2018.

51 This application of the immunity to the suspects of international crimes is controversial even among academics; Dapo Akande, 'The Legal Nature of Security Council Referrals to the ICC and its Impact on Al Bashir's Immunities' (2009) 7 *Journal of International Criminal Justice* 333–352; but see Paola Gaeta, 'Does President Al Bashir Enjoy Immunity from Arrest?' (2009) 7 *Journal of International Criminal Justice* 315–332.

52 *The Prosecutor v Omar Hassan Ahmad Al Bashir*, ICC-02/05-01/09, <https://www.icc-cpi.int/darfur/albashir> (accessed 30 July 2023).

53 Assembly of the Affrican Union, 'Decision on the Application by the International Criminal Court, (ICC) Prosecutor for the Indictment of the President of the Republic of the Sudan', adopted 12th Ordinary Session at Addis Abba (Ethiopia), Assembly/AU/Dec.221(XII), February 2009.

54 Assembly of the Affrican Union, 'Decision on the Report of the Commission on the Meeting of African States Parties to the Rome Statute of the International Criminal Tribunal (ICC) – Doc. Assembly/AU/13 (XIII)', adopted 13th Ordinary Session at Libyan Arab Jamahiriya (Libya), Assembly/AU/Dec.245(XIII) Rev.1, July 2009.

began revising the statute on the African Court on Human and Peoples Rights.[55] Consequently, AU enacted a new protocol at the 32nd AU Assembly held in Malabo. This new protocol, the Protocol on Amendments to the Protocol on the Statute of the African Court of Justice and Human Rights (hereinafter, Malabo Protocol), established international criminal jurisdiction.[56] According to Article 28(A) of the Malabo Protocol, in addition to four core crimes targeted by ICC, the African Court also has jurisdiction over the following 10 crimes: crimes of unconstitutional change of government, piracy, terrorism, mercenarism, corruption, money laundering, trafficking in persons, trafficking in drugs, trafficking in hazardous wastes, and illicit exploitation of natural resources.[57]

Given this, the ten additional crimes become subject to regional universal jurisdiction in Africa, since they could be prosecuted and punished by the Regional Court. However, according to Article 46(E), the precondition for the Court to exercise its jurisdiction is the acceptance of states who actually have jurisdiction according to the territoriality, personality, and protective principles. Moreover, Article 46(A) bis provides that the Court cannot exercise its jurisdiction over individuals who enjoy immunities. Therefore, unlike the ICC, the African Criminal Court only exercises the jurisdiction conferred to it by member states. Therefore, its jurisdiction is not based on universal jurisdiction in a strict sense. However, as defined by the article, if universal jurisdiction were understood as a jurisdiction exercised by an entity with no nexus with targeted crimes, the jurisdiction exercised by the African Criminal Court would fall within the scope of universal jurisdiction.

---

55 Assembly of the Affrican Union, 'Decision on the Implementation of the Assembly Decision on the Abuse of the Principle of Universal Jurisdiction – Doc. Assembly/AU/3 (XII)', adopted 12th Ordinary Session at Addis Ababa (Ethiopia), Assembly/AU/Dec.213(XII), February 2009.

56 Assembly of the Affrican Union, 'Decision on the Draft Legal Instruments – Doc. Assembly/AU/8(XXIII)', 23rd Ordinary Session in Malabo (Equatorial Guinea), Assembly/AU/Dec.529(XXIII), June 2014.

57 Protocol on Amendments to the Protocol on the Statute of the African Court of Justice and Human Rights (Malabo Protocol), Art 28 (A) <https://au.int/sites/default/files/treaties/36398-treaty-0045_-_protocol_on_amendments_to_the_protocol_on_the_statute_of_the_african_court_of_justice_and_human_rights_e.pdf> (accessed 30 July 2023); Jalloh classifies the crimes provided in Article 28(A) in the following four categories: (1) international crimes, (2) transnational crimes, (3) partly international crimes and (4) partly transnational crimes; Charles C Jalloh, 'A Classification of the Crimes in the Malabo Protocol', in Charles C Jalloh, Kamari M Clarke, and Vincent O Nmehielle (eds), *The African Court of Justice and Human and Peoples' Rights in Context: Development and Challenges* (Cambridge University Press 2019) 225–256, 238–239.

3.2 *Asian Practices*

China is among the Asian states targeted by the Spanish exercise of universal jurisdiction. In 2005, a Spanish national of Tibetan origin filed, with the assistance of non-governmental organizations (NGO), a criminal lawsuit against eight Chinese leaders for genocide, crimes against humanity, torture, and terrorism committed against Tibetans.[58] The following year, in 2006, the Spanish *Audiencia Nacional* rendered admissible a complaint against former Chinese President Jang Zemin, and six other high-ranking officers.[59] Furthermore, Spanish authorities also exerted efforts to hold Jian Zemin and others criminally responsible for crimes against humanity and torture against Falun Gong practitioners.[60]

Facing such prosecutions against its own leaders, China interposed two counter-arguments. First, it denied the facts that could be used as basis for prosecution, especially those against Falun Gong which the Chinese government had labelled as an illegal sect.[61] Second, China claimed that it had absolute sovereignty over its nationals and foreign States could not intervene under the guise of human rights protection.[62] China's position is not unique when compared to that of other Asian states. According to a survey conducted by Xing Yun, Asian states are reticent towards universal jurisdiction,[63] especially over GHROs. Although two practices are involved in the exercise of universal

58 Trial International, *Universal Jurisdiction Annual Review 2016* (2016) 43 <https://trialinternational.org/wp-content/uploads/2022/09/UJAR-2016.pdf> (accessed 30 July 2023).

59 Christine A E Bakker, 'Universal Jurisdiction of Spanish Courts over Genocide in Tibet: Can it Work?' (2006) 4 *Journal of International Criminal Justice* 595–601, 595.

60 Trial International (n 58) 46.

61 Embassy of the People's republic of China in the Republic of Latvia, 'Outlawing Falun Gong Cult', <http://www.china-embassy.org/eng/zt/ppflg/> (accessed 30 July 2023).

62 Mugambi Jouet, 'Spain's Expanded Universal Jurisdiction to Prosecute Human Rights Abuses in Latin America, China, and Beyond' (2007) 35 *Georgia Journal of International and Comparative Law* 495–537, 525–526.

63 Xing Yun, 'Asia's Reticence Towards Universal Jurisdiction' (2016) 4 *Groningen Journal of International Law* 54–67. China once said '[u]niversal jurisdiction was currently only an academic concept and did not yet constitute an international legal norm'. 'Summary record of the 12th meeting', UN Doc A/C.6/64/SR.12, 25 November 2009, para. 48; Guo and Ireland-Piper pointed the discrepancy within China towards the notion of universal jurisdiction between the acadmics and government officials; Sanzhuan (Sandra) Guo and Danielle Ireland-Piper, 'China and Extraterritorial Criminal Jurisdiction' in Danielle Ireland-Piper (eds), *Extraterritoriality in East Asia: Extraterritorial Criminal Jurisdiction in China, Japan, and South Korea* (Edward Elgar 2021) 48–77, 75; As one of the scholary articles on universal jurisdiction, see Ma Chengyuan, 'The Connotation of Universal Jurisdiction and its Application in the Criminal Law of China' in Morten Bergsmo and

jurisdiction by Asian states, both practices are related to criminal proceedings for piracy and not GHROs.[64]

Asian states are also not supportive of the ICC. As of April 2024, 124 states are parties to the ICC. According to the United Nations Regional Group, only 19 of the total number come from the Asia-Pacific region.[65] Takemura points out that the Asia-Pacific region is reluctant to accept the ICC due to its massive population.[66] According to Noguchi, the former chair of the ICC's Board of the Directors of the Trust Fund for Victims and a former Supreme Court Chamber Judge of the Extraordinary Chambers in the Courts of Cambodia, the reluctance can be attributed to four reasons. First, law is not the primary guiding principle in many parts of Asian culture. Second, the criminal justice system in some Asian states have problems (e.g. corruption) and therefore is not supported by their nationals. Third, most Asian states believe criminal matters are domestic issues, and such, external intervention is uncomfortable. Fourth, since the Asian region is very diverse, it would be difficult for all of them to share a single international or regional criminal justice.[67]

Some states, when targeted by ICC, have similar resistance to that of the African region. A typical example is the Philippines which ratified the Rome Statute in 2011. Given that only two of the 10 Association of Southeast Asian Nations member states – Cambodia and the Philippines – were state parties, the Philippines was labelled as pro-ICC, especially among States in Southeast Asia. However, after Rodrigo Duterte became president and initiated the so-called 'war on drugs', the relationship between the ICC and the Philippines changed. As argued by several NGOs, this change in the relationship is due to the 'war on drugs', wherein the Filipino government has allegedly killed

---

Ling Yan (eds), *State Sovereignty and International Criminal Law* (Torkel Opsahl Academic EPublisher 2012) 149–189.

64 One is the Atan Naim et al. case rendered by the Chinese municipal court. As for this case, see Yao Huang, 'Universal Jurisdiction over Piracy and East Asian Practice' (2012) 11 *Chinese Journal of International Law* 623–655, 651–652. The other is the Guanabara case rendered by the Japanese Court. See Shuichi Furuya, Makoto Seta and Kenta Hirami, 'International Law and Organizations [Developments in 2013]' (2015) *Waseda Bulletin of Comparative Law* 84–88; Jun Tsuruta, 'The Guanabara Case' (2014) *Journal of East Asia and International Law* 243–248.

65 International Criminal Court, 'The States Parties to the Rome Statute', <https://asp.icc-cpi.int/states-parties> (accessed 15 April 2024).

66 Hitomi Takemura 'The Asian Region and the International Criminal Court' in Yumiko Nakanishi (ed), *Contemporary Issues in Human Rights Law: Europe and Asia* (Springer 2017) 107–125, 107–108.

67 Motoo Noguchi, 'Criminal Justice in Asia and Japan and the International Criminal Court' (2006) 6 *International Criminal Law Review* 585–604, 587–592.

more than 10,000 nationals, which constitutes human rights violations.[68] Furthermore, in February 2018, Mrs. Fatou Bensouda, the ICC's prosecutor released a statement regarding opening preliminary examinations into the situation in the Philippines.[69] Opposing this, the Philippines withdrew from the Rome Statute in March, just one month later. It made things official the following year, in March 2019. Similarly, when ICC investigated Myanmar, the latter criticized the ICC and emphasized that it was not a state party.[70] Interestingly, however, the National Unity Government Myanmar, a group of parliament members and government staff, ousted in the 2021 Myanmar coup d'état, accepted the ICC's jurisdiction.[71] Furthermore, it is worth noting that Malaysia deposited the instrument of accession to the ICC Statute on 4 March 2019, but only one month later, on 5 April 2019, it withdrew from the Statute.[72]

4 How Universal Jurisdiction Would Be Exercised

4.1 *Conflicts between Global Justice and Regional Justice*

In Section 3, the backlash against the universal jurisdiction exercised by states and the ICC was confirmed.[73] Additionally, as shown in Section 2, from both

68 See, for example, Human Rights Watch, *Human Rights Watch World Report* (2018) 429–430, <https://www.hrw.org/sites/default/files/world_report_download/201801world_report_web.pdf> (accessed 30 July 2023); Amnesty International, *Amnesty International Report 2017/2018: The State of the World's Human Rights* (2018) 299, <https://www.amnesty.org/en/wp-content/uploads/2021/05/POL1067002018ENGLISH.pdf> (accessed 30 July 2023).

69 The Office of the Prosecutory (ICC), 'Report on Preliminary Examination Activities 2018', para 19, <https://www.icc-cpi.int/itemsDocuments/181205-rep-otp-PE-ENG.pdf> (accessed 30 July 2023).

70 'Myanmar says International Criminal Court has no jurisdiction in Rohingya crisis', <https://www.reuters.com/article/us-myanmar-rohingya-icc/myanmar-says-international-criminal-court-has-no-jurisdiction-in-rohingya-crisis-idUSKCN1LN22X> (accessed 30 July 2023).

71 National Unity Government Myanmar, 'The National Unity Government of the Republic of the Union of Myanmar accepts the jurisdiction of the International Criminal Court' (20 August 21), <https://twitter.com/NUGMyanmar/status/1428739347717648389> (accessed 30 July 2023); See also Special Advisry Council for Myanmar, 'Myanmar and the International Criminal Court', (2022) 6, <https://specialadvisorycouncil.org/wp-content/uploads/2022/12/SAC-M-Briefing-Paper-ICC-ENGLISH-1.pdf> (accessed 30 July 2023).

72 Coalition for the International Criminal Court, 'Malaysia backtracks on accession to the Rome Statute' (11 April 2019), <https://www.coalitionfortheicc.org/sites/default/files/cicc_documents/CICC%20Press%20Release-%20Malaysia%27s%20Withdrawal%20from%20the%20Rome%20Statute.pdf> (accessed 30 July 2023).

73 As Handmaker and Arts indicated, this paper also uses the concept of 'global justice' as focusing on criminal justice and ending impunity; Jeff Handmaker and Karin Arts,

practical and theoretical perspectives, a region can establish universal jurisdiction and can justify it on the basis of regional justice.

On this point, even if the justice among regions and states differs, parts of justice supporting universal jurisdiction seem to be shared worldwide, irrespective of region. This is strongly confirmed by African practices. In its model law on universal jurisdiction and the constituent instrument of the criminal section of the African Court, genocide, crimes against humanity, and war crimes are provided for in the same way as under the ICC Statute. This shows that African states also consider GHROs being subject to universal jurisdiction due to their heinous character.[74] It should be noted that Gambia, an African state, exerted efforts to hold Myanmar responsible for genocide against Rohingya before ICJ.[75] Therefore, there is no difference between global justice and African justice when it comes to the targeted crimes, which are provided for in substantive law. The only difference apparent between global justice and African justice seems to be in procedural law. While justice that puts an end to immunity prevails on the international level, the African region is keener on respecting immunity in order to maintain regional order.[76]

For Asian states, their values are diversified and difficult to present uniformly. However, some states who are against ICC do not consider immunity from GHROs as acceptable. For example, China did not ratify the Rome Statute, because there was dissatisfaction with the rules on war crimes and crimes against humanity. Regardless, China does not grant immunity to GHROs. This is confirmed by China's positive participation in the Rome Conference.[77] The Philippines, the sole Asian state that withdrew from the Rome Statute, also believes GHROs should be punished. In fact, in 2009, the Philippine Congress enacted Republic Act No. 9851. This law criminalized genocide and other

'Mobilising International Law as an Instrument of Global Justice: Introduction', in Jeff Handmaker and Karin Arts (eds) *Mobilising International Law for 'Global Justice'* (Cambridge University Press 2018) 1–21, 9.

74 Model National Law, (n 40) para 1 of the Preamble; Malabo Protocol, (n 57) paras 9 and 12 of the Preamble.

75 *Application of the Convention on the Prevention and Punishment of the Crime of Genocide (The Gambia v. Myanmar), Application Instituting Proceedings and Request for Provisional Measures* (11 November 2019), <https://www.icj-cij.org/sites/default/files/case-related/178/178-20191111-APP-01-00-EN.pdf> (accessed 30 July 2023).

76 Assembly of the Affrican Union, 'Decision on International Jurisdiction, Justice and the International Criminal Court (ICC)', adopted 21st Ordinary Session at Addis Abba (Ethiopia), Assembly/AU/Dec.482(XXI), May 2013.

77 Lu Jianping and Wang Zhixiang, 'China's Attitude towards the ICC' (2005) 3 *Journal of International Criminal Justice* 608–620.

international crimes.[78] This demonstrated that the Philippines does not recognize immunity granted to perpetrators of GHROs.

Unlike Africa, it is difficult to pinpoint what Asian values and justice are.[79] Nonetheless, as demonstrated above, Asian justice still would not deviate from the core elements of global justice.[80] One of the possible differences is also a procedural aspect, namely the priority of sovereignty. This is a concept emphasized by Asian states.[81] Given this, it can at least be concluded that no state can officially uphold GHROs and accept the immunity of perpetrators of such crimes.[82]

4.2 *Global Constitutionalism and Global Justice*

As the previous section illustrated, some states are against the exercise of universal jurisdiction by other states, and have gone to the extent of withdrawing from the ICC. Nevertheless, it does not necessarily follow that Asian or African states do not support global justice and international criminal law. Quite the opposite, these states actually share the same intention but their manner of realizing justice is different. Some states in Asia and Africa give priority to their sovereignty and immunity. The opposing views on procedural law resemble a situation where European values conflict with the universal norm, which was debated from the perspective of global constitutionalism.[83] This tension arose because the universal norm imposed by the Security Council did not pay enough attention to human rights, which is unacceptable for European constitutionalism.[84]

---

78 An Act Defining and Penalizing Crimes against International Humanitarian Law, Genocide and Other Crimes against Humanity, Organizing Jurisdiction, Designating Special Courts, and for Related Purposes (Republic Act No. 9851) <https://www.lawphil.net/statutes/repacts/ra2009/ra_9851_2009.html> (accessed 30 July 2023).

79 Sovereignty plays a more critical role in Asian States; Makoto Seta, 'The Asian Contribution to the Development of International Law: Focusing on the ReCAAP' (2019) 25 *Asian Yearbook of International Law* 65–83, 65.

80 Palmer argues that localization of international criminal justice is found in States in Southeast Asia; Emma Palmer, *Adapting International Criminal Justice in Southeast Asia: Beyond the International Criminal Court* (Cambridge University Press 2020) 10.

81 Noguchi (n 67) 589–90, fn 67.

82 Philippe (n 16) 385.

83 Takao Suami, 'Global Constitutionalism and European Legal Experiences: Can European Constitutionalism Be Applied to The Rest of The World?', Takao Suami, Anne Peters, Dimitri Vanoverbeke and Mattias Kumm (eds), *Global Constitutionalism from European and East Asian Perspectives* (Cambridge University Press 2018) 123–167.

84 N Türküler Isiksel, 'Fundamental Rights in the EU after Kadi and Al Barakaat' (2010) 16 *European Law Journal* 551–577, 557; Gráinne de Búrca, 'The European Court of the

The difference between universal vs. European and universal vs. Asia and Africa, may be the treatment of human rights enjoyed by individuals. In the EU, as Prof. Mogami indicates, UN security council sanctions were resisted for the purpose of protecting the fundamental rights of individuals.[85] Therefore, the conflict seemed to be resolved, as the Security Council accepted the EU's arguments and provided procedures to protect human rights.[86] However, the situation in Asia and Africa might not be similarly solved, because it is the regional side that does not respect human rights. Therefore, global constitutionalism may be limited to only solving this problem directly. This is because human rights and democracy are equally emphasized in the theory of global constitutionalism.[87] Democracy is mostly manifested through general elections. However, this does not prevail in some states within Asia and Africa. Although, even a State where a general election is held, such as Philippines, a president who poetizes public order (states interest) to human rights (individual interest) was elected.[88] This simply indicates that the global justice pursued by universal jurisdiction might not be commonly shared among Filipino people. For them at least, security from drug prevalence is more important to the extent that they accept the coincidental deprivation of their rights.

Considering the European experience wherein judicial dialogue is important,[89] the judicial divisions of each Asian and African state would also be very important. In fact, judicial division has played an important role in solving tension between public order and respect for human rights in the Asian and African regions. For example, in Africa, South Africa tried to withdraw from the ICC. However, the High Court of South Africa ruled that the government's attempt to withdraw was both illegal and invalid. This changed the mind of the

---

Justice and the International Legal Order After Kadi' (2010) 51 *Harvard International Law Journal* 1–50.

85 Toshiki Mogami, 'Towards *Jus Contra Oligarchiam*: A Note on Critical Constitutionalism' (2012) 55 *Japanese Yearbook of International Law* 371–402, 394–395.

86 Devika Hovell, *The Power of Process: The Value of Due Process in Security Council Sanctions Decision-Making* (Oxford University Press 2016).

87 Antje Wiener, Anthony F Lang, James Tully, Miguel Poiares Maduro, and Mattias Kumm, 'Global Constitutionalism: Human Rights, Democracy and the Rule of Law' (2012) 1 *Global Constitutionalism* 1–15.

88 As for Duterte's policy, see Julio C Teehankee, 'Duterte's Resurgent Nationalism in the Philippines: A Discursive Institutionalist Analysis' (2016) 35 *Journal of Current Southeast Asian Affairs* 69–89.

89 Anthony Arnull, 'Judicial Dialogue in the European Union' in Julie Dickson and Pavlos Eleftheriadis (eds), *Philosophical Foundations of European Union Law* (Oxford University Press 2012) 109–133.

government.[90] In the case of Phillippine, the Supreme Court did not successfully change the government's mind, which decided to withdraw from the ICC and not cooperate with its investigation.[91] However, the ruling of the Supreme Court that the Philippines remains obliged to cooperate with the ICC for its investigations, which was initiated when the Philippines became a member,[92] indicates that universal value may be strongly shared among judiciaries all over the world.

Currently, exercising universal jurisdiction cannot be regarded as absolute justice, especially by people unfamiliar with international law. Rather, the value of universal jurisdiction is relative and is challenged by other values. However, given the general acceptance of the values embodied in substantive law, the regionalization and consequent fragmentation of justice will not be possible. Following World War II, human rights issues were brought into the international sphere. As such, international law arose to regulate it. Since this time, the value rooted in global constitutionalism has grown. If these trends continue, as Elderink indicates, the ICC would exercise its jurisdiction more widely. Even the third states would be able to exercise universal jurisdiction more often.[93]

5 Conclusion

What makes Professor Mogami a distinguished and special academic in this field is not only his academic achievement, as frequently referred to in this book, but also his dedication to ordinary Japanese citizens who are unfamiliar with international law. I personally knew him through his famous book *United Nations and the United States*, which was written for the general public. When the general public learns how international law provides global justice, they

---

90 Maxdu Plessis and Guénaël Mettraux, 'South Africa's Failed Withdrawal from the Rome Statute Politics, Law, and Judicial Accountability' (2017) 15 *Journal of International Criminal Justice* 361–370, 362.

91 Presidential Communications Office (Philippines), 'PBBM: We're done with the ICC', <https://pco.gov.ph/news_releases/pbbm-were-done-with-the-icc/> (accessed 30 July 2023).

92 *Pangilinan v Cayetano* (G.R. No. 238875, G.R. No. 239483, and G.R. No. 240954, 16 March 2021) <https://lawphil.net/judjuris/juri2021/mar2021/gr_238875_2021.html> (accessed 30 July 2023).

93 Rupert Elderkin, 'The Impact of International Criminal Law and the ICC on National Constitutional Arrangements' (2015) 4 *Global Constitutionalism* 227–253, 251–252.

can advocate for a democratic State, which commits to international criminal law and accepts universal jurisdiction.

As the previous sections illustrated, the value of universal jurisdiction has been widely accepted among international lawyers because of their education, training, and experiences. Therefore, the knowledge of international law is essential for pursuing global justice through the exercise of universal jurisdiction. This is comparable to Root's argument in the very first paper published in *American Journal of International Law* that the knowledge of international law is crucial for maintaining peace.[94] To enhance the knowledge among the general public, international lawyers should pursue the democratization of international law for years to come. In such pursuit, international criminal law and global justice can truly be shared by the people across the globe.[95] The democratization of international law should be the central pursuit of every future international lawyer.

---

94 Elihu Root, 'The Need of Popular Understanding of International Law' (1907) 1(1) The American Journal of International Law, 1–3.

95 Rankin emphasized the role of private non-State actors as *de facto* international prosecutors to put an end to impunity; Melinda Rankin, *De facto International Prosecutors in a Global Era: With My Own Eyes* (Cambridge University Press 2022) 11; Palmer also indicates the vital function of civil societies in realizing international criminal justice; Palmer (n 80) 243–244.

Index

Aesthetics 22–25
affected stakeholders 170–171
African Charter on Human and Peoples' Rights (ACHPR) 59*n*2, 80, 91, 92–101, 106, 107, 123*n*27
African Commission on Human and Peoples' Rights (African Commission) 91–94, 97– 99, 101, 106–109
African Court on Human and Peoples' Rights (ACtHPR) 91, 97, 101–103, 107–109
African Union (AU) 91, 94, 196, 238, 239*n*42, 240n49 n. 49–50
Agreement on the Settlement of Problems Concerning Property and Claims and the Economic Cooperation Between the Republic of Korean and Japan 52
all-affected principle 175
Annexation of Korea 51*n*52, 53
Arms Trade Treaty (ATT) 137
Arrest Warrant Case 197*n*42, 230, 235, 237
ASEAN Human Rights Declaration (AHRD) 80, 91, 103, 104, 106

Beijing Platform for Action 64
Belated justice 36–56
Brussels Declaration of 1874 147

Caribbean Community (CARICOM) 55
Carty, Anthony 17*n*9, 21–22, 30
CEDAW General Recommendation 64*n*24
comfort women 4, 39, 43–44, 54
Committee on the Elimination of Discrimination against Women (CEDAW Committee) 63, 67, 75, 76*n*105
Comprehensive Nuclear Test Ban Treaty (CTBT) 129
Conduct of Hostilities paradigm 143, 150–161
Constitutionalism 165–214
Constitutionalization of international law 186, 187–188, 191, 213
Convention on the Elimination of All Forms of Discrimination against Women (CEDAW Convention) 64–65, 70, 73, 76*n*105
Convention on the Prohibition of Anti-Personnel Mines 116
Convention on Cluster Munitions 116
Conversion Theories 153–156
Core Crimes 196*n*38, 230–231, 241
Court of Justice of the European Union (CJEU) 169, 178–184
Council of Europe Convention on preventing and combating violence against women and domestic violence (Istanbul Convention) 59*n*2, 71, 74–76
Cuban Missile Crisis 121
cultural imperialism 118
culture of peace 87, 88, 116, 137–141
culture of war and violence 113, 116, 117–119, 124, 139

d'Aspremont, Jean 17*n*9, 20, 21, 24, 180*n*66
Declaration and Program of Action on a Culture of Peace 139
Declaration on the Elimination of Violence against Women (DEVAW) 64
Declaration on the Rights to Peace 89, 124*n*28
democratic control 165–185
Discrimination 37, 39, 56, 63, 64, 66, 67, 73, 102, 124*n*28, 129
Dispute settlement 26
Domestic violence 59*n*2, 64*n*30, 77, 78, 106
Due diligence 76
Durban Conference 37, 38

'either or' theory 152–153
Epoché 17, 21, 22
Equality 2, 44*n*27, 65, 72–73, 75, 79, 84, 89, 94, 102, 198*n*42, 223, 226
Eurocentrism 118
European Court of Human Rights (ECtHR) 5, 177, 178, 191
European Court of Justice (ECJ) 5, 180*n*66, 192

European Union (EU) 108, 166, 179, 182, 183, 187

Feminist international law/feminist approaches to international law 59, 60, 62, 77, 78
Feminist judgments in international law 60*n*4, 79
four freedom 136
Fourth World Conference on Women (Beijing, 1995) 64
franc-tireurs 147–148

Gaza Strip 142, 143, 155, 159, 160
Gender 59–79
Gender-based violence against women (GBVAW) 9, 59–79
Geneva Convention III of 12 August 1949 148, 149, 150, 154, 157
Geneva Convention IV of 12 August 1949 145, 150, 153
Genocide 37*n*7, 55, 228, 230–237, 242, 245
Global constitutionalism 6, 11, 12, 165–185, 186–214, 246–248
global contestatory democracy 166, 173–174
Global Justice 38, 244–248
global warming 119

Hague Regulations of 1899/1907 146–147
historiographical turn 41
human security 10, 113–137
humanistic approaches 125–127
Husserl, Edmund 15, 21, 22, 25, 28, 30, 31

indiscriminate view of war 118, 119
Industrial revolution 119
Injustice 9, 10, 36*n*3, 38*n*10, 60, 67–69, 113–137, 171
intercontinental ballistic missiles (ICBM) 121
Intermediate-Range Nuclear Forces (INF) Treaty 113, 125
International armed conflict (IAC) 156–160
International Campaign to Abolish Nuclear Weapons (ICAN) 115
international conferences on the 'humanitarian impact' of nuclear weapons 127
international constitutionalism 5–7, 11, 136*n*58, 191*n*21
International Court of Justice (ICJ) 38*n*10, 54, 113, 125, 205, 224, 230, 233, 235, 240, 245
International Covenant on Civil and Political Rights (ICCPR) 44*n*27, 98
International Covenant on Economic, Social and Cultural Rights (ICESCR) 67*n*53
International Criminal Court (ICC) 8, 135*n*54, 137, 156*n*40, 196*n*36, 196*n*38, 204*n*62, 231–248
International criminal justice 33, 71, 187, 195–199
International Group of Eminent Persons for a World without Nuclear Weapons (IGEP) 138
International Law Commission (ILC) 56, 81
International organization 187, 200, 211, 212, 219, 220, 222, 235
International Women's Year, 1975 63
inter-organizational contestation 173, 174, 175–185
Irish Resolution 121

Jump Theory 155–156
jus ad bellum 134
Jus cogens 12, 192*n*27, 199*n*46, 231
jus in bello 134
Just War Theory 118, 133

Law Enforcement paradigm 143, 150–156, 160, 161
Legal (non-)judicial control 208–210
Lethal Autonomous Weapons Systems (LAWS) 139
levée en masse 149
Lieber Code of 1863 145

military sexual slavery 39
Model Nuclear Weapons Convention 126
multilateralism 2, 3–5, 6*n*22, 7, 11, 114*n*3, 115, 137, 214, 218, 225, 227–229

Nairobi Forward-Looking Strategies for the Advancement of Women 63
New Strategic Arms Reduction Treaty (New START) 113

Non international armed conflict (NIAC) 155, 157–160
Non-discrimination 66, 73, 74, 89
Non-judicial control 11, 210
norm contestation 11, 166, 170, 171, 174, 181
North Atlantic Treaty Organization (NATO) 132
NPT regime 120–122, 124, 131, 137–139
NPT Review Conference 125, 126, 127, 139
nuclear deterrence 10, 117, 129, 132
nuclear era 114, 123
Nuclear Hegemony System 113, 120–122
nuclear umbrella 116–117, 131–132, 134
nuclear winter 119

occupied Territory of Palestine 143
Organisation of African Union (OAU) 91, 93, 94, 97, 98, 100
Oxford Manual of 1880 147–148

Palestine 143, 157, 159–160, 205
Peacekeeping operations (PKO) 62*n*16, 87, 218
Prague Speech 125
Prisoners of war 148–149, 157
Protocol Additional to the Geneva Conventions of 12 August 1949, and relating to the Protection of Victims of International Armed Conflicts (API) 148, 149, 154
Protocol on Amendments to the Protocol on the Statute of the African Court of Justice and Human Rights (Malabo Protocol) 241*n*57
Protocol to Prevent, Suppress and Punish Trafficking in Persons Especially Women and Children (Palermo Protocol) 71
Protocol to the African Charter on Human and Peoples' Rights on the Rights of Women in Africa (Maputo Protocol) 59*n*2, 80, 91, 94–97, 101, 106

Responsibility to protect 101, 136*n*58, 187, 199–201, 210
right of last resort 210, 211–212
right to live in peace 84, 101, 104, 115, 116, 136
Right to Peace 3, 7, 9, 10, 80–81, 83–93, 95–97, 100–119, 123*n*27, 124*n*28
Rome Statute of International Criminal Court 71
Russian-Ukrainian war 142
Ryuku Shobun (Ryukyu Disposition) 46, 48, 49

Sex discrimination 64, 66, 74
Sliding Scale Theory 153–155
Soft law 70, 76, 167
Special Tribunal for Lebanon 198
step-by-step approach 132–133
Structural inequality 75
structural rights 124
structural violence 4, 7, 60, 114, 119, 124, 135
subcritical experiments 129
Subsidiarity 202–204
Substantial equality 77
Sustainable Development Goals (SDGs) 115, 228

Targeted sanctions 5, 166, 179–185, 191–195, 199, 208, 214
Technological revolution 119
The rule of law 1, 4, 10, 87, 89, 102, 114*n*3, 165, 182, 188, 191*n*20, 208–209, 213, 214*n*94
Thirty Years' War 118
Transformative approaches to gender-based violence against women 73–76
Transformative equality 72–73, 79
Transitional Justice 36
trans-temporal justice 43, 49
Treaty for human security 115
Treaty on the Prohibition of Nuclear Weapons (TPNW) 8, 10, 113–141

UN Charter 1, 3, 81, 86, 87, 92, 93, 97, 100, 107, 108, 167, 169, 172, 186–188, 192, 194, 195*n*34, 199, 202–205, 217–218, 223–229
UN Decade for Women, 1976–1985 63
UN Educational, Scientific, and Cultural Organization (UNESCO) 140
UN General Assembly 64, 80, 82–84, 121, 123, 125–127, 131, 137, 139, 224
UN Human Rights Committee 44*n*27, 192
UN Human Rights Council (HRC) 46, 64, 81, 82–84, 124*n*28, 208, 217
UN Sanctions Committee 184, 193, 194*n*32
UN Security Council 1–5, 11, 89, 120, 167, 186–212, 218, 223, 239, 240, 246–247

UN World Conference against Racism, Racial Discrimination, Xenophobia and Related Intolerance 37
Unilateralism 3, 8, 11–13, 217–227
Universal Declaration of Human Rights (UDHR) 4, 67, 68, 89, 92, 103, 123, 194
Universal Jurisdiction 12, 230–248
Universal value 93, 107, 222–223, 248

Vienna Declaration and Programme of Action 63
Violence against women 9, 44, 59–78

War Crimes 54, 71*n*78, 141, 230, 233, 245
war in Ukraine 113
Westphalia System 117–119
Women's human rights 60, 65–67, 75
Women's rights 63, 65, 66, 68, 72, 73, 76, 94–97
Working Group of Experts on People of African Descent 56
World Conference on Human Rights (Vienna, 1993) 63, 103
World Law 113–137

Yesh Din v. Israel Defense Forces (IDF) Chief of Staff 142–143, 151, 154

www.ingramcontent.com/pod-product-compliance
Lightning Source LLC
LaVergne TN
LVHW010626300926
849162LV00001B/74